How to Prepare a Results-Driven Marketing Plan

How to Prepare a Results-Driven Marketing Plan

Martin L. Bell

American Management Association

This book is available at a special
discount when ordered in bulk quantities.
For information, contact Special Sales Department,
AMACOM, a division of American Management Association,
135 West 50th Street, New York, NY 10020.

Library of Congress Cataloging-in-Publication Data

Bell, Martin L.
  How to prepare a results-driven marketing plan.

  Bibliography: p.
  Includes index.
  1. Marketing. I. Title.
HF 5415.B4285 1987   658.8'02   87-47717
ISBN 0-8144-7690-2

Printing number

10 9 8 7 6 5 4

All the material in this manual is designed to support a central concept: *The purpose of planning is not to produce a plan. The purpose of planning is to produce results.*

Preface

This book contains a complete description of the marketing planning process. It has been prepared primarily for persons responsible for marketing planning, such as product managers, advertising agency account executives, and general marketing managers. People in these positions typically have as their primary responsibility the design and implementation of marketing plans for their respective products, services, or market areas. However, numerous other functions and individuals are involved in the marketing planning process as well. Therefore, the material in this book should also be of interest to persons in marketing services, sales, advertising, and marketing research areas. And, because the boundary between marketing and the general management of a business is often hard to identify, general managers of small businesses or decentralized business units of larger corporations will find very helpful information in this book.

The book is in the nature of a procedures manual. It contains a step-by-step description of the marketing planning procedure, together with worksheets and comments bearing on the activities involved in each phase of the process. Its basic purpose is to guide the marketing planner through the entire procedure, suggesting not only the sequence of activities but the rationale for each and its relationship to the overall marketing management task. If you will thoughtfully (rather than mechanically) follow the procedures outlined in this book, not only will a useful marketing plan be developed but you will become a better informed and more productive contributor to the overall performance of the organization.

Contents

Part I: Before the Planning Begins   1

    1. Marketing and the Marketing Plan   3
    2. Plan Your Planning   13
    3. Prerequisites for Marketing Planning   19

Part II: The Marketing Planning Process   41

    4. The Situation Analysis   43
    5. The Analytic Summaries   100
    6. Developing a Marketing Strategy   144
    7. Tactics, Implementation, and Control   194

Part III: Beyond the Planning Process   247

    8. Financial Aspects of Marketing Planning   249
    9. The Personal Side of Planning   286
  10. Pitfalls in Planning   303

  Appendix 1:   Situation Analysis Questionnaire   306
  Appendix 2:   A Selective Bibliography on Marketing Planning   312

  Notes   317

  Index   319

  About the Author   325

Part I
Before the Planning Begins

The major portion of this book is devoted to a discussion of steps in the marketing planning process. However, before delving into the details of developing a marketing plan, there are a few important preliminaries that need to be taken care of. The three short chapters that follow deal with these matters. Chapter 1 presents some basic definitions: What is marketing? What is a marketing plan? What are the general roles of the various levels of management? Although much of this information will be familiar to marketing professionals, it provides a useful reminder and a framework for later discussion, as well as a critical introduction for those new to the field.

Chapter 2 poses the challenge: Have you planned your planning? The marketing plan is the outcome of a large number of actions taken by a considerable number of people. To make sure that the right kind of plan materializes, on time, is the purpose of planning the planning. After all, what better place to begin planning than with your own marketing plan?

Chapter 3 describes what must occur *before* you can start the planning process. Your work as a marketing planner requires that you have some very important information to get started. We call these inputs the *planning prerequisites*. For the most part these prerequisites are met by top management, and you have a right to them before you begin. This chapter should help you identify those necessary requirements and tell you how you go about obtaining them.

1
Marketing and the Marketing Plan

Before starting a discussion of marketing planning, we need to agree on what marketing actually is. The term has been defined many times and in various ways, and there is no point in simply adding another definition. It is important, though, to point out what needs to be addressed in your marketing plan.

What Is Marketing?

Some people tend to equate marketing with a number of functions or activities that really are only part of marketing. For example, we may hear somebody say, "Marketing is sales." Or, "Marketing is introducing new products." Perhaps you may encounter this viewpoint: "Marketing is advertising and promotion." Marketing is all of these and yet is none of them exclusively. And it should be viewed more broadly than as a set of activities performed in the "marketing department."

How broadly? you may ask. Broadly enough to include all those activities in the business that are necessary to serve customers profitably. This includes activities that normally are outside the traditional boundaries of the marketing department. Consider, for example, whether marketing occurs in the following areas:

Manufacturing. Unless the manufacturing department can make the product, on time and according to specification, there is nothing to sell, nothing to deliver, nothing with which to satisfy the customer. Every time a decision is reached in manufacturing, it almost inevitably influences in some way the organization's ability to serve its customers. The same applies in a service organization—a bank, for example. When decisions are made concerning bank operations—say, the hours during which the bank will be open—the bank's customers are directly affected. To this extent, then, these really are marketing decisions even though they are made by operating managers.

Quality Control. The determination as to whether a product is ready for delivery to the customer is a marketing decision, but it is usually made by people over whom marketing managers have little or no authority. *Quality* is defined as conformance to standard. But whose standard? The quality control manager may quickly answer, "Why, the engineering standard, of course." But this is not strictly so. A quality product is one that meets the customer's expectations. Quality control is essentially a marketing concern, and those people who are responsible for it need to see their responsibility from that point of view.

The Warehouse. Does marketing take place in the warehouse? Of course. If the right product isn't shipped, if the warehouse staff can't find it, if it isn't there at all—these are all marketing mistakes. Planning inventories and filling orders are important inputs to the servicing of customers.

Accounting and Finance. Do financial policies and procedures have marketing implications? Often they do. For instance, credit and collection activities involve direct customer contact. They can either enhance or disrupt the orderly development of an ongoing relationship with customers. These are important customer-contacts, as well as vital aspects of an organization's financial operation. Clearly, marketing is involved, and the marketing plan may well embrace customer relations initiated in the accounting and finance departments.

In addition, the finance group performs a vital role in budgeting and controlling marketing expenditures. Marketing programs, in common with all other business activities, involve costs—both capital expenditures and operating expenditures. Accounting or financial decisions that limit or direct the manner in which funds are employed will directly affect the marketing plan. In addition, because marketing is the primary producer of funds *into* the business, accounting and financial managers are often involved in the forecasting process and even in the selection of strategy, since the ultimate internal test of marketing's effectiveness is how well it performs financially. There may be no area outside of marketing where more critical decisions affecting marketing strategy are made.

Other Departments and Functions. There is practically no department or function in a business that does not have some impact on that business's relations with its customers. Personnel—or human resource management, as it is frequently called—makes decisions that affect customers when it determines the number, kind, and compensation of people who serve customers. Hiring practices, training programs, and supervisory practices may all play a part in improving or worsening customer relations.

The legal department can have considerable impact, too. There are many laws and judicial precedents that govern the way in which companies perform the marketing task. The law sets the boundaries within which a firm can operate, and it is not uncommon for the legal staff to be involved in the development of strategy. For example, an acquisition that may be very desirable from a marketing-strategy point of view may not be possible. When Pepsi-Cola was considering the purchase of Seven-Up, it backed away from the move because of the antitrust implications. Certain areas of tactical marketing, especially pricing and advertising, are so tightly constrained by the legal framework that the legal department is often required to approve day-to-day marketing decisions, such as reviewing price quotations and advertising copy.

Since such activities affect an organization's ability to serve its customers, they can (and often do) influence the kinds of programs that can be considered. And often they are critical forces in the implementation of marketing plans. True, marketing managers seldom have direct authority over these activities, but they usually must work closely with the managers of these departments in the design and implementation of a marketing plan.

Peter Drucker, the renowned management expert, has said that a business has only two functions: marketing and innovation. He has also noted that the purpose and function of every business is to create customers.[1] Extending Drucker's concept, we can say that marketing is the process of serving today's customers. Innovation is the act of getting ready to serve tomorrow's customers.

There is no more important management viewpoint. It is sometimes thought that the purpose of a business is to make a profit, to obtain a fair return on the shareholders' investment. Important as this goal may be, it does not define the purpose of the business. And it provides no indication of the direction that its managers should take. Profit is the reward for serving customers well. It may be the factor in deciding which customers to serve and which strategy to employ, but profit itself does not define the function of a business.

As Drucker implies, there are both short- and long-term marketing assignments. In the short run, the function of a business is to serve its present customers. In the long run, changes will occur. The customer base may change. Customer needs will become different. And the technical means by which those new needs can be served will change. The management process by which adaptation to the future takes place is innovation. We often think very narrowly about innovation, equating it with research and development. But R&D is only one part of the process. The future environment of the business must be anticipated. Changes in the structure of the market must be predicted. Alterations in the competitive climate must be anticipated. New objectives that are consistent with these anticipated developments must be set, and strategies to attain them must be approved. Ultimately, the entire resources of the business—including research, finance, manufacturing, and marketing—must be committed to these new goals. This is the broader meaning of innovation.

As a marketing planner, don't be reluctant to adopt this broad concept of marketing. At first it may seem to complicate your assignment, but when you have completed a plan that incorporates all the customer-serving forces in the organization, you will have much improved prospects of achieving the plan's objectives.

Marketing is the whole business seen from the point of view of its final result—that is, from the customer's point of view. Concern and responsibility for marketing must, therefore, permeate all areas of the business. Carrying out the marketing task is the responsibility of the entire company. Creating a customer is everybody's job. Since the marketing task pervades the whole business, we will direct our attention to three organizational levels, starting at the top.

Top Management's Role in Marketing

The president and executive staff decide the basic direction a company should take, and marketing vision should provide that direction. According to the head of one executive search firm, his company's clients are increasingly asking to locate CEO candidates with "savvy marketing skills and vision." John Bassler reports that "profitability-minded boards of directors want CEOs who can establish a strong marketing focus and strategy and clearly communicate it to all reporting managers throughout the company."[2] The trend seems to be accelerating. A 1985 report indicated that, whereas in 1983 only 29 percent of the chief executives responding to a survey believed that marketing was the most important management area, two years later 64 percent held that view. Coopers and Lybrand, sponsors of the study, stated: "Strategic marketing, marketing strategies, and marketing plans which help corporations hold or develop a competitive advantage have become paramount management challenges and major unresolved business issues."[3]

Top managers determine the kind and size of a company. In the very broadest sense, the chief executive officer must answer the question, "Who is our customer—now and in the future?" By defining the customer, it is possible to make plans to provide specific goods and services. That customer information enables top management to determine which ventures to support and which to abandon. We refer to such marketing-oriented decisions as *corporate strategic planning*.

Top management also gives specific marketing-oriented direction to those at lower levels in the company, so that these people can develop appropriate programs to carry out the company mission. Top management establishes objectives for its various divisions. It also may set policies that guide operating people in making lower-level decisions. Finally, of course, top management establishes an organization capable of carrying out the company's mission and creates a climate conducive to effective performance. To illustrate how important this kind of leadership can be to a company, consider the situation at Apple Computer. Apple was a company born of the technological wizardry of its founders. But when faced with the reality of a hostile and rapidly changing market, the company recruited John Sculley, former president of Pepsi-Cola and a recognized wizard in the field of marketing, for its president's office.[4]

Divisional Management's Role in Marketing

In decentralized companies, the second tier of management often is called the divisional, or Strategic Business Unit (SBU), level. The divisional level may be an entire company, such as a subsidiary of a large parent corporation. In smaller firms, the second level might be a group of similar products managed by a divisional vice president. Regardless of nomenclature, a hierarchy exits, and this next lower management level has its particular marketing role. The divisional manager is responsible for developing a strategy consistent with the company's mission—one that will achieve the objectives assigned to the division. A strategy is a long-range plan, which usually involves programs lasting from three to five years. Marketing is an important element in a division's overall plan.

At this level, the marketing strategy is aimed at a particular group of potential customers—a market segment. It includes decisions in the four critical areas of marketing management: products, distribution, promotion, and pricing. Decisions in these areas are integrated carefully into a total strategy—the marketing mix. It goes without saying that this marketing strategy is not developed until exhaustive research concerning the consumer, the competition, and all other external influences has been completed. Obviously, the division must have a total strategy involving more than marketing. Manufacturing, financial, and work-force plans also are needed. But the principal thrust of a division's program almost always is marketing, because the basic purpose of a company—its very reason for existing—is to create customers and provide customer satisfaction. All of a division's plans are aimed at this goal.

As companies have grown, especially through acquisition or by diversification, it has become useful to define another level of strategic management. Within the division or business group there may exist a number of strategic business units. These business units are operated more or less like individual companies, and their managers have considerable authority over the manner in which they seek to achieve their objectives. This is the level of management at which specific decisions are made about the products or services to be offered and the markets to be served. If a strategic business unit has more than one product or market, it may organize itself around the nexus of these products and markets. It may have several products or markets in its portfolio of offerings. These product markets are usually directed by middle managers known as product or market managers. While these managers do not have as far-reaching authority as do divisional or even SBU managers, they are often responsible for developing the entire marketing program, including those activities performed outside the marketing department.

Functional Management's Role in Marketing

At the operational level, almost every business is organized along functional lines. That is, a division or strategic business unit normally is divided into at least three specialized areas: manufacturing (or operations), marketing, and finance. These functional departments are managed by persons who develop detailed programs necessary to carry out the divisional strategy. We call these action-oriented programs *tactics*, and we usually associate them with the short run, a period of one year or less.

The marketing department is the key functional group in a company's effort to implement its overall business strategy. It contributes in two very important ways. First, as a functional department specializing in marketing, it has the responsibility of working out tactical details of a division's long-range marketing plan. Managers of specialized marketing activities, such as product planning, advertising, and sales management, develop short-run programs for their areas. The manager of the marketing department makes sure that these various tactical plans are integrated.

The marketing department's second contribution to the company's overall marketing effort is in its role as an intelligence-gathering arm of the firm. Corporate strategic planning and divisional and SBU long-range planning require information about customers, competition, and social, economic, and political developments. Similarly, information about the company's past sales and profits is required. It is often the responsibility of the marketing department to gather this information from external and internal sources. The subfunction of the marketing department that typically collects

such data is called *marketing research.* Very large companies, with extensive and sophisticated marketing intelligence needs, expand the function into a complete marketing
information and control system.

In carrying out these two important responsibilities, the marketing department
becomes the key group in a company. But it does not run the company, nor do marketing managers intrude on the domains of other functional managers, dictating how
their jobs should be done. Marketing gives purpose and direction; and a company
operates best not when marketing people run it, but when all those making business
decisions do so from a marketing point of view.

Marketing Is Not a Panacea

The preceding discription of how the marketing-oriented company operates may seem
logical and quite simple. In practice, however, it is difficult and only a relatively few
companies seem to do it very well. The obstacles are considerable. Regrettably, not all
managers accept the idea that the purpose of a company is to satisfy its customers.
Some still cling to the outmoded notion that the purpose of a business is to manufacture
and sell products. Production orientation is a fatal deterrent to effective marketing.

Even the marketing-oriented manager faces serious problems. There are other
forces to be satisfied—employees, shareholders, and creditors. Resources are always
limited. No company can do everything. Some customer wants must go unsatisfied
because demand always exceeds supply. Moreover, there is an impressive list of things
that can go wrong with the development and execution of a marketing program. The
information a company needs may not be available. Data that it does collect may be
obsolete or inaccurate. The market is constantly changing. The wrong strategy may be
selected and the tactics poorly chosen. There is always the uncertainty of what the
competition is going to do. Add to these the increasing external pressure from the
government and from consumer activists, and you can see that the marketing-oriented
manager faces a most difficult task. But it is not an impossible assignment, and this
book is intended to demonstrate just how a marketing-oriented business can be managed effectively.

Marketing, thus, is the driving force within an organization. It is the eyes and ears
of the business. It is the integrating element that focuses the attention of the entire
organization on the company's basic purpose: serving its customers profitably. And
so, we arrive at the definition of marketing that underlies our discussion of marketing
planning. *Marketing is a total process involving all business activities necessary to identify
customer wants and to satisfy them profitably.**

---

* This definition does not exclude not-for-profit organizations. While "profit" *per se* may not be relevant,
operational efficiency and long-term survival certainly are. Marketing adds value to a product or service,
and its total cost must be covered—if not by consumers, then by others who support the activity. Winning
that support is a major marketing task in the so-called not-for-profit organization. Many not-for-profit
marketers have successfully used the planning procedures described in this book.

What Is a Marketing Plan?

According to the Conference Board, a marketing plan is "an organized, documented, written communication that sets forth business goals and action programs required to achieve those goals for a twelve-month period."[5] Thus, in effect, a marketing plan is a statement of how an organization intends to accomplish its marketing objectives. More specifically, a marketing plan does these things:

Analyzes the business situation—where it has been, where it is now, and where it is likely to be in the future *- ABS*

Identifies the opportunities and problems facing the business *I O P*

Sets forth specific and realistic business objectives *S RBO*

Defines marketing strategy (that is, the long-term direction of the company)

Defines marketing tactics (that is, short-term action programs) to implement the strategy

Specifies individuals responsible for the execution of programs

Creates schedules and controls for the execution of programs

Provides forecasts and budgets that provide a basis for planning by other departments of the organization

Provides for periodic review of performance under the plan and for instituting modifications of it, as necessary

Provides a contingency plan to deal with developments, the occurrences of which are uncertain but which would have an important impact on the organization

Does your company's plan look like this? Companies have been preparing what they call "marketing plans" for a good many years. The fact is, however, that very few of these plans conform to the description just presented. Even if your company has been preparing marketing plans for a long time, one of the very first things you should do in getting ready to prepare your next plan is to check how closely those previous plans conform to this list. Do not be overly concerned if the organization of the plan differs, as long as the contents are similar. What is contained in the plan is more important than the way in which its contents are arranged.

If you find some disparity, decide ahead of time just what changes you want to make. Discuss these changes with others who are involved and make sure everyone is in agreement. You don't want your plan rejected simply because it "doesn't look right."

The Purposes of Planning

It is not the purpose of planning simply to produce a marketing plan. There are three important goals of planning. First, and foremost, a marketing plan should *produce results*—it should achieve whatever objectives have been set. Second, a marketing plan should enable the marketing manager to exercise some control and discipline over the marketing effort. That is, a marketing planner, although far removed from the field (and without any direct authority over the activities that take place there), can have a profound impact on the marketing success of an organization. This is partially addressed by the third major purpose of the marketing plan: to communicate. The marketing plan sets forth the goals of a business and the programs that will be employed to achieve them. It becomes the basis for obtaining top management approval, and it is the source of all implementation. Once the plan has been prepared and properly distributed to those involved, it becomes a powerful and important communications tool. It is with the expectation of what the marketing plan can accomplish that the planning process should commence.

Marketing Planning and the Rest of the Organization

The marketing planner, whether a marketing director, a product manager, or an account executive in an advertising department or agency, has the basic responsibility to see that an overall marketing plan is developed. To do this properly, however, the planner must obtain the support of other parts of the business. Some of these parts will be in the marketing area; others, outside. For example, a marketing planner will often require the assistance of people in marketing research, customer service, sales, or one of the other functional marketing specialties. But the need for information or approval may also involve nonmarketing functions such as research and development, logistics, or production scheduling. It is the marketing planner's responsibility to establish good working relations with all individuals whose cooperation is essential to the successful development and execution of the marketing plan.

The overall marketing plan, and the functional plans (that is, for advertising, sales, product development, and the like) which flow from it, must be linked to the organization's overall business strategy. To assure that this occurs, it is important the marketing planning process be tied to the corporate planning procedure. Market planners should provide essential information to the corporate planners, and the corporate strategists must define the organization's long-range objectives, which, in turn, provide the starting point for the development of marketing strategy and tactics. Obviously, the more market-driven the organization, the closer will be the linkage between corporate and marketing planning.

Exhibit 1.1 presents four levels and types of marketing planning. At the top is long-range corporate strategic planning, which defines the mission and overall strategic thrust of the business. Divisional or business-unit management designs long-run (three to five years) business plans. Functional managers develop strategies needed to implement the long-run business plan. Subfunctional managers design action programs (tactics) to carry out the strategy.

Consider the example of a company that developed a system of marketing planning as the means of implementing a major turnaround strategy. For almost 75 years, Pet Milk Company relied almost exclusively on a single product—the one contained in its name, milk—as the basis of its steady growth. Unfortunately, by 1960, the consumption of evaporated milk, the company's mainstay, had declined so seriously that the com-

Exhibit 1.1. Types and levels of marketing planning.

Management Level	Type of Planning	Time Frame
Top management	Corporate strategy	5 or more years
Divisional or strategic business unit (SBU) management	Business plan	3 to 5 years
Functional management (e.g., marketing)	Strategy	1 to 3 years
Subfunction management (for example, advertising, sales, and so on)	Tactics	1 year or less

pany's prospects were seriously in doubt. A comprehensive audit by a management consulting firm identified the need for new product development and diversification programs. Thus emerged a new strategic direction for Pet Milk Company, which subsequently changed its name to Pet, Inc., to reflect its long-term commitment to a wide variety of consumer and industrial products. The company was organized into major product groups, each with its own divisional president. Grocery Products assumed the responsibility for the mature evaporated milk line, as well as a number of new offerings developed internally or acquired. A Frozen Foods division was created. Its initial product, Pet Ritz frozen pies, was quickly augmented by other frozen specialty products. Product managers were assigned the responsibility for specific brands, such as Sego Diet Food in the Grocery Products area and Downyflake frozen breakfast items in the Frozen Foods division. Advertising agencies assisted the product managers in developing promotional campaigns to support their brands. Thus, over time, the kind of hierarchical arrangement illustrated in Exhibit 1.1 materialized at Pet, Inc. In a general way, this is the manner in which most modern business planning systems have developed.

The hierarchy need not be limited to three levels, depending on the size and scope of the organization. Divisional (business-unit) plans can be broken out further by program units, such as products, brands, or markets. Functional planning can take place at any level of the business—even in the president's office in a small firm. The important point to remember is that marketing planning at every level of an organization is necessarily linked with the planning that is done above and below it in the organization.

In the planning steps presented in the following pages, note at what points the marketing planner interacts with the planning in other functions and at other levels of management. This integration of planning efforts is seldom easy to achieve, but it is imperative if the planning process is to produce marketing plans that get things done.

The Unique Role of the Marketing Planner

As a marketing planner you have one of the most fascinating and challenging jobs in the entire area of business management. Not only is your work critically important, but it demands a blend of talents not often found in one individual. This may best be explained by looking at the extreme contrasts found in selected aspects of the marketing planner's job.

On the one hand, the planner is a thinker—a researcher, an analyst. On the other hand, he or she must be a doer—making sure that the planning tasks are completed. The planner is also both problem finder and problem solver, with each assignment demanding somewhat different skills and perspectives. The marketing planner must be a strategist, thinking about long-range, competitive positioning. Yet he or she is simultaneously a short-term tactician, concerned with programs to produce immediate results. He or she has widely diverse decision-making and decision-taking roles. From one vantage point, the planner makes important top-level decisions, notably those involving the strategic direction of the business. From another perspective, the marketing planner is fairly low in the marketing hierarchy and must respond to the suggestions and dictates of executives higher up the organizational ladder. In short, the marketing planner's job is often to find ways to implement someone else's strategy.

2
Plan Your Planning

Developing a marketing plan is not appreciably different from other management tasks that a marketing executive is asked to perform. The factors that make planning particularly challenging are the uncertainties involved, the number of subtasks to be performed, the considerable involvement of those outside the traditional marketing department, and the limited time and resources with which to accomplish those tasks. The first of these is addressed by becoming better informed about the marketing circumstances affecting the marketing plan. Since this in itself is a part of the planning process, it will be discussed in a subsequent section. The limitations posed by the diversities of tasks, the involvement with nonmarketing functions, and the lack of time and resources can be addressed by planning the planning and by following the procedure faithfully.

A Plan for Planning

The most effective way to make sure that your planning efforts bear fruit is to prepare a plan for developing your marketing plan. There are two aspects to this process. First, it is important that you anticipate exactly what will emerge at the end of the planning process. Planning is a discipline. It involves an integrated set of activities necessary to create a marketing plan. While it is not possible, or even correct, to anticipate the precise *content* of the marketing plan, its scope and organization can be determined in advance. This done, coupled with an understanding of the audiences to which the plan is directed, you will be able to prepare a plan that produces its desired results and is appropriate to the circumstances in which it is presented.

It is important to stress at this point that more than one marketing plan may prove necessary. This is certainly true of marketing plans prepared for diversified businesses. In general, a marketing plan must be prepared for each major market segment. Thus, if a company is marketing to both original equipment manufacturers (OEMs) and aftermarket customers (maintenance and replacement), very different marketing programs will probably be required and separate plans will need to be prepared. Also, as we shall see, marketing plans differ significantly depending on the management level for which they are prepared. Generally, strategic plans are prepared for presentation to top management while action plans are prepared to guide those who are responsible for implementing the strategy. Thus, it is not uncommon to find that the overall planning output is actually a set of plans involving long- and short-range marketing plans for several market segments.

Requirements of Your Plan for Planning

Your plan for planning should be written down. You will need to refer to it, and your superiors may require you to prepare a marketing planning proposal. The plan for planning should be relatively brief, but comprehensive. Every important planning step or activity, every input from an external source, and every review and approval stage should be included. It should be flexible. You may have to make changes in procedure, in format, and in schedule. Anticipate where such changes may have to be made, and be ready for them. Above all, never lose sight of what marketing planning is all about. Its purpose is not to write a plan; it is to produce results. This is too important an assignment not to plan it carefully.

The Process of Marketing Planning

The marketing-planning process involves 14 steps, a few of which can be performed simultaneously, but most of which must take place in the order described. These steps fall logically into three distinct phases. Phase I includes Steps 1 through 5—the analysis. Phase II covers Steps 6 through 9—the development of the marketing plan. Phase III includes Steps 10 through 14—the finalization, including tactics, implementation, and control.

Exhibit 2.1 depicts this planning process. It also indicates three other pertinent items of information regarding each step:

1. The need or usefulness of assistance or cooperation from persons outside the marketing department. Where the specific need can be anticipated in advance—as, for example, from the production planning department—the specific individual or department should be noted on the schedule.
2. The need to obtain advance approval for any particular program or activity, and specifically from whom this approval must be obtained.
3. The requirement to make a formal presentation of the planning work accomplished to date. Note that the opportunity to present some phase of the plan occurs several times during the planning process. It is not simply something that is done after the plan has been completed.

Exhibit 2.1. Steps in the marketing planning process.

Typical Schedule	Planning Step	External Input Required	Approval Required	Presentation
	Phase I Analysis			
4/1–4/15	1. Review last year's plan	No	No	Yes
4/15–5/15	2. Satisfy the planning prerequisites	Yes	Yes	No
5/15–6/1	3. Decide on the product/market focus	Yes	No	No
6/1–7/15	4. Prepare a situation analysis	Yes	No	No
6/1–7/15	5. Prepare an analytic summary	No	No	Yes
	Phase II Development			
7/15–8/1	6. Finalize marketing objectives	Yes	Yes	No
8/1–9/1	7. Identify marketing strategy alternatives	Yes	Yes	Yes
9/1–10/15	8. Develop the marketing mix	Yes	Yes	No
10/15–11/1	9. Select a strategy option	Yes	Yes	Yes
	Phase III Finalization			
11/1–12/1	10. Design the tactics	Yes	Yes	No
12/1–12/15	11. Present the plan	No	No	Yes
11/1–12/15	12. Write the plan	No	Yes	Yes
1/1–12/31	13. Implement the plan	Yes	No	No
2/1–12/31	14. Measure, evaluate, and control	Yes	No	Yes

Critical Steps in Planning the Plan

There are five critical actions in planning your marketing plan.

Identify What Needs to Be Done

This task involves an understanding of the steps in the planning process. These are the steps described in Exhibit 2.1., but they may have to be adapted to your particular planning assignment. As you outline the steps that must be taken, don't be reluctant to go into detail. In fact, the more specific your plan for planning is, the less likely you will overlook some important element. At this stage, don't attempt to organize the many activities. Don't attempt to schedule them or even worry about who will perform them. Simply write them down. You will organize them into a logical sequence later.

How do you know what needs to be done? Experience, of course, can be of great benefit. But if this is your first pass at preparing a plan, you will have to "go it alone," except for advice you can solicit from more experienced planners. However, don't be surprised if these "old hands" aren't very helpful. Relatively few people have good planning plans, keep adequate records of what they have done, or give much thought to ways in which their planning effectiveness might be improved. Resolve not to join this fraternity. Plan your planning, and work on developing your plan. Keep a journal or diary of what you do. Record the time spent. Make notes of ways to improve or expedite the process. Then, next time around, your past experience will guide you.

One surefire way to identify what needs to be done is to take each step in the planning process and expand it into a larger number of specific tasks. Do this by asking the questions "how?" and "how else?" For example, one of the planning process steps involves determining marketing objectives. The marketing planner who understands the character and function of objectives will have little difficulty answering the questions "how?" and "how else?" For example, suppose you are considering the planning task: State the Marketing Objectives. You would ask yourself, "How do I determine our marketing objectives?" This answer might come to mind: Review the SBU business plan. Then you might ask the question, "how else?" and another approach might occur to you; for example: Discuss marketing objectives with the SBU general manager.

And so you would continue this process, generating several more ways of identifying marketing objectives. These might include:

- Discussing the situation with other functional managers, such as the sales manager and the manager of marketing services
- Reviewing prior years' objectives and how well they were met
- Studying opportunities from the situation analysis

Of course, stating marketing objectives is only one of many planning tasks. Very quickly you will assemble a long list of things that must be done to prepare the marketing plan.

Decide Who Will Be Responsible for Each Task

For every task listed, an individual must be responsible for completing it. This involves much more than simply putting somebody's name beside a given task. The designated individual must be competent to undertake the task, be willing to do so, and be able to commit sufficient time and effort to perform it satisfactorily. The assignment should be stated clearly; critical scheduling dates must be agreed upon; and any expenses should be budgeted in advance. For example, if one task involves a marketing research survey, all of these task specifications would need to be worked out in advance to make sure you will obtain the information at the right time and in a form that is applicable to your planning task.

Determine When Each Planning Task Must Be Started and Completed

You cannot get everything going at once, because planning involves a sequence of steps. Some steps cannot be begun until others have been completed. For example, you cannot identify problems and opportunities until the situation analysis has been finished. Strategies are pointless unless objectives have been defined.

You will always be pressed for time, so an early start is desirable. But, regardless of how early or late you begin, you must finish all the steps on time and in the proper sequence.

The best way to do this is to apply the basic scheduling procedure known as PERT (Program Evaluation and Review Technique). It involves:

- Determining the steps necessary to complete each task as well as the key component activities of each
- Arranging the tasks sequentially, noting wherever unrelated tasks can be carried on simultaneously, but always making sure that all tasks are arranged in the proper order so that activities that need to precede others are placed early in the sequence
- Preparing a schedule of specific starting and completion dates for each task, working backwards from the date when the plan is to be completed
- Preparing some type of chart of the planning activities so that you can visually check your progress, determine if the overall schedule is being met, and spot potential problems and their impacts before they occur.

Identify the Expected Specific Outcome of Each Planning Task

This critical aspect of planning is sometimes neglected or misunderstood. It may appear obvious that performing a particular task produces a predictable result, but this is not necessarily so. Unless a task is very tightly defined, the outcome can vary considerably, depending on the approach taken by the planner and the way the results are presented.

For example, suppose you ask another person (perhaps somebody in the marketing research department) to "prepare an economic forecast" in connection with a plan for marketing diesel fuel to the agricultural market in the Midwest. Unless you specify exactly what you want, you are likely to get almost anything from a discussion of political conditions in the petroleum-producing regions of the Middle East to an estimate of the number of diesel-powered Volkswagen Rabbits in Kansas.

If you need this particular information, fine. But chances are, you really want an estimate of diesel fuel sales to large Kansas wheat farmers, presented in thousands of gallons by three-month periods for the years 1988–1990. It is this kind of specific outcome that needs to be identified for each task.

It is important to require tangible evidence of task outcomes. Insist on written reports, thoroughly documented. Subsequently, you may want to rely heavily on these task results. You want the results to be reliable, and you want evidence to support their validity.

Estimate the Funds (Budget) Necessary to Complete the Planning Tasks

This is most likely to be important for planning activities that are assigned to outside sources, such as marketing research firms and advertising agencies. Make sure you understand the various billing arrangements these organizations employ. This may even be important when such tasks are performed internally. For instance, a number of marketing research departments "sell" their services to other arms of the company.

Assuming that funds are available, don't be reluctant to "go outside" for planning assistance. Your time is valuable. Actually, it may be more economical to hire external help than to do everything yourself. Besides, an outside view is often fresh and objective. Your advertising agency is a potential source of external planning assistance, for example. Of course, there are always management consultants ready to go to work, and if your company is a subsidiary of a larger corporation, its planning staff may be of considerable assistance.

Equally important is not becoming bogged down with paper-and-pencil work. Be sure you have a capable assistant who can handle the data gathering and maintain a good filing system to keep track of the considerable amount of information that will be collected. Of course, you cannot delegate critical analytic work, but you will find that a capable assistant will free you up to do the analysis and thinking that are so critical to the preparation of a good marketing plan.

3
Prerequisites
for Marketing Planning

The marketing planner cannot suddenly decide, "Today I'm going to start my plan." Several steps need to be taken and a number of prerequisites must be satisfied before you can begin. This is primarily because of the derivative character of a marketing plan. As we have seen, it does not, and cannot, stand alone. The marketing plan is developed out of the business plan, and the business plan finds its origin in the organization's overall strategic plan. This linkage must be clearly established. Likewise, a functional plan (such as a product-line marketing plan or an advertising campaign) must be recognized as one of the means by which higher-order plans are implemented.

Let us return briefly to the Pet, Inc. example presented in the previous chapter. The company president, heeding the advice of the management consultants, determined to change the basic strategic direction of the business. New businesses were to be developed and acquired in order to assure long-term growth and improved profitability. Within the Grocery Products area, an entirely new product concept was developed—the 400-calorie liquid diet food. The strategic purpose of this business was to utilize the company's capability in serving an emerging market—the diet-conscious consumer. Marketing plans for the development, testing, and introduction of the new product were formulated. The critical decision to position the new product as a "food" and not as a pharmaceutical led to developing an advertising campaign featuring the Sego Girl, who epitomized the copy line "For the Joy of a Slender Figure." Later, when the Food and Drug Administration banned the use of cyclamates, Pet repositioned its offering in the form of Sego Bars, adapting to the changing environment in which the company operated but keeping the Sego Girl as the spokesperson for the brand. In a very real sense, the advertising campaign was simply an extension of the corporate strategy. Thus, the marketing planning at each level of the business was linked closely to the programs at other levels.

Unfortunately, this clear linkage is not always so well established. Even if not, the marketing planner still must have input from upper management before the planning process can begin. We call these upper-management inputs the *planning prerequisites.*

The Statement of Corporate Mission

The statement of corporate mission defines the market domain within which an organization seeks to attain its objectives. It describes the nature of the business, primarily by identifying the types of customers the company has elected to serve.

The next aspect of a corporate mission is the determination of the kinds of products and services that the company intends to offer its customers. It is best to think in generic terms here, rather than in specific products. A good way to do this is to define the mission in terms of benefits it will offer. This frees the planner from the myopic viewpoint that ties his or her view of a company mission to a particular product. For example, consider how important it has been for AT&T to shed its view of itself as a "telephone" company. It is really in the information-movement business.

A third dimension to the corporate mission concerns the level of technological development at which the company intends to operate. Obviously, this dimension differs considerably from one company to the next, and an illustration of its application, together with the other two dimensions of corporate mission, may be helpful. Exhibit 3.1 shows a three-dimensional chart of the corporate mission of Federal Express at two different points in its development. Initially, the company served a very limited customer base—businesses in selected U.S. city pairs—and offered only delivery of medium-size packages by company truck. Later, Federal Express expanded its customer base to include individuals and businesses throughout the U.S. and Canada. Its offerings were expanded to include overnight delivery of letters and packages by fleets of trucks and planes. In a still later stage of its evolution, Federal Express explored an entirely new technology: the electronic delivery of encoded materials. Unable to compete with established communications companies, Federal Express withdrew, at least temporarily, from this business in 1986.

A worksheet for recording the statement of corporate mission is found in Exhibit 3.2. Ideally, there should already be a company document that sets forth the information required. If not, you should discuss the company's mission with senior and peer executives who can contribute to a clear statement of the scope and purpose of the business.

A blank chart for preparing a diagram similar to the Federal Express corporate mission chart is found in Exhibit 3.3. You will probably find it very useful in graphing both your company's present mission, as well as future missions your management might consider. A good rule of thumb in constructing such a chart is to keep the most basic and familiar markets, offerings, and technologies closest to the center of the diagram. Thus, as you expand the corporate mission, you address customers, products, and technologies with which you are less and less familiar. The chart can also be used to diagram the decision to narrow, rather than to expand, a company's mission. Another interesting use is to plot the company's major competitors on similar diagrams and overlay them upon each other to determine the extent of direct overlap with your

(text continues on p. 24)

Exhibit 3.1. The corporate mission of Federal Express.

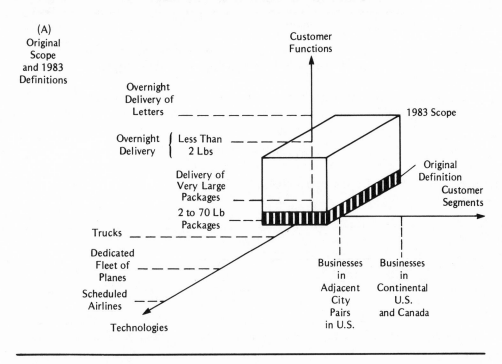

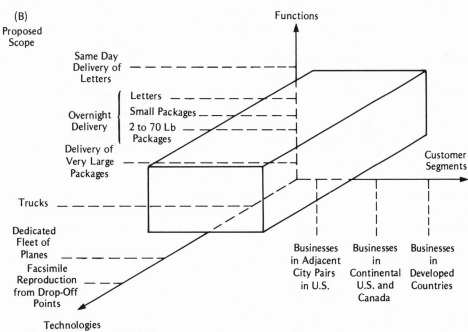

Source: Day, George. *Strategic Market Planning* (St. Paul, Minn.: West Publishing Company, 1984), p. 21.

Exhibit 3.2.   Corporate mission statement worksheet.

Complete this worksheet in four stages:

1. Provide the information requested for the business as it now operates.
2. Provide the information requested for the business as it might operate by changing its mission.
3. Write short mission statements to summarize the information provided.
4. Construct the mission charts as provided for in Exhibit 3.3.

The Business Today

1. List the major types of customers that your company presently serves:

   _____

   _____

   _____

2. List the major types of products that your company presently offers to the customers listed above:

   _____

   _____

   _____

3. List the levels of technology that your company employs in serving its present customers:

   _____

   _____

   _____

   _____

MISSION STATEMENT: _____

_____

_____

Exhibit 3.2. Continued.

The Business in the Future

1. List the major types of customers that your company could serve if it changed its mission:

   _____

   _____

   _____

   _____

2. List the major types of products that your company would have to offer to the customers listed above:

   _____

   _____

   _____

   _____

3. List the levels of technology that your company would have to employ to serve the customers listed above:

   _____

   _____

   _____

   _____

MISSION STATEMENT: _____

_____

_____

_____

_____

_____

Exhibit 3.3.   Corporate mission chart worksheet.

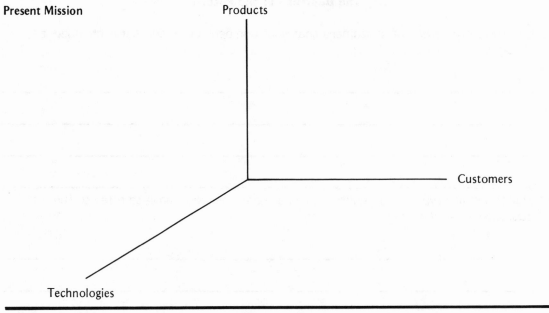

Present Mission

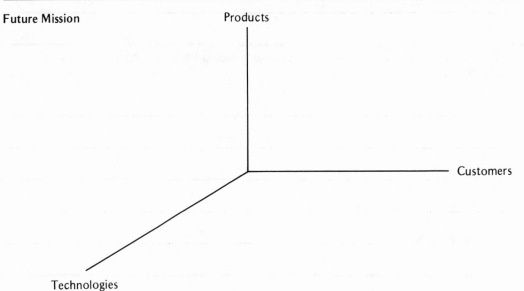

Future Mission

company and with each other. Changing a company's mission does not occur frequently, but when it does it has a dramatic impact on the way in which the company
operates. Consider these examples:

1. Sears expands its merchandising from its traditional lines into real estate, insurance, and financial services.

2. At the same time, J.C. Penney sheds many of its hard lines, such as lawn and garden supplies, tools, and appliances, to concentrate on merchandising soft goods.
3. Spiegel, the old general-merchandise catalog house, completely redirected its efforts to cater to upscale, professional women with lines of high-fashion apparel and home furnishings.
4. Burroughs (now merged with Sperry to form Unisys), Zenith, NCR, and other firms have gone into the computer business with the intent of leaving behind older, mature businesses in favor of growth in newer, high-technology markets.

Only One Mission

It should be very obvious. A company can have only one mission statement. Sometimes, when the mission is not clear and various planners in the company state their own versions of what they think that mission to be, very different perspectives materialize. All marketing planners must function under the same overall statement of corporate mission if their various programs are to be consistent and synergistic. Thus, it becomes the prime responsibility of top management to provide this prerequisite for the marketing planning process.

Division and Product Area Charters

The statement of corporate mission gives overall direction to the marketing planner, but in a decentralized organization, it is usually too general to offer specific guidance in developing a product-line marketing plan. Instead, marketing planners look to divisional or business-unit charters. For example, a large agribusiness has several very large business units. They include:

fertilizer and agricultural chemicals
feed and animal health products
petroleum products
farm equipment and supplies
consumer packaged-good products

A charter should clearly define the scope of activity for each of these business units. The preferable method is to distinguish them according to their products (or services) and the markets served. Other bases might be according to customer type—a version of market focus—or by geographical coverage.

A business unit such as the petroleum products in the example just given can be further divided into program units—for instance, refined fuels and tires, batteries, and accessories. Most marketing planning is done at the program-unit level, as for specific products or brands. The planning that is done at the business-unit level is usually broader in scope and is properly viewed as *business planning*.

Exhibit 3.4. Business unit charter worksheet.

Complete this worksheet in three stages:

1. Provide the information requested for the business unit as it now operates.
2. Provide the information requested for the business unit as it might operate by changing its charter.
3. Write short charter statements to summarize the information provided.

The Business Unit Today

1. List the major types of customers that your business unit presently serves:

_____

_____

_____

_____

2. List the major types of products that your business unit presently offers to the customers listed above:

_____

_____

_____

_____

3. List the levels of technology that your business unit employs in serving its present customers:

_____

_____

_____

_____

CHARTER STATEMENT: _____

_____

_____

_____

Exhibit 3.4.   Continued.

The Business Unit in the Future

1. List the major types of customers that your business unit could serve if it changed its charter:

    _____

    _____

    _____

2. List the major types of products that your business unit would have to offer to the customers listed above:

    _____

    _____

    _____

3. List the levels of technology that your business unit would have to employ in order to serve the customers listed above:

    _____

    _____

    _____

CHARTER STATEMENT: _____

_____

_____

_____

Marketing planners should not have to "create" charter statements. These should be provided by upper management. Hence statements of corporate mission and charters are properly viewed as prerequisites for marketing planning.

A worksheet for recording the divisional or strategic business-unit charter is found in Exhibit 3.4. Ideally, there should be a company document that sets forth this information. If not, you should discuss the charter statement with other executives, especially those in other divisions whose activities might overlap with yours.

Objectives and Subobjectives

The ultimate objective of any business (except not-for-profit organizations, which present a special case) is to provide an acceptable return on the organization's investment while simultaneously addressing its underlying purpose of serving customers. Profit is the reward for doing this well, and a company may correctly view its long-run earnings as an indication of how well it has served the market.

Requirements of Objectives

According to Philip Kotler, the statement of a company's objectives must meet four requirements.[1]

Above all, *the objective must be stated quantitatively*—in terms both of what is expected and when it must be achieved. If you encounter a statement such as, "The objective of this company is to grow significantly and to attain a position of leadership in the industry," you can be sure that this first requirement has not been met. The growth is not specific with respect to either volume or rate, nor has the time period during which this growth is expected been made explicit. The term *leadership* is not defined and might not refer at all to becoming the share leader, although this is what one would ordinarily assume.

Second, *an objective must be realistic*. That is, the company must be capable of achieving it with existing resources or with resources it can afford to acquire. There is no place in formal marketing plans for the "good old college try." In a paraphrase of the familiar expression, one might well say, "The path to marketing failure is paved with unrealistic objectives." Necessity is not the mother of invention. Opportunity is. The test of realism for any objective must be based on two facts: (1) There is a valid opportunity and (2) the company has the capabilities necessary to exploit that opportunity properly. For this reason, it may not be possible to assess the realism of any particular objective until the marketing situation analysis has been conducted.

Third, *any set of company objectives must be consistent*. Two elements are involved. First, marketing objectives must be consistent with those established in manufacturing, finance, research and development, and so on. This consistency is absolutely necessary if proper coordination within the business unit is to be achieved. An even more basic aspect of consistency is the importance of setting objectives that do not work against each other. For example, it is virtually impossible to increase market share and short-term profits at the same time. In a much tighter context, imagine the dilemma of a marketing manager who is asked to build volume on a new product without cannibalizing sales of a similar product in the company's product line. For example, how does Coca-Cola build demand for Diet Coke without adversely affecting sales of Tab?

The fourth requirement is that *objectives be linked hierarchically*. That is, there should be a relationship between the objectives set at any level of the business and the objectives established for the levels both above and below it in the organization. This becomes especially difficult, since the way in which goals are stated often differs from one organizational level to the next. The following example shows the linkage among objectives that are stated at different levels and the manner in which each objective is correspondingly changed.

Let us assume that the president of a major food products company recognizes the importance of improving that company's financial performance. Earnings must be improved, and the measure by which this is to be determined is earnings per common share. An objective of $5 per share has been set and approved by the board of directors. Let us also assume that, in view of general economic conditions and the very competitive nature of the markets in which the company operates, this will not be an easy goal to attain.

How does the company president proceed? He uses the tools of planning that are available. He looks to the next lower level in the management hierarchy—to the several divisions that make up the company. Some of these divisions offer greater prospects for improving earnings than do others, but all must have some part to play. Suppose, for example, that one of the company's largest business units is its coffee division, a fully integrated business that grows, processes, and markets various brands of coffee for consumers and institutional use. The president feels that this business unit is in a good position to bear the lion's share of the profit improvement. He calls the vice president of the coffee division to his office and tells him something like, "Jim, you'll be glad to know that I've worked out a strategy to achieve the goal of improving earnings to $5 a share. You and your people will do it. Next year, I want the coffee division to post earnings of twenty-five percent on employed assets. How you do it is entirely up to you and your team."

The vice president returns to his office, thinking about the ways in which his division can improve its profit performance. He naturally reviews in his mind the situations faced by the two major product groups in his division: retail brands and institutional coffee. He knows that the institutional business is highly competitive and not particularly brand loyal. The way to pick up earnings is to improve the market share in the consumer end of the business. Following through with this idea, he asks the marketing manager for consumer brands to stop by his office. In much the same way that the president talked to him, Jim says to his subordinate manager, "Bill, you'll be interested to know that I've worked out a plan to achieve the twenty-five percent ROI that the front office has asked us to produce next year. I'm expecting you and your brand managers to do the job. Overall, I want you folks to improve our share of the retail coffee business to forty percent."

The marketing director understands that the ball is now in his court. What should his strategy be? Simple enough. He already knows that some of the consumer brands are growing, others are fairly stable, and some have actually begun to lose ground. To improve the market share, his various brand managers are all going to have to perform well, each pursuing a strategy appropriate for the circumstances faced by his or her brand.

The manager knows that the best hope of a substantial improvement in overall share lies with the growth brands. So he asks the brand manager of the company's new decaffeinated coffee line to come to a strategy session. The marketing director starts the meeting this way. "Joan," he says, "you're in charge of the hottest product we have in this brand group. Overall, we're looking for a substantial improvement in market share, and I want you to lead this effort by boosting your new 'decaf' to the dominant share spot in the trade. Specifically, I want to see your share figures go up by at least fifty percent next year. Any ideas on how you'll go about that?"

The brand manager is on the spot. It appears that the whole burden of improving earnings has come down on her shoulders. "Not to worry," she responds. (Chances are, however, that a cold shudder went down her spine.) "We have just completed some new research that suggests a great new creative approach. We really believe that we can reposition our 'decaf' right in on top of the regular coffee brands and come out on top. It's a matter of taste and perception. Our taste tests prove we have the equal of any brewed regular coffee. All we have to do is convince people that 'decaf' isn't just for invalids and health freaks. Give me the ad budget to achieve the reach and frequency we need, and I'll deliver the share points."

With a little less assurance than her words implied, the "decaf" brand manager goes back to her office to firm up her ideas on the marketing program for her brand. She decides to call a meeting of the brand team for the next morning. This team, composed of the brand manager, the sales manager, a representative from manufacturing, and the account executive from the ad agency, meets the following morning. Joan opens the meeting this way. "Okay, this is how it is. We're shooting for thirty-two share points in the 'decaf' market and, what is more important, for a ten percent share of the total coffee business. Sales must convert that goal into specific targets for all major territories and accounts. I want the agency to think in terms of achieving a significant shift in consumer perception. By year end, I want at least half of all heavy coffee drinkers to be convinced that 'decaf' is real coffee for everyday coffee drinkers and to associate that new idea with our brand. I want media back here in two weeks with reach and frequency goals, and I want creative in here with testable concepts by the end of the month. Okay, everybody—go to it."

Finally, something is going to happen. People who do things in the business have assignments. The plan to achieve earnings of $5 per share has been initiated.

To review briefly, the hierarchy of objectives just described is pictured as an inverted staircase, as shown below.

Level	Statement Form	Example
Corporate objective	Earnings per share	$5
Divisional objective	Return on investment	25%
Product area	Market share	40%
Brand	Market share	10%
Sales	Volume	50% increase
Advertising	Cognitive change	Awareness = 50%

One moves down this staircase of objectives by asking how the goal at each level is to be accomplished. The answer provides the objective for the next level lower in the hierarchy. For example, the objective of achieving $5 earnings per share is to be met by having one (among several) division earn an ROI of 25 percent. The advertising objective of achieving 50 percent awareness stemmed from the brand objective of winning a 10 percent market share, which, in turn, emanated from the overall 40 percent market share objective. The sales management objective was similarly derived. And, of course, all these marketing objectives were determined by the divisional objective of attaining a 25 percent ROI. Ultimately, the corporate objective set the pace for the rest of the organization.

Of course, this example is extremely oversimplified. It may take many weeks for this linkage to be established. Moreover, what has been illustrated is simply one strategic path down through an organization. It is highly unlikely that only one division, one business group, or one brand would be singled out for attention. In practice, the president would issue instructions to each of several divisional vice presidents. Divisional heads would develop plans for a number of business groups. Marketing directors would initiate plans for each and every brand. So what looks at first like a staircase turns out to be only one face of a multisided pyramid. Each side represents a different planning hierarchy, with each contributing in its own way to the achievement of the overall company objective.

In practice, it is even more complex than the pyramid example implies, for there are horizontal relationships involved, too. For example, several brand managers may use the same sales organization. The products of more than one division may be made in the same factory or stored in the same warehouses. Integrating these relationships is no simple task. But the harsh reality is that, unless the hierarchy of objectives is worked out, the possible conflicts and need for integration and cooperation may never be realized.

Traditionally, most marketing planning was functional—that is, sales, advertising, and the like—and the tradition still influences planning in some companies. The result is a multiplicity of plans all moving in different directions. The planning is driven from the bottom, rather than the top. It *should* work the other way around. Thus, while the functional planner (such as an advertising or sales manager) may be sorely tempted to set functional goals, pretty much ignoring the system of objectives higher up in the hierarchy, this practice is not only wrong, it is dangerous. Sales or advertising is never an end in itself; its purpose is first to support the larger marketing strategy and, ultimately, to contribute to the economic success of the company as a whole.

The worksheet displayed in Exhibit 3.5 can be adapted to your planning situation. Its purpose is to help you outline the planning hierarchy by having you identify the various organizational levels involved in the development of plans that impact on marketing. Starting at the top, you will identify overall company objectives and the business strategies that have been developed to achieve them. Then note in the right-hand column whether these objectives meet the four requirements given earlier: quantitatively stated, realistic, consistent, and hierarchically linked.

The most interesting aspect about this worksheet is how it visibly demonstrates that the strategies at one level identify the objectives at the next lower level in the

Exhibit 3.5. Worksheet for identifying the hierarchy of objectives.

	Requirements Met?			
	Obj. "a"		Obj. "b"	
	Yes	No	Yes	No

Top level (corporate): _____ (name)
   1. Objectives:

	Yes	No	Yes	No
Quantitative	—	—	—	—
Realistic	—	—	—	—
Consistent	—	—	—	—
Hierarchical	—	—	—	—

     a. _____

     b. _____

  2. Strategies (as they involve the next
     lower level planning units):

     a. _____

     b. _____

Second level (SBU) _____ (name)
  1. Objectives:

	Yes	No	Yes	No
Quantitative	—	—	—	—
Realistic	—	—	—	—
Consistent	—	—	—	—
Hierarchical	—	—	—	—

     a. _____

     b. _____

  2. Strategies (as they involve the next
     lower level planning units):

     a. _____

     b. _____

Third level (marketing) _____ (name)
  1. Objectives:

	Yes	No	Yes	No
Quantitative	—	—	—	—
Realistic	—	—	—	—
Consistent	—	—	—	—
Hierarchical	—	—	—	—

     a. _____

     b. _____

hierarchy. This is why arrows are drawn from the strategy section at each level (except the last) to the objective section at the planning level below it. It suggests a very useful way to identify your objectives: Discover them in your boss's strategy. This will enable you to make sure that the marketing program you eventually develop will be related properly to strategies higher in the hierarchy.

Exhibit 3.5.   Continued.

	Obj. "a"		Obj. "b"	
Requirements Met?	Yes	No	Yes	No

2. Strategies (as they involve the next
   lower level planning units):

   a. _____

   b. _____

Fourth level (product/market) _____ (name)

1. Objectives:

   a. _____

   b. _____

2. Strategies (as they involve the next
   lower level planning units):

   a. _____

   b. _____

	Obj. "a"		Obj. "b"	
Quantitative	__	__	__	__
Realistic	__	__	__	__
Consistent	__	__	__	__
Hierarchical	__	__	__	__

Fifth level (marketing function) _____ (name)

1. Objectives:

   a. _____

   b. _____

2. Strategies (as they involve the next
   lower level planning units):

   a. _____

   b. _____

	Obj. "a"		Obj. "b"	
Quantitative	__	__	__	__
Realistic	__	__	__	__
Consistent	__	__	__	__
Hierarchical	__	__	__	__

To discover this linkage properly, *do not* go to your superior and ask, "What are my objectives for next year?" Instead ask, "What is your strategy for next year and what role do you see my department playing in its implementation?" The answer to this question will tell you exactly how your program should link up with the next higher level and, therefore, what your objectives should be.

Exhibit 3.6. Worksheet for identification of objectives in the absence of a top-down hierarchy.

Requirements Met?

	Obj. "a"		Obj. "b"	
	Yes	No	Yes	No

Top level (corporate): _____ (name)

1. Objectives:

    a. _____

    b. _____

2. Strategies (as they involve the next lower level planning units):

    a. _____

    b. _____

	Yes	No	Yes	No
Quantitative	___	___	___	___
Realistic	___	___	___	___
Consistent	___	___	___	___
Hierarchical	___	___	___	___

Plant Manager 1
1. Objectives:

    a. _____

    b. _____

2. Strategies:

    a. _____

    b. _____

Plant Manager 2
1. Objectives:

    a. _____

    b. _____

2. Strategies:

    a. _____

    b. _____

Controller
1. Objectives:

    a. _____

    b. _____

2. Strategies:

    a. _____

    b. _____

Requirements Met?

	Obj. "a"		Obj. "b"	
	Yes	No	Yes	No

Marketing

1. Objectives:

    a. _____

    b. _____

2. Strategies:

    a. _____

    b. _____

	Yes	No	Yes	No
Quantitative	___	___	___	___
Realistic	___	___	___	___
Consistent	___	___	___	___
Hierarchical	___	___	___	___

Because of the great value that understanding these relationships can add to your own planning efforts, this worksheet should be prepared as soon as the situation analysis has been completed.

You may encounter some difficulty in identifying the various levels in the hierarchy, but in organizations with some semblance of vertical structure, a logical flow of planning responsibility can usually be detected. If it cannot, then you may have discovered a critical internal weakness that needs to be corrected. Consider this dilemma. You are a sales manager in a business that does not have a clear sense of marketing direction. There are two plant managers, and your sales force sells the outputs of both plants. The company's business plan is basically a financial one. The company controller believes his or her job is to protect the owners' equity. As a sales manager, you might be given objectives from all three of these executives, and their objectives are quite likely to conflict with one another. Each plant manager would probably want to maximize sales volume of the products his or her factory makes, up to capacity. If cutting price is necessary to generate volume, this is probably what each plant manager would recommend. The controller, on the other hand, wants to maximize profits. To do this, he or she would want to keep prices up and marketing costs down. In such a situation, the hierarchical arrangement breaks down, and the planner must employ a worksheet that models the situation as it actually is. Using the example just mentioned, the chart might look like the one that appears in Exhibit 3.6. It should be readily apparent from this exhibit that the suboptimizing that is going on not only places the sales department in an almost impossible position but produces a set of objectives for the company that fails to meet the requirements.

Company Policies

Top management has the prerogative of establishing rules for the conduct of the business. Some of these rules may affect marketing, either directly or indirectly. For example, a company policy may dictate the use of a logo or slogan. Less obvious, perhaps, is a policy based on a philosophical viewpoint that all customers, regardless of size or cost of service, should be treated equally.

A major chemical company, which traditionally had limited itself to the development and marketing of commodity and specialty chemicals for industrial use, developed a remarkably effective laundry detergent and decided to get directly involved in consumer marketing. The effort was very successful, and within a few years this chemical company had gained a substantial share of the market. Over this same period, the company began to experience a softening in sales of its basic chemicals to other companies that also made laundry detergents. Eventually, the profits from the detergent business were insufficient to compensate for the loss of the industrial chemical sales. The solution was to get out of the consumer end of the business and stick to the company's core business of industrial chemicals. To avoid other costly ventures of this sort, the company established a firm policy that it would never compete directly with its own customers. (Not a bad rule for most companies to follow!)

Exhibit 3.7.   Policy worksheet.

List below the policies (standing rules) that you must keep in mind as you develop your marketing plan. These may be written policies from a company policy manual, or they may be generally understood rules that marketing planners in the organization are expected to obey. In preparing this list it is a good idea to make sure that (1) you have stated the policy correctly and (2) the policy is still in effect.

	Policy	Source	Current? (check when confirmed)
1.	_____	_____	[ ]
	_____		
2.	_____	_____	[ ]
	_____		
3.	_____	_____	[ ]
	_____		
4.	_____	_____	[ ]
	_____		
5.	_____	_____	[ ]
	_____		
6.	_____	_____	[ ]
	_____		
7.	_____	_____	[ ]
	_____		
8.	_____	_____	[ ]
	_____		
9.	_____	_____	[ ]
	_____		
10.	_____	_____	[ ]
	_____		

Another fairly common company policy dictates how much business a company wants to do with any given customer. For example, for many years Levi Strauss limited its volume with any one retailer to about 5 percent of total sales. The reason? To avoid the devastating impact that the loss of any one account could have on total company volume.

To be sure, most policies are restrictive, indicating what a marketing planner *cannot* consider in developing a strategy. Sometimes, however, a policy may actually force consideration of innovative and worthwhile opportunities. For example, one well-known company has a policy which requires that each operating unit introduce at least one new product every year.

Exhibit 3.7 is a worksheet for summarizing the various policies you need to keep in mind as you develop your marketing plan. These policies may come from different sources in the organization. Sometimes they are formalized in a company policy manual. More often, they are found in various memoranda, issued from time to time as the need arises. Often, however, they are simply part of the company culture—rules that are not formally recorded but that everybody understands must be obeyed.

Periodically, you should update this worksheet. Whenever a new rule is promulgated, record it in your planning documentation. And, from time to time, confirm that the policies you have on your worksheet are still in effect. Your worksheet should indicate the individual who or department which has issued the policy. When you have confirmed its current status, check the appropriate box on the worksheet. Of course, any old policies that have been reversed should be eliminated from your list.

Organization

Marketing plans ordinarily should be written for organizational components that are capable of carrying them out. This is especially true of tactical plans. If this were not the case, the basic purpose of planning could not be achieved. This means, in general, that your marketing plan is not the place for recommendations regarding major organizational changes. Of course, minor adjustments in organization in order to implement a proposed strategy are often necessary. In situations in which an otherwise viable strategy may require a major organizational change, deal with this issue early in the planning stages so that the necessary structural modifications can be instituted before the plan is put into place.

Because of its pervasive character, marketing responsibility is often rather widely dispersed across an organization. Many departments outside the marketing group may be intimately involved in the development of marketing plans. In general, though, the marketing staff is ultimately responsible for its development. This poses a distinct challenge. The responsibility for developing the plan is there, but the authority to command the involvement of nonmarketing areas seldom is. This is the classic paradox of product management: a system with managers who cannot manage because they do not have authority commensurate with their responsibility. Fortunately, many marketing planners have learned to live with this situation, substituting other leadership skills for the formal authority they do not possess. This topic is considered in more detail in Chapter 9.

Exhibit 3.8.   Organization charts.

On this worksheet (or as many as required), draw the organization charts that describe the various parts of the company and/or business unit. Shade or color all those positions that are involved in the preparation and/or implementation of your marketing plan.

It is important at this preliminary stage of the planning process to become familiar with the organizational structure through which you will produce and implement your marketing plan. Develop organization charts that identify the various positions or departments that will be involved in the marketing planning process (see Exhibit 3.8). Since marketing issues carry all the way to the top of an organization and affect almost every other function in a business, you should start with an organization chart of the entire company. Next you want a chart of your division or strategic business unit. Finally, you need a chart of the marketing department. As you move down the company hierarchy, your charts will necessarily become more detailed. Ideally, the business unit and marketing department charts should identify every individual with whom you will be working in developing and implementing the marketing plan.

Business Strategy

We've already referred to the overall business plan as the immediate source of marketing objectives. It is necessary here only to point out that the overall marketing strategy included in the business plan, together with the supporting analysis, should provide the point of departure for product-line marketing planning.

Regrettably, in many companies the overall business plan does not contain sufficient information. The marketing situation analysis is seldom complete, and the strategy statements are often too general to provide good marketing direction. Business plans are often restricted to financial matters, with insufficient attention to strategic issues.

The various marketing planning steps described in the next three chapters include some activities that might be considered part of an overall business planning process. However, because many business plans are essentially financial planning documents and do not contain the marketing information necessary to develop marketing strategy, the planning process described in these chapters requires the development of marketing strategy before the details of the tactical annual plan are considered.

Part II
The Marketing Planning Process

Part II contains a complete description of the marketing planning process. The preparatory steps have been taken. You have a broad understanding of what marketing is. You understand the scope and content of a marketing plan. You have planned your planning, and you have seen that the planning prerequisites have been satisfied. You are ready to get started.

As pointed out in Chapter 2, the marketing planning process involves 14 steps. They have been broken into three groups, or phases. Phase I comprises the analysis steps and is covered in Chapters 4 and 5. The steps in developing marketing strategy are contained in Phase II, the subject of Chapter 6. Phase III, the finalization steps, is addressed in Chapter 7. These four chapters provide the specifics of marketing planning. They are long chapters. Take each in stages, breaking at the end of major sections, to make sure you understand the process as it unfolds.

Each step is carefully described and its relationship to the marketing management task is explained. When you have finished reading these chapters, you should know how to prepare a marketing plan. You will also have a much deeper appreciation of the thought processes that go into its development. Numerous exhibits and examples are provided, together with worksheets that you can use in preparing your own plan.

4
The Situation Analysis

This chapter begins the discussion of the marketing planning process. In it, we cover four of the five Phase I steps, numbers 1 through 4. These are, as you recall from Exhibit 2.1:

1. Review last year's plan
2. Satisfy the planning prerequisites
3. Decide on the product/market focus
4. Prepare the situation analysis

Step 1:
Reviewing the Previous Year's Planning Effort

There is really no termination point to the planning process. It is a cycle in which the results of one planning exercise become input to the next. So, as you begin to think about preparing a new plan, your first step is to review the previous year's efforts and their results. Focus on these points:

Compare Results to Objectives

Since the purpose of planning is to produce results, the first point of concern is to answer the question, "How well did the plan work last year?"

The proper procedure is to refer to the previous year's plan (as amended, of course), and note every statement of a major objective or subobjective in the document. If properly stated, these objectives were expressed quantitatively with respect both to amount and time frame, and so comparisons of them to measured results should be relatively easy. Don't be overly alarmed if objectives and results did not perfectly agree. No plan is perfect. Circumstances change. But if there was a significant variance, you should endeavor to uncover the reasons for it. This will help you better understand the planning challenge and enable you to reduce the error in the next plan.

Evaluate the Accuracy of Assumptions and Analysis

Closely related to variance analysis is a review of how well last year's plan dealt with the expected marketing situation. Did the intervening months reveal any important errors in the situation analysis? Were most of the critical factors properly identified and assessed? Were the planning assumptions about the economy, competition, and the like essentially correct? How accurate was the sales forecast? If the forecast missed badly, what was the reason? Was something left out? If so, could it have been spotted? How?

Review the Planning Document

The only residual evidence of a planning exercise is the written marketing plan. It was the basis for implementation and control. It remains the only permanent record of the facts and the reasoning behind the strategies and tactics that were employed. Before beginning a new planning effort, review the documents that the previous year's planning exercise produced. This review might address these points:

1. Was the plan appropriate and adequate? Did it address the most important issues thoroughly and correctly?
2. Was the plan sufficiently flexible? Was there enough pliability in the plan to permit its adaption to changes in the external environment?
3. Was the plan sufficiently implementable? This question covers a wide range of concerns, but its basic purpose is to determine if the company was able to undertake the activities necessary to put the plan into action.

How Well Was the Plan Implemented?

Execution must follow planning, or the planning will have been a waste of time and effort. In part, this is related to how well the plan could be implemented. But it is also a matter of the willingness and ability of people in the organization to use the plan.

Review all materials that were developed as a part of the plan. This includes such elements as marketing research projects, advertising and sales promotion programs, and the like. Unfortunately, these materials are frequently scattered throughout the company as they are developed and used. It is a good idea for you to keep copies of all advertisements, schedules, promotions, and other implementation materials for this planning review stage. This examination should focus on the quality of these tactical materials and their consistency with the overall marketing plan.

Exhibit 4.1. Planning review summary.

Problem/Deficiency	Changes to Be Made This Year

I. The Planning Process:

_____

_____

_____

_____

II. The Document:

_____

_____

_____

_____

III. Implementation:

_____

_____

_____

_____

IV. Results:

_____

_____

_____

_____

Was the Planning Procedure Utilized and Did It Work Satisfactorily?

The final aspect of this first step of the planning sequence involves a review of the planning procedure used the previous year. There are two considerations: (1) How faithfully was the planning procedure followed? (2) Were these procedures appropriate to the particular marketing situation?

It is usually desirable to produce a summary of the outcome of Step 1. Exhibit 4.1 is a worksheet for this purpose. It is set up in two columns. In the left-hand column, record the most serious problems you have found with last year's planning, the plan itself, its implementation, and its results. In the right-hand column you will note the changes to be made in this year's plan. Space is provided for only four items on each list. If more room is needed, additional sheets can be added. Keep this summary evaluation close at hand as you proceed to develop the next plan. There is no excuse for not correcting deficiencies in procedure. To the extent that these mistakes are corrected, next year's plan and its results should be substantially improved.

Step 2:
Making Sure the Planning Prerequisites Have Been Satisfied

Chapter 3 described six important planning prerequisites:

1. Statement of corporate mission
2. Division and SBU charters
3. Objectives and subobjectives
4. Company policies
5. Organization
6. Business strategy

None of these inputs is the direct responsibility of the marketing planner. They are determined or performed at higher levels of the company and, in some cases, even outside the mainstream of the marketing function.

Obtaining these inputs will not always be easy because other persons may not perceive the importance of this information or understand why you need it. As the marketing planning culture becomes more firmly established, these obstacles become less frequent and less serious. If you do fail to obtain these inputs, you will have to proxy for them by making plausible assumptions. Worksheets for recording these prerequisites were provided in Chapter 3.

Step 3:
Identifying the Product/Market Focus

Marketing plans must be prepared in ways that encourage implementation and produce the best possible results. This is partially a matter of organization. Plans must be prepared for every important organizational unit that has marketing responsibility. Most companies are organized into broad product categories, with product (or brand) subdivisions within each commodity area.

Marketing planning is normally done in each of these product subdivisions. Sales planning tends to be by major commodity groups and by geographical area. Advertising and promotion planning usually responds to the needs of both products and territories.

While organizationally convenient, product-line planning tends to neglect market segmentation strategy. Plans are executed by an organization, but they are directed at people—at target markets. It is just as important for the plan to be focused on a specific target market segment as it is for it to be properly related to one of the company's products. Unfortunately, this fit is seldom perfect. In general, the market served by any one product is actually composed of a number of market segments, several of which are usually of sufficient importance to require individual planning efforts.

There are numerous bases on which overall markets might be segmented. Take diesel fuel, for example. First, there are farm and nonfarm segments. Within the farm market, there may be numerous subsegments. Among these subsegments are geographical location, type of agriculture, size of farm, characteristics of buyers, and so on. Depending on the number of segments and their relative importance, a marketing planner may decide to focus on a few high-potential or major-problem segments. This premise then governs all the remaining steps of the planning process, because the complete planning process must be applied to each segment for which a plan is needed.

There is probably no other single aspect of marketing planning as important as selecting the correct target market and then positioning correctly against it. Matching the marketing program with the needs and nature of the targeted customer is the essential step in planning. The trick is to zero in tightly on the target. To overreach the target market is wasteful and frequently generates irritation on the part of those who are exposed to the program but who are not its intended prospects. It is equally wrong to underreach the market. The most serious blunder, of course, is to miss the target market altogether.

Mismatching can occur in any part of the marketing program. The price can be wrong. The product may be in the wrong stores. The package may be improperly designed. Doing all these things correctly depends first of all upon the proper selection of the target market. Hence the importance of this step in the planning procedure.

The selection of a target market may not be possible until after the situation analysis has been completed. One of the outcomes of the situation analysis is a target market matrix. With the information in this matrix, you should be able to select one or more product/market segments as strategic targets. A number of criteria can be employed in selecting market targets:

1. The segment must be specifically identified and measured. You must know who belongs in the segment and be able to measure the segment's demand.
2. The segment must evidence adequate potential. This requirement can be satisfied by comparing the segment's potential with the objective of your marketing strategy.

3. The segment must be economically accessible. This means that there must be some cost-effective means of reaching the segment.
4. The segment must react uniquely to marketing inputs. Whatever segment (or combination of segments) is eventually selected, it must be composed of potential customers who will react in similar and predictable ways to your marketing efforts. Unless this requirement holds, there is no purpose in segmenting.
5. A segment must be reasonably stable over time. Since a marketing strategy is a long-range plan that projects over a period of three to five years, it is highly desirable for there to be reasonable prospects for target market stability over the same time frame.

The marketing planner must evaluate each of the segments identified in the target market analysis and select the ones that appear to present the best targets of opportunity. In general, it is best not to select more than three or four separate segments. The reason for this is that a separate marketing plan must be developed for each target segment chosen.

Each target market that has been selected must be profiled. A general description of the target market should be included in the strategy statement; and a detailed profile, including both demographic and psychographic descriptors, should be documented.

Step 4:
Conducting the Situation Analysis

The situation analysis is an organized and comprehensive investigation of all those internal and external factors that can be expected to influence the outcome of your marketing program. To cover all this ground is an extremely ambitious undertaking. It implies that you will explore every facet of your company's marketing operation.

The situation analysis should focus primarily on those factors that are expected to influence *significantly* the marketing effort. This means that you will not be concerned with trivial information. You must identify, in advance, those elements that deserve inquiry and restrict your investigation to them.

Information Requirements for Marketing Planning

What kinds of information are pertinent for developing your marketing plan? It is the purpose of this chapter to answer this question. However, it may be useful to generalize about the types of information usually needed, and to review how these data are assembled and accessed in a marketing information system.

- Information About Customers and Markets. This information is absolutely critical in marketing planning. It is sourced through primary research projects and external data bases.

- Sales Information. The analysis of past sales and the forecast of future sales yield critical information for evaluating past performance and planning future strategy.
- Cost and Profit Information. Income and cost information, especially related to the products and programs for which the planner is responsible, is obtained from financial accounting reports, as well as special diagnostics involved in marketing cost and profitability analysis.
- Environmental Information. The marketing information system should contain data about the overall economic situation, the industry in which the firm operates, its channels of distribution, and its competitors.

Philip Kotler defines a marketing information system as follows:

> A marketing information system is a continuing and interacting structure of people, equipment, and procedures to gather, sort, analyze, evaluate, and distribute pertinent, timely, and accurate information for use by marketing decision makers to improve their marketing planning, implementation, and control.[1]

The marketing information system is composed of several subsystems. They are: (1) the internal data base, (2) the external data base, (3) the marketing research system, and (4) the decision support system. Let us consider each of these in turn.

Internal Data Base. This is the depository of all pertinent information generated within the company. Much of it comes from the accounting department, but it also comes from sales, manufacturing, and materials management.

External Data Base. This contains information obtained from sources outside the company. For example, an organization may subscribe to one or more external information services.

Marketing Research System. In contrast to the internal and external data bases, which contain information flowing into the system on a more or less regular schedule, marketing research information typically is generated on an "as needed" basis. However, once the research has been completed, the findings become an important source of information for future use.

Decision Support System. Shifts in technology and terminology are gradually taking place. The marketing information system is being brought closer to the day-to-day needs of the marketing planner by the use of the desktop personal computer and the development of decision-oriented software. The older designation—marketing information system—is being replaced by the term *decision support system* (DSS). The MIS really hasn't changed as much as the use of it has. Instead of having to go to a programmer in the data processing department to have information extracted and processed, the marketing planner can directly access the data base, download information to a personal computer, and then analyze it with one or more software packages.

How the Marketing Information System Works

A model showing the relationship between the flow of information and the processes of planning and controlling is found in Exhibit 4.2. Two flow lines are shown. The solid

Exhibit 4.2.   The marketing information system.

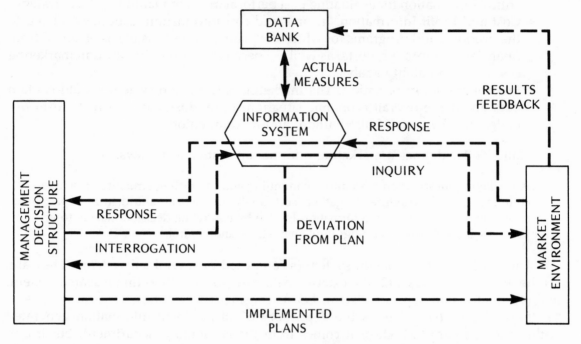

Source: Amstrutz, A. E. "The Marketing Executive and Management Information Systems," in R. M. Haas (ed.), *Science, Technology, and Marketing.* (Chicago: American Marketing Association, 1966), p. 85.

line depicts the flow of information required in the development of the marketing plan and its implementation. The dotted lines show the feedback required to evaluate performance and to initiate adjustments in strategy and tactics.

The process begins with the flow of information from the environment to the information system. The data may be generated routinely, or may be collected at the request of a marketing planner. This information, in relation to the needs of the company, leads to setting objectives which, in turn, drive the marketing planning process. After approval, the marketing plan becomes the basis for issuing implementation instructions. It also becomes part of the information system, where it becomes the basis for exercising control. Results feedback originates in the environment and flows back to the information system for analysis, particularly for comparison to the content of the marketing plan. From this evaluation of performance in relation to plan, exception (variance) reports are issued. Routine adjustments are initiated. If the variances persist, modifications to tactics or strategy may have to be made.

The Computer and Your Marketing Plan

No one in marketing is more dependent upon or can take such advantage of the information system as the marketing planner. Information is the raw material of the marketing plan. The data base is its source. Analytic software is the means by which the planner captures the information needed to make forward decisions.

The computer, whether mainframe or personal, is at the center of the information revolution. The capacity of the computer to store, process, and distribute information is tremendous, and growing rapidly. It is useful to describe briefly the ways in which marketing planners can make use of the two major systems.

The tradition of business computing has been the centralized data processing facility. The staff of a data processing department is made up of technicians who keep the machine running and programmers who assist users in inputting and withdrawing information from the computer. This is still the type of computer arrangement in many companies. The marketing planner relies primarily upon reports issued by the MIS department. A number of extremely useful analytic computer programs are available. Among these are statistical packages, such as the widely used SPSS (Statistical Package for Social Sciences) and SAS (Statistical Analysis System) programs.

The next generation of data analysis programs falls into the general category of decision support software. These programs permit the user to access the mainframe data base and employ simulation models with which to explore the possible outcomes of various decisions. Although the routines take some time to learn, the typical marketing manager could master the use of the software, and some of the programs are extremely user friendly.

Some decision support software permits the marketing planner to model his or her decision. The user imputs decision information and controlling assumptions. The computer generates an outcome, perhaps a comparison of the profitability of two or more alternative courses of action. Another type of decision support software enables the user to specify the model and then to analyze data to obtain insight on a particular issue. One of the best known and widely used is the Interactive Financial Planning System (IFPS), developed by Execucom. This particular program permits three kinds of model manipulation. The first is called "goal seeking." Using this routine, the planner can stipulate an outcome and, given the parameters of the model, the system will specify how the decision variables need to be changed to achieve the goal. Another is a "what if?" capability. Here the planner specifies a change in one or more variables, and the model estimates what the effect on the outcome will be. Finally, the program permits the planner to identify the combination of decision variables that will produce the best, or "optimal," solution. This is powerful analytic assistance, and the marketing planner should recognize its tremendous value. As is true of much of the software that has been developed, IFPS is fairly expensive, but not out of line with other packages available on the market.

The personal computer is a fixture on the desks of managers interested in harnessing the power of the computer to enhance their own productivity. In less than half a decade, as much progress has been made in the capability of personal computers as was accomplished in 20 years with their big brothers, the mainframes. Today, an IBM XT can store more data and perform more functions faster than the IBM 650 introduced just about 30 years ago. The remarkable thing about the evolution of the personal computer is that the development of software has kept pace with improvements in the computer itself. Today there are literally hundreds of software packages available for the marketing manager.

The personal computer can serve two uses for the marketing planner. First, in most cases the device can be used as a terminal to access a mainframe computer. This can be accomplished by direct networking or by the use of a modem. Using the personal computer this way, the analyst utilizes the data stored in the mainframe as well as the programs it contains. Personal files can be maintained on the large computer, or data can be downloaded to the PC and stored locally. The second use is the one for which the personal computer was designed—as a free-standing data storage and analysis device. Data can be entered directly from the keyboard, from a diskette, or downloaded from the mainframe or other data base. Once loaded, the manager utilizes software to which he or she has personal access. In comparison to the mainframe, the personal computer's limitations are in terms of storage capacity and speed of processing. However, for most of the work that a marketing manager performs, the typical personal computer has more than enough capacity and handles almost all the routines available on the mainframe.

The heart of your personal-decision support system is the data base. As mentioned above, you will enter data in an appropriate format into the memory of your computer. This may come from various sources. One of the first pieces of software you will use will enable you to properly load data into your machine. This software will enable you to maintain data bases and files in which you can store the results of your analyses. Data base and file management systems provide the input to the various analytic software programs that you will use. There are over 100 such systems available. One of the best known is Ashton-Tate's dBase, which is now in its third version.

There are three types of analysis software that might be included in a decision support system. The first of these is the electronic spreadsheet. According to one source, in 1983 there were already 46 different spreadsheet packages available. A spreadsheet is a matrix on which information can be displayed in two dimensions. It resembles a columnar accounting sheet, on which financial data for different years might be displayed. The typical program permits any number of data manipulations, including the standard mathematical and some statistical procedures. Some of the programs, such as IFPS and Lotus 1-2-3, include graphics and other convenient routines.

Several of the mainframe statistical packages have been converted to use on the personal computer. SPSS and SAS are available, as are a considerable number of customized statistical packages available from other trade sources.

There are a number of management functions for which specialized software has been developed. Planning is, of course, one of these functions. Others deal with specific aspects of the overall planning process. There are a number of forecasting programs available. Project management, including the construction of time line charts, Gantt charts, and PERT and CPM networks have been developed. There are programs that integrate a number of management decision areas.

For the marketing planner, it is useful to be able to integrate these analytic packages with a word processing software package. There are many in use and, aside from the ability to integrate them with the analytic packages, the differences among them lie largely in the complexity—and therefore the task diversity—of the programs. Much of the marketing planning task involves writing. The word processor adds tremendous power to the plan writer because of its ability to rearrange, add, and delete text with ease.

The marketing plan must be in writing. A good way to prepare it is to start with an outline of the major and minor sections in the plan. These might come from your company's planning manual, from a standardized version, or from one of the planning software packages. The process of plan writing, then, involves adding textual content to the outline. If your system does not permit the direct insertion of data or graphs from other software, you can at least provide space in your manuscript where these exhibits will later be inserted. Editing is facilitated. Corrections are easy to make. You can print a hard copy of any part or all of the document at any point you desire. Most word processing systems include routines for checking spelling. Some will evaluate the text for syntax, grammar, and style.

When the time comes for you to present your marketing plan, you will find the presentation software packages very useful. There are several that are available. Pictureit from General Parametrics permits the construction of several different types of presentation slides—word displays, line charts, pie charts, bar charts, flow diagrams, organization charts, Gantt charts, and so on—all in a variety of formats, colors, typefaces, and so forth. Another, Storyboard, permits the inclusion of animation. Aside from the original cost of the software, and some hardware that may be required, the presentation materials are quite inexpensive. For example, if your department produces as many as 1,000 presentation slides a year, the average cost of a 2" × 2" color transparency generated by Pictureit is under $2. If you can access an electronic projection system for your presentation, the out-of-pocket cost is miniscule.

The ideal decision support package for the marketing planner is one that integrates the various data processing and word processing functions. Some approach this. Lotus 1-2-3 has spreadsheet, data processing, a file management system, and graphics. At present it does not have its own word processor, but some word processing systems are equipped to merge spreadsheets and text. Symphony, Javelin, Context MBA, and Framework are comprehensive packages.

It isn't appropriate in this book to evaluate the various decision support packages that are available. New software is constantly being introduced, and existing ones improved. You need to make your own selection, based on your needs, what you can afford to spend, and how deeply you want to get into the use of a personal computer. There is little doubt that eventually every marketing planner will be a dedicated user of a personal computer. If you are not already using this powerful companion, perhaps now is the time to look into it.

The Situation Analysis Procedure

There is no single, established procedure for conducting a situation analysis. However, there is considerable agreement among practitioners as to what should be covered. There are four major steps:

1. Identify the factors to be analyzed. The situation analysis focuses only on those factors that are expected to influence the outcome of your marketing strategy in an important way. How do you determine in advance what these factors should be? This

is not to suggest that you must possess a crystal ball, but you should have some concept of what it is that makes marketing work, and what the external forces are that affect its performance.

In general, the situation analysis should include a description of the product/market, information on the company's position in it (that is, share and share trend), and an explanation of the factors that will have the greatest impact on the company's ability to maintain or strengthen its position.

2. Develop a plan for the analysis. The situation analysis is an organized and comprehensive study. It needs to be planned carefully. The general areas of investigation will have been identified. It remains to design an investigative process to gather information on each of the important impact factors. One very commonly used approach is to employ a set of fairly specific questions that, when answered by those qualified to do so, will provide the necessary information. A number of lists of questions for this purpose have been developed. A comprehensive set of situation analysis questions is included in the Appendix 1.

3. Conduct the situation analysis. The analysis of the marketing situation involves obtaining answers to the questions identified in the preceding step. Of course, in many instances, the desired information is statistical and can be obtained from the company's records. Examples include sales by product line, by sales region, and by customer type; market share; profit and margin contribution; production; inventory; and so on. In addition, statistical information is often obtained from secondary sources or from syndicated data sold by major research organizations.

It should be apparent that the process of asking questions, gathering data, and recording information is time consuming. The situation analysis stage cannot be completed swiftly. A "quick and dirty" scan of the situation may be sufficient for some purposes, but it seldom provides the depth of knowledge required in the development of really sound marketing plans.

4. Prepare analytic summaries. After the data have been assembled, it is necessary to summarize the findings in ways that can be employed directly in the development of marketing strategies. This summary can take several forms, the most common of which is the Strength-Weakness-Opportunity-Problem (SWOP) statement discussed in Chapter 5.

The Analytic Perspectives

When you consider how many different factors or circumstances have a bearing on the outcome of your marketing program, you may feel overwhelmed and discouraged at the prospect of investigating and understanding all of them. Fortunately, the task is made manageable by classifying the areas of inquiry that are likely to be most fruitful. We call these *analytic perspectives*—that is, different ways to view the marketing situation.

Exhibit 4.3 depicts the situation analysis and the various analytic perspectives that can be taken from it. The concentric circles surrounding your marketing plan represent the analytic modes on which it will be based. It is readily apparent that much analytic

Exhibit 4.3. The analytic perspectives.

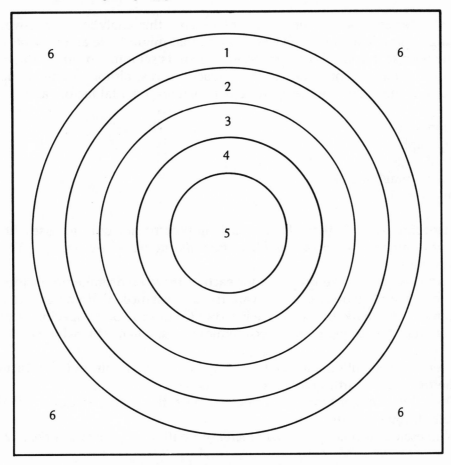

1. The Macroenvironment
2. The Industry
3. The Competitors
4. The Customers
5. The Company
6. Economic Analysis

work is focused outside the marketing function—even outside the company. It should be so, since marketing itself represents an outreach from the firm to the marketplace. However, the external analysis is never at the expense of a thorough appraisal of the company's internal strengths and weaknesses. These, after all, determine how effective an organization can be in attempting to address the marketing opportunities that one or more of the external perspectives reveals.

As indicated in the exhibit, there are a number of important analytic perspectives. These are the macroenvironment, the industry, the competition, the customers, and the company itself. We will consider the various aspects of each of these in turn for the balance of the chapter.

The Macroenvironment

Sometimes referred to as an "environmental scan," this analytic perspective involves a sweeping review of aggregate external forces that might have an effect on your program. The term *scan* is employed purposely. There is seldom a need for the marketing planner to explore in depth most of these macro forces, although one or more could be exceedingly important. Some of these macroenvironmental factors are:

> economic
> demographic
> technological
> social/cultural/life-style
> legal/political

When inspecting each of these factors, it is important not only to assess its current status, but to attempt to *forecast its likely effects during the future period with which your plan is concerned.*

A worksheet should be prepared for each of these environmental factors. See Exhibit 4.4 for a sample worksheet. The various circumstances that you expect will affect the outcome of the marketing plan are listed in Column 1. Be as specific as you can in describing them. For example, under economic factors, you might include the following:

- Interest rates will remain stable throughout the first half, but rise fractionally in the third and fourth quarters of next year.
- The value of major foreign currencies against the American dollar will rise gradually throughout the year.
- Wholesale and retail prices will increase by 10 percent over the next 12 months.

Suppose, however, that you are not sure about the way in which these external factors will behave. A useful means to determine whether the impact of these macroenvironmental factors needs to be incorporated in the marketing plan is to position each on an opportunity/threat matrix such as the one shown in Exhibit 4.5. The first step in doing this is to estimate the level of impact each of the individual factors is likely to have. Use a scale from 0 to 10, in which 0 indicates almost no impact and 10 indicates the most serious impact predictable. These numbers are inserted beside each listed item in Column 2 of the worksheet.

Next, estimate how likely it is that the level of impact indicated in Column 2 will actually occur. To do this, employ a concept known as *subjective probability.* For example, people are quite used to estimates of the probability of rain or snow. Weather people say, "The chances are 60 percent that it will rain today." You do more or less the same thing with each of the external factors. If you are absolutely sure the factor will have an impact, assign a probability of 100 percent. On the other hand, if you are quite certain it will not have an impact, assign a low probability, say 5 or 10 percent. These occurrence probabilities are inserted on the worksheet in Column 3, beside each of the factors.

Exhibit 4.4.   Environmental analysis worksheet.

Economic Factors

Circumstances	*Importance*	*Probability of Occurrence*
1. _____	_____	_____
_____	_____	_____
2. _____	_____	_____
_____	_____	_____
3. _____	_____	_____
_____	_____	_____
4. _____	_____	_____
_____	_____	_____
5. _____	_____	_____
_____	_____	_____
6. _____	_____	_____
_____	_____	_____
7. _____	_____	_____
_____	_____	_____
8. _____	_____	_____
_____	_____	_____
9. _____	_____	_____
_____	_____	_____
10. _____	_____	_____
_____	_____	_____

Exhibit 4.5.   Opportunity-threat matrix.

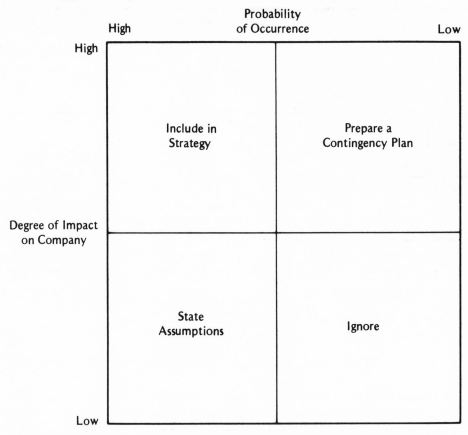

Source: Adapted from an exhibit in Kotler, Philip. *Marketing Management*, 5th Edition
(Englewood Cliffs, N.J.: Prentice-Hall, 1984), p. 42.

Each of these factors should then be plotted on the matrix shown in Exhibit 4.5. Any factor that falls in the upper left-hand cell of the matrix must be dealt with in the marketing strategy. A high-impact event that has a low probability of occurring should be dealt with on a contingency basis. Low-impact events with high-probability threats and opportunities are dealt with as part of the macroenvironment in which the marketing strategy must operate. Low-impact events with low-probability threats and opportunities can be ignored for the present. However, any given factor can change its character quite suddenly. It is important to scan the macroenvironment periodically to make sure that any shifts in impact level or probability have been taken into account. And, of course, new events can materialize at any time.

Industry Analysis

Your industry can be considered as the set of competitors that collectively addresses a more or less common group of customers. There is an incorrect tendency to think of an industry as a group of firms operating in the same way (automobile companies or hotel chains, for example) or as a group of firms offering more or less the same kinds of products or services. These views are inferior to the first, because they may very well exclude important generic competitors, and thus omit a very important part of the overall marketing situation. However, from a practical point of view, the analyst must use industry data in the form in which it is available. Industry factors that the marketing planner should investigate include: (1) demand conditions and trends, (2) supply conditions, and (3) trade channel arrangements.

Demand Conditions and Trends

Historical data on industry sales should be studied carefully. To do this properly, collect annual industry sales data for the recent past and for selected prior years.

The most common method of reporting sales is in terms of current dollars. This is a useful and obviously convenient means, but it seldom measures very precisely what is actually happening. Change in price level is the major culprit, and screening out the effects of price-level changes is not easy. However, a number of economic research companies and the federal government regularly publish indexes that can be used to adjust current dollars to constant dollars. Recording and reporting sales in physical terms (gallons, units, tons, cases, and so on) eliminates the problem, but it makes aggregation in industry statistics almost impossible. How, for instance, do you add gallons of gasoline and cases of motor oil to obtain a total demand for petroleum products? Notwithstanding, some industry data are reported in physical units, and these figures do eliminate the necessity of adjusting current sales for changes in price level.

The overall sales figures for an industry should be broken down further by specific product types or groups. For industrial products this breakdown is usually done by Standard Industrial Classification (SIC). See Exhibit 4.6 for a worksheet to use in assembling this information.

Consumer product sales typically are reported at several levels—manufacturing, wholesale, and retail. Manufacturing sales are usually broken down by category, such as canned or frozen vegetables. Wholesale and retail sales are reported by type of product and location.

Industry sales are often available for industrial markets. The most obvious classification is geographical, such as by region or state. Industrial sales, classified according to the SIC designation of the buying establishments, are often employed.

Once the historical data have been assembled, it is possible to perform a number of statistical analyses to better understand the demand conditions in the industry. Called *time series analysis*, these routines enable the marketing planner to identify the effects of several kinds of fluctuations that are typically embedded in all historical data. These are:

seasonal fluctuations
cyclical movements
changes owing to long-run trend—for example, the growth rate
random variations

Exhibit 4.6. Industry sales worksheet.

Customer Classification (SIC)	Last Year Dollars	%	Next Year Dollars	%
_____	_____	____	_____	____
_____	_____	____	_____	____
_____	_____	____	_____	____
_____	_____	____	_____	____
_____	_____	____	_____	____
_____	_____	____	_____	____
_____	_____	____	_____	____
_____	_____	____	_____	____
_____	_____	____	_____	____
_____	_____	____	_____	____
_____	_____	____	_____	____
_____	_____	____	_____	____
_____	_____	____	_____	____
_____	_____	____	_____	____
_____	_____	____	_____	____

Refer to any basic statistics textbook for a description of these procedures.[2] These routines are available on a number of software programs. SPSS (Statistical Package for the Social Sciences) and SAS (Statistical Analysis System) are well-known mainframe programs. Time series analysis is also feasible on a personal computer. SPSS, SAS, and Statgraphics, for example, provide PC-ready software for making these kinds of analyses.

One of the most important aspects of demand analysis is the estimation of market potential. Market potential is the industry sales level that exists when all firms in the industry are operating at maximum efficiency. It is limited only by the ability of the market to absorb increasing amounts of the product. It is very important to define the industry carefully when estimating its market potential. For example, when estimating the potential for trucks, should the demand for all trucks, even pickups and panel vehicles, be included? To do so might give a very misleading picture to a marketing planner at a firm like Navistar, which is primarily interested in over-the-highway, tractor-trailer rigs. On the other hand, a fabricator of camper tops would be interested only in the potential for pickups. Naturally enough, market potential differs considerably from one market area to the next. Thus, not only does market potential give an idea of the size of a total market, but it shows how to allocate resources to different regions or other market segments.

There are several methods of measuring market potential. Direct measurement is seldom feasible, although there are exceptions. Sales of some products, such as motor vehicles and liquor, which must be reported to government agencies, are easy to track. Often, both competitors' sales as well as total sales can be obtained from public records. For most products, however, indirect measurements must be made.

There are a number of indirect methods that can be employed to estimate market potential. These are:

surveys
market indexes
syndicated data services
chain ratio
census of business

Survey Methods. It is practical to estimate potential by using a survey when the industry is made up of a limited number of customers. For example, it is common for a sales manager to ask regional sales offices to obtain information on annual usage from all customers and prospects. Since the reliability of the sales force in providing this kind of information is somewhat questionable, some firms prefer to use the services of a commercial research house, such as the F. W. Dodge division of McGraw-Hill. Using an industry-wide survey, a company can estimate quite accurately the size of a market and also identify any trends that are taking place.

Market Indexes. A market index is a number that indicates the proportion of total demand that can be expected in a particular market area. By far the best known and most widely used of the commercially available market indexes is *Sales Management*'s annual "Survey of Buying Power." This publication provides three single-factor indexes: (1) population, (2) effective buying (disposable) income, and (3) retail sales. An example of a single-factor index, based on population, is found in Exhibit 4.7. It shows the distribution of total retail sales in nine geographic regions and the index that results from this distribution. In addition, the report provides three composite indexes.

1. The Buying Power Index (BPI). This is a weighted index in which a weight of 0.5 is given to an area's percentage of total U.S. effective buying income, a weight of 0.3 to its percentage of U.S. retail sales, and a weight of 0.2 to its percentage of the total population of the United States. Index values for two metropolitan areas are shown in Exhibit 4.8. Comparing the two buying power indexes of Philadelphia and Kansas

Exhibit 4.7.   Single-factor market index.

Region	1986 Retail Sales (in $ Millions)	Index
New England	88,113	6.3
Middle Atlantic	208,627	15.0
East North Central	232,746	16.7
West North Central	104,482	7.5
South Atlantic	238,701	17.1
East South Central	74,388	5.3
West South Central	153,939	11.0
Mountain	76,021	5.5
Far West	218,226	15.6
Total	1,395,243	100.0

Source: "Survey of Buying Power," *Sales Management* (July 28, 1986).

City, it is very apparent that the overall potential of Philadelphia is almost three times that of Kansas City. It is simply a bigger metropolitan area.

2. The Sales Activity Index (SAI). This is a measure of the per capita retail sales of an area compared with that of the nation. See Exhibit 4.9. It is computed by dividing an area's percentage of retail sales by its percentage of U.S. population. The SAIs for the Philadelphia and Kansas City metropolitan areas are shown. From a comparison of these two SAIs, it is apparent that although Kansas City is much smaller, it has disproportionately more sales activity. Presumably, Kansas City attracts more retail business from people who reside outside the area, possibly tourists or people from outlying rural areas. Of course, Kansas Citians could simply consume more or have more money to spend. In any event, Kansas City has a significantly higher sales activity index than does Philadelphia.

3. The Quality Index (QI). This compares the buying power per capita of an area to the corresponding figure for the country as a whole. It is computed by dividing an area's Buying Power Index (BPI) by its percentage of the U.S. population. The calculations for Philadelphia and Kansas City in Exhibit 4.10 show that Philadelphia's Quality

Exhibit 4.8.   Buying power index in two markets.

Metropolitan Area	Percent Effective Buying Income (w = .5)	Percent Retail Sales (w = .3)	Percent Population (w = .2)	Index (w = 1.0)
Philadelphia	2.117	2.035	1.997	
× weight	1.059	.611	.399	2.029
Kansas City	.708	.752	.622	
× weight	.354	.227	.124	.701

Source: Calculated from data in "Survey of Buying Power," *Sales Management* (July 28, 1986).

Exhibit 4.9. Sales activity index of two markets.

Metropolitan Area	Percent Retail Sales	Percent U.S. Population	Index 100(A/B)
	(A)	(B)	
Philadelphia	2.035	1.997	102
Kansas City	.752	.622	121

Source: Calculated from data in "Survey of Buying Power," *Sales Management* (July 28, 1986).

Exhibit 4.10. Quality index.

Metropolitan Area	Buying Power Sales	Percent U.S. Population	Index 100(A/B)
	(A)	(B)	
Philadelphia	2.069	1.997	104
Kansas City	.701	.622	113

Source: Calculated from data in "Survey of Buying Power," *Sales Management* (July 28, 1986).

Index is 104 and Kansas City's is 113. Thus both cities are above par for the nation as a whole, but Kansas City enjoys a somewhat higher overall rating.

A great deal of useful information is found in market indexes such as these. For instance, these estimates can be used in the selection of test markets, the allocation of the sales force, the appointment and location of distributors, the selection of advertising media, and the allocation of the advertising budget.

4. The Brand Development Index (BDI) is another useful diagnostic tool. An example showing how it is constructed is found in Exhibit 4.11. The index is the ratio of

Exhibit 4.11. Brand development index.

Region	(Col. 1) Retail Sales	(Col. 2) Sales Potential Index	(Col. 3) Company Dollars	(Col. 4) Sales %	(Col. 5) BDI 100×(4/2)
New England	88.1	6.3	1.4	4.0	63
Middle Atlantic	208.6	15.0	4.5	13.0	87
East North Central	232.7	16.7	4.2	12.0	72
West North Central	104.5	7.5	2.5	7.0	93
South Atlantic	238.7	17.1	7.7	22.0	129
East South Central	74.4	5.3	2.1	6.0	113
West South Central	153.9	11.0	4.2	12.0	109
Mountain	76.0	5.4	1.4	4.0	73
Pacific	218.2	15.6	7.0	20.0	128
Total	1,395.1	100.0	35.0	100.0	100

Source: Calculated from data in "Survey of Buying Power," *Sales Management* (July 28, 1986).

a company's proportion of its sales in a given market area to the market potential in the same area. Exhibit 4.11 uses the single-factor index (Column 2) from Exhibit 4.7 and a comparable distribution of a company's sales (Column 4). Column 5 displays the BDI ([Column 4 ÷ Column 2] × 100). The company in this example has been much more successful in penetrating the South and West than it has the North Central and Northeast regions. The low-indexed areas appear to have been neglected. Possibly this was intentional, the target market having been defined as California and the south-eastern Sunbelt. On the other hand, it may indicate a failure of the company to adapt its program sufficiently to be effective in the areas where its BDI is low.

A worksheet to use in constructing your own BDI index is found in Exhibit 4.12. Enough space has been provided for selecting twenty market areas or segments. Make your own selection. Determine the single- or multiple-factor weighted index that you believe best reflects the demand for your company's products. Insert the index numbers for each of the markets. Next, fill in your company's sales for a recent period of time. Calculate the percentages. Finally, as shown in Exhibit 4.11, divide the percentage of sales by the percentage of market demand and multiply by 100 to determine the BDI for each area or segment.

Syndicated Data. There are two general types of syndicated data bases that consumer packaged-goods marketers can employ. One is based on retail sales; the other is based on warehouse withdrawals. Manufacturers, especially of packaged consumer goods, have learned that statistics of their own sales can provide a very misleading picture of actual demand. The principal reason is the lag between the time a manufacturer sells products and the time those products are purchased by consumers or industrial end users. This bulge in manufacturer's sales is often referred to as "pipeline" filling. It is illustrated in Exhibit 4.13. The manufacturer's sales in six successive periods are shown by the lighter bars. Sales to end users of the product are shown by the darker bars. Note how considerable distortion occurs when you look simply at the manufacturer's shipment record.

The best-known firms supplying this kind of information are the A. C. Nielsen Company and SAMI (Sales Area Marketing, Inc.). Nielsen maintains a panel of representative food and drug outlets from which it collects information on product movement. Historically, this was done by stock audits. Today, most of the data are collected from the electronic scanners. SAMI data are collected at the wholesale or warehouse level. These figures are now being supplemented with point-of-sale data obtained by checkout scanners. Both of these services are fairly costly, but the value of the data cannot be underestimated.

Chain Ratio. Market potential can be estimated by applying a series of usage ratios to an estimate of total demand. Suppose that the Stupendous Snacking Cake Company is interested in estimating the number of cake mixes it might sell. The starting point is the entire population aged six years and over. This number would be multiplied by the per capita consumption of cakes to determine the total number consumed in a year. Since some desserts are not eaten at home or are bought already baked from retail shops, the total number of cakes must be multiplied by the percentage of cakes prepared at home. Of those cooks who prepare cakes at home, some (a given percentage) work from scratch. Only a portion use a prepared mix, and only some of these people prepare

Exhibit 4.12. Brand development index worksheet.

Area	Market Index	Company Sales	Percent	BDI
_____	_____	_____	_____	____
_____	_____	_____	_____	____
_____	_____	_____	_____	____
_____	_____	_____	_____	____
_____	_____	_____	_____	____
_____	_____	_____	_____	____
_____	_____	_____	_____	____
_____	_____	_____	_____	____
_____	_____	_____	_____	____
_____	_____	_____	_____	____
_____	_____	_____	_____	____
_____	_____	_____	_____	____
_____	_____	_____	_____	____
_____	_____	_____	_____	____
_____	_____	_____	_____	____
_____	_____	_____	_____	____
_____	_____	_____	_____	____
_____	_____	_____	_____	____
_____	_____	_____	_____	____

Exhibit 4.13.   "Pipeline" vs. end user sales.

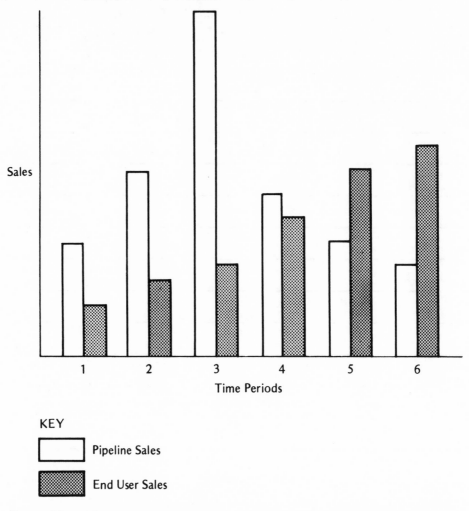

Source: Adapted from an exhibit in Bell, Martin L. *Marketing: Concepts and Strategy* (Boston: Houghton Mifflin Company, 1979), p. 152.

a snacking cake. Exhibit 4.14 illustrates how this chain of ratios was worked out by a product manager responsible for a line of cake mixes.

Census of Business. Market potential for an industrial products company can be estimated from data available in the *Census of Manufacturers.* Exhibit 4.15 shows how a paint manufacturer might estimate the market potential in various states. The first step in such an analysis is to determine the type of industries (by SIC code) that are heavy users of paint. The company's own sales records might provide this information or perhaps a trade association might publish the data. It is also necessary to ascertain how much money each type of customer spends on paint. This information is probably obtained from the same sources. Next, the marketing planner must determine where these prospective buyers are located. Along with a great deal of other data, the Census of Manufacturers reports the purchase of materials by SIC code for each state and metropolitan area. To determine the potential in a particular state, such as Illinois or Georgia, multiply the paint purchase rate by the value of materials purchased for each SIC code. These values are totaled to obtain an estimate of potential in the state. In the example in Exhibit 4.15, the paint manufacturer might expect to obtain some share of a market potential in either Illinois or Georgia. It is doubtful, because of the lack of an industrial base in Montana, that the company would make any serious attempt to develop sales there.

Supply Conditions

Industry supply refers to the ability of an industry to satisfy demand. A number of factors are involved. First and foremost is industry capacity.

Industry capacity is a measure of the output potential of the firms in the industry. Data on capacity is not as readily available as sales information, but is referred to frequently enough in the trade press to obtain estimates needed for planning purposes. This is also true of changes in capacity, which can be estimated from reports of firms entering or leaving the market.

Just as important as capacity is the rate of capacity utilization. Capacity utilization has several important effects on industry supply. Obviously, it sets a ceiling on the volume of goods or services that can be offered. If demand exceeds this amount, the short- and long-term implications are serious. In the short run, a seller's market prevails. Prices tend to be high, and competitive pressures are low. It may even be necessary to put customers on allocation. Demarketing (the use of marketing tools to decrease demand) may be required. In the long run, capacity will be increased either by existing firms or by newcomers entering the industry. If the barriers to entry are low, new entrants are bound to appear, attracted by high profits and low levels of competitive

Exhibit 4.14. Chain ratio calculation of market potential.

Population age 6 and over	230 million
× per capita consumption of cakes	3.3
= number of cakes consumed per year	759 million
× percent of cakes consumed at home	75%
= number of cakes consumed at home	569 million
× percent of cakes prepared at home	72%
= number of cakes prepared at home	410 million
× percent prepared with a mix	80%
= number cakes prepared with a mix	328 million
× percent preparing a snacking cake	15%
= number of snacking cakes prepared	49 million
× Stupendous Snacking Cake Company market share	20%
= market potential for Stupendous Snacking Cake Company	9.8 million

Exhibit 4.15. Using the census of business to estimate potential for industrial paint in three states.

States	Purchases ($ Mill.)	Paint Purchases $ of Purchases	Potential ($ Mill.)
Illinois			
SIC 24 Lumber & Wood Products	374.3	.019	7.1
SIC 25 Furniture & Fixtures	523.5	.021	11.0
SIC 34 Fabricated Metal Products	4,016.3	.004	16.1
SIC 35 Machinery (Exc. Elec.)	8,007.8	.002	16.0
SIC 36 Elect./Electronic Equip	4,467.4	.003	13.4
SIC 37 Transportation Equip	3,274.1	.004	13.1
Total			76.7
Georgia			
SIC 24 Lumber & Wood Products	867.2	.019	16.5
SIC 25 Furniture & Fixtures	178.5	.021	3.7
SIC 34 Fabricated Metal Products	649.1	.004	2.6
SIC 35 Machinery (Exc. Elec.)	408.7	.002	.8
SIC 36 Elect./Electronic Equip	456.1	.003	1.4
SIC 37 Transportation Equip	3,453.2	.004	13.8
Total			38.8
Montana			
SIC 24 Lumber & Wood Products	33.2	.019	.6
SIC 25 Furniture & Fixtures	2.4	.021	.1
SIC 34 Fabricated Metal Products	16.5	.004	.1
SIC 35 Machinery (Exc. Elec.)	8.3	.002	—
SIC 36 Elect./Electronic Equip	8.3	.003	—
SIC 37 Transportation Equip	6.0	.004	—
Total			.8

Source: *1977 Census of Manufacturers* (Washington, D.C.: U.S. Government Printing Office, 1981).

activity. This threat may be sufficiently strong to impel existing firms to expand to prevent loss of market share. Almost inevitably, capacity and output increase, prices fall, and the competitive climate becomes more active.

Excess or underutilized capacity poses equally serious planning problems. A buyer's market prevails. Customers can pick and choose. Competition for the existing demand is intense. Price discounting is common. Large marketing budgets are required. Because overhead is fixed, unit costs go up with decreased output. Profits decline. Now the process is reversed. Some companies close plants and others leave the industry. Eventually, supply is adjusted to demand. Meanwhile, of course, each competitor develops plans appropriate to the industry and each's competitive position.

Exhibit 4.16. Resellers of automotive aftermarket products.

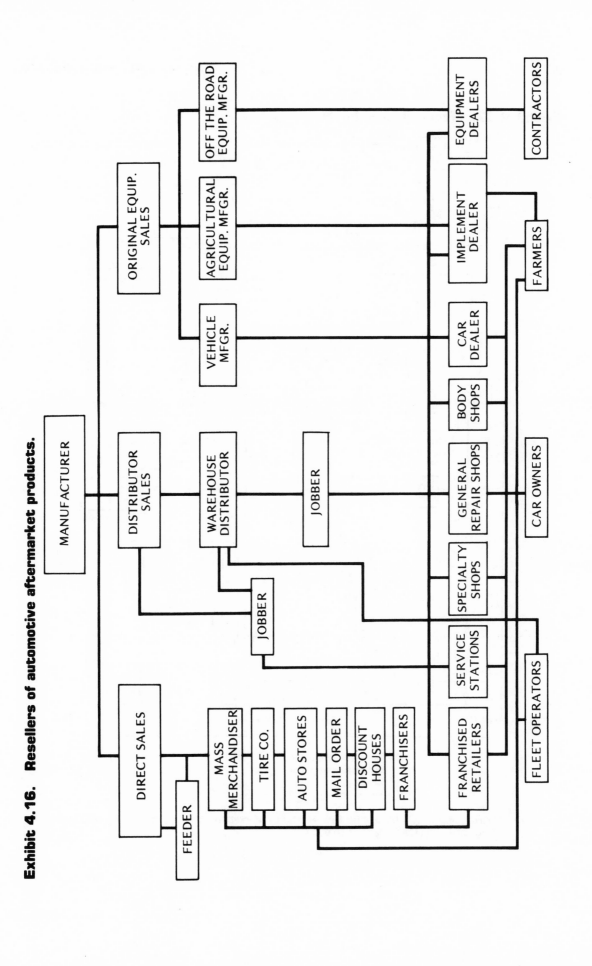

Exhibit 4.17. Trade channel for brake fluid.

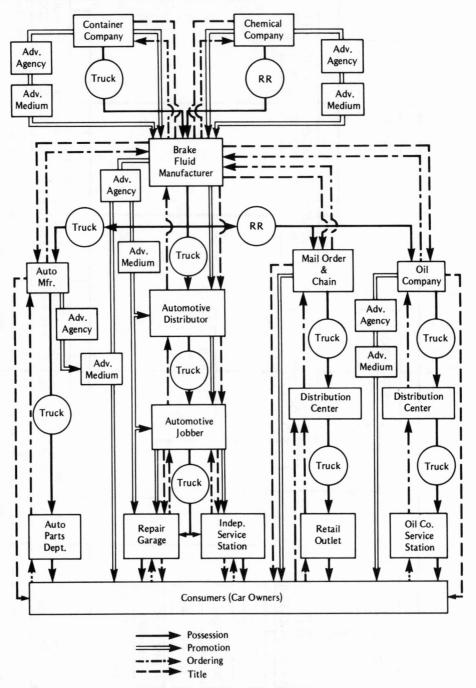

Source: Instructor's Manual for Bell, Martin L. *Marketing: Concepts and Strategy* (Boston: Houghton Mifflin Company, 1979), p. 27.

Trade Channel Arrangements

This industry factor refers to the types of middlemen and facilitating agencies typically used in the industry. Of course, not all firms use the same channels, and even if two competitors use the same *type* of channel, they usually employ different middlemen. However, it is very useful to understand the general trade channel arrangements that exist and the ways in which these systems operate and are managed.

Trade channel arrangements can be extremely complex. Consider the example in Exhibit 4.16. It displays the various channel options open to a manufacturer of an automotive aftermarket product, such as brake fluid or front-end replacement parts. This exhibit contains only those channel components that resell the product. But the trade channel includes other marketing agencies as well. Exhibit 4.17 illustrates a somewhat simpler trade channel, but does include facilitating agencies that may also be important in the design and implementation of the marketing plan. You should chart your present and potential channel options. Begin with a blank flowchart, such as in Exhibit 4.18, and prepare a worksheet for each major channel you use. Fill in the blanks

Exhibit 4.18. Trade channel options.

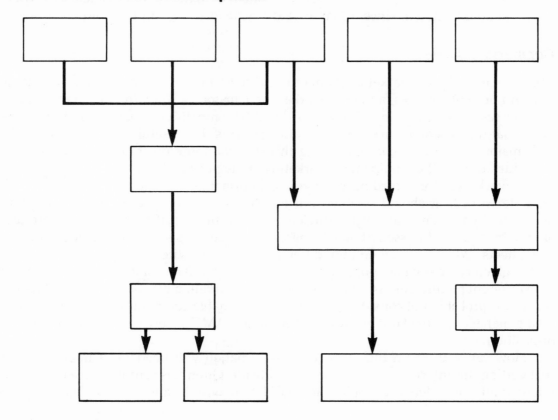

and add others as necessary. In doing so, consider the following:

1. What is its function? Exactly what distributive services does this component provide? How does it do this? How efficiently does it function?
2. What margin or cost is involved? Some channel components take title to goods and resell them. If so, what markups are involved? Others, such as agents and brokers, work on commission. Some have flat fees; others have variable rates. Ultimately, these charges become marketing costs.
3. What conflicts of interest exist? Channel components are usually independent businesses whose own interests may conflict with those of others in the channel. Problems arising from conflicts of interest need to be anticipated and plans made to minimize their impact.
4. What arrangement is best? A smoothly functioning trade channel provides any company with a decided competitive edge. Additionally, some channel arrangements are more efficient and therefore less costly than others. Usually, channel components are in closer contact with end users than the manufacturer is. A retailer, for example, which serves its customers well and understands their buying needs and behavior, can be a fruitful source of planning information.
5. What other useful information should be considered? Like every other facet of marketing, channel components are constantly changing. Any new, useful information relating to a particular component or to the channel system as a whole should be noted, since it may herald a needed change in distribution strategy.

Competitor Analysis

At bare minimum, the marketing planner needs to know who the competitors are, their past and present volumes, and their market share histories. Knowing the strengths and weaknesses of specific competitors helps identify competitive problems and opportunities that the evolving marketing plan must address. It is useful, also, to be aware of each major competitor's core marketing thrust. Even more desirable, if obtainable, is some idea of the other companies' marketing strategies for the future.

A worksheet for recording competitive information is found in Exhibit 4.19. A separate worksheet should be filled out for each major competitor. The assumption here is that your plan will cover a single product or market. If more than one product or market is to be addressed, it may be necessary to develop separate sets of competitor worksheets. Why? First, an entirely different set of competitors may be involved. Second, a given company may pose quite different competitive problems or opportunities with different products or markets. For example, a marketing planner for the Ford Escort car would probably not consider AMC a very formidable competitor. However, a marketing manager for the Ford Scout would recognize AMC's Jeep as its most threatening opposition.

How can you obtain the competitive information you need? You might suspect that getting this information could be very difficult. Often it is, but it is easier than you might think, provided you don't want the data overnight and from a single source.

Exhibit 4.19. Competitor analysis worksheet.

Name of Competitor: _____

1. Provide this competitor's sales and market share data for the past five years:

	Current Year	−1	−2	−3	−4	−5
a. Sales volume	_____	_____	_____	_____	_____	_____
b. Market share	_____	_____	_____	_____	_____	_____

2. Estimate this competitor's sales for each year as follows:

Region	Current Year	−1	−2	−3	−4	−5
_____	_____	_____	_____	_____	_____	_____
_____	_____	_____	_____	_____	_____	_____
_____	_____	_____	_____	_____	_____	_____
_____	_____	_____	_____	_____	_____	_____
_____	_____	_____	_____	_____	_____	_____
_____	_____	_____	_____	_____	_____	_____
_____	_____	_____	_____	_____	_____	_____

Product Line	Current Year	−1	−2	−3	−4	−5
_____	_____	_____	_____	_____	_____	_____
_____	_____	_____	_____	_____	_____	_____
_____	_____	_____	_____	_____	_____	_____
_____	_____	_____	_____	_____	_____	_____
_____	_____	_____	_____	_____	_____	_____
_____	_____	_____	_____	_____	_____	_____
_____	_____	_____	_____	_____	_____	_____

3. List this competitor's business strengths:

_____

_____

_____

_____

Exhibit 4.19. Continued.

4. List this competitor's business weaknesses:

_____

_____

_____

5. What is this competitor's present marketing strategy?
   a. Product strategy: _____

   _____

   b. Distribution: _____

   _____

   c. Promotion: _____

   _____

   d. Price: _____

   _____

6. What changes in strategy are expected?
   a. Product Strategy: _____

   _____

   b. Distribution: _____

   _____

   c. Promotion: _____

   _____

   d. Price: _____

   _____

You will need to build a competitor data base over a period of time and utilize many different sources.

While it is true that information about specific companies is regarded as proprietary, eventually almost everything you need to know can be discovered or deduced. Much of it is actually published. The rest can be gained by observation, research, and reasoning. Some sources of published competitor information are:

1. Information reported to the government and either published or available through the freedom of information privilege
2. Reports to the Securities and Exchange Commission, including annual reports and the details for various lines of business found in 10K reports
3. Syndicated financial reporting services such as Moody's and Standard & Poor's
4. Syndicated marketing information from services such as Simmons Market Research Bureau and Leading National Advertisers
5. Information on major companies, such as the list of Fortune 500 companies, published periodically
6. Ad hoc reports of in-depth studies of particular industries or companies in such publications as *The Wall Street Journal, Fortune,* and *Business Week*
7. Noteworthy developments at particular companies as reported in the daily newspapers and the business press; a clipping service is a useful way of covering this source
8. Confidential competitor reports prepared by third parties, notably Dun & Bradstreet's well-known "D & Bs"
9. Company publications, such as annual reports, product catalogs, price sheets, capability brochures, company histories, advertisements
10. Publicly accessible data bases, including research libraries and computer-based information data banks

A few nonpublished sources of competitive information are:

1. Your own company's salespeople
2. Customers you share with the competitor
3. Consultants, including privately commissioned research people
4. Competitors' employees
5. Casual public conversations

Customer Analysis

No element in the external environment is more important than the ultimate customer. Marketing exists solely to locate and serve this potential customer. Malcolm McNair, in the introduction to one of the early editions of the Harvard Business School's marketing casebook, included this quotation from Rudyard Kipling's *The Elephant's Child:*

> I keep six honest serving men
> (They taught me all I knew);
> Their names are What and Why and When
> And How and Where and Who.

Thus, McNair identified the customer information that the marketing planner requires before trying to design a marketing strategy. These "honest serving men" apply

Exhibit 4.20. Example of SMRB data—female users of hair conditioners.

	Total U.S. '000	All Users A '000	B % Across Down	C %	D Indx	Heavy Users A '000	B % Across Down	C %	D Indx	Medium Users A '000	B % Across Down	C %	D Indx	Light Users A '000	B % Across Down	C %	D Indx
Total females	82524	39069	100.0	47.3	100	7893	100.0	9.6	100	13278	100.0	16.1	100	17899	100.0	21.7	100
Female homemakers	74975	34549	88.4	46.1	97	6619	83.9	8.8	92	11838	89.2	15.8	98	16093	89.9	21.5	99
Employed mothers	17362	9365	24.0	53.9	114	2133	27.0	12.3	128	3087	23.2	17.8	111	4145	23.2	23.9	110
18–24	14314	8196	21.0	57.3	121	2376	30.1	16.6	174	2516	18.9	17.6	109	3304	18.5	23.1	106
25–34	18104	10524	26.9	58.1	123	2187	27.7	12.1	126	4028	30.3	22.2	138	4309	24.1	23.8	110
35–44	12982	6449	16.5	49.7	105	1301	16.5	10.0	105	1973	14.9	15.2	94	3175	17.7	24.5	113
45–54	12039	5301	13.6	44.0	93	1024	13.0	8.5	89	1764	13.3	14.7	91	2513	14.0	20.9	96
55–64	11092	4588	11.7	41.4	87	*513	6.5	4.6	48	1323	10.0	11.9	74	2752	15.4	24.8	114
65 or older	13993	4012	10.3	28.7	61	*492	6.2	3.5	37	1674	12.6	12.0	74	1846	10.3	13.2	61
18–34	32417	18719	47.9	57.7	122	4563	57.8	14.1	147	6544	49.3	20.2	125	7613	42.5	23.5	108
18–49	51303	27811	71.2	54.2	115	6463	81.9	12.6	132	9407	70.8	18.3	114	11941	66.7	23.3	107
25–49	43125	22273	57.0	51.6	109	4512	57.2	10.5	109	7764	58.5	18.0	112	9997	55.9	23.2	107
35–49	18885	9092	23.3	48.1	102	1900	24.1	10.1	105	2864	21.6	15.2	94	4328	24.2	22.9	106
Graduated college	9780	4495	11.5	46.0	97	858	10.9	8.8	92	1579	11.9	16.1	100	2058	11.5	21.0	97
Attended college	13001	6719	17.2	51.7	109	1506	19.1	11.6	121	2274	17.1	17.5	109	2939	16.4	22.6	104
Graduated high school	34120	16782	43.0	49.2	104	3276	41.5	9.6	100	5637	42.5	16.5	103	7869	44.0	23.1	106
Did not graduate high school	25623	11072	28.3	43.2	91	2253	28.5	8.8	92	3787	28.5	14.8	92	5033	28.1	19.6	91
Employed	39817	20298	52.0	51.0	108	4491	56.9	11.3	118	6769	51.0	17.0	106	9039	50.5	22.7	105
Employed full-time	30636	15406	39.4	50.3	106	3547	44.9	11.6	121	5067	38.2	16.5	103	6792	37.9	22.2	102
Employed part-time	9182	4892	12.5	53.3	113	943	11.9	10.3	107	1702	12.8	18.5	115	2246	12.5	24.5	113
Not employed	42707	18771	48.0	44.0	93	3402	43.1	8.0	83	6509	49.0	15.2	95	8860	49.5	20.7	96
Professional/manager	10178	4739	12.1	46.6	98	1081	13.7	10.6	111	1575	11.9	15.5	96	2082	11.6	20.5	94
Clerical/sales	16374	8789	22.5	53.7	113	1964	24.9	12.0	125	2704	20.4	16.5	103	4121	23.0	25.2	116
Craftsmen/foremen	745	*442	1.1	59.3	125	**100	1.3	13.4	140	**105	.8	14.1	88	**238	1.3	31.9	147
Other employed	12521	6328	16.2	50.5	107	1346	17.1	10.7	112	2385	18.0	19.0	118	2598	14.5	20.7	96
Single	13803	7443	19.1	53.9	114	2039	25.8	14.8	154	2513	18.9	18.2	113	2891	16.2	20.9	97
Married	50050	23612	60.4	47.2	100	4229	53.6	8.4	88	8194	61.7	16.4	102	11189	62.5	22.4	103
Divorced/separated/widowed	18670	8014	20.5	42.9	91	1625	20.6	8.7	91	2571	19.4	13.8	86	3819	21.3	20.5	94
Parents	32034	17088	43.7	53.3	113	3688	46.7	11.5	120	5951	44.8	18.6	115	7449	41.6	23.3	107
White	71667	32767	83.9	45.7	97	6787	86.0	9.5	99	10989	82.8	15.3	95	14990	83.7	20.9	96
Black	9349	5709	14.6	61.1	129	995	12.6	10.6	111	1964	14.8	21.0	131	2750	15.4	29.4	136
Other	1508	*594	1.5	39.4	83	**110	1.4	7.3	76	**324	2.4	21.5	134	**159	.9	10.5	49
Northeast-census	18147	8062	20.6	44.4	94	1541	19.5	8.5	89	3088	23.3	17.0	106	3433	19.2	18.9	87
North Central	20352	9605	24.6	47.2	100	1841	23.3	9.0	95	3046	22.9	15.0	93	4718	26.4	23.2	107
South	27078	13065	33.4	48.2	102	2191	27.8	8.1	85	4507	33.9	16.6	103	6367	35.6	23.5	108
West	16947	8337	21.3	49.2	104	2319	29.4	13.7	143	2636	19.9	15.6	97	3382	18.9	20.0	92
Northeast-mktg.	19685	8760	22.4	44.5	94	1596	20.2	8.1	85	3283	24.7	16.7	104	3881	21.7	19.7	91
East Central	12246	5588	14.3	45.6	96	938	11.9	7.7	80	1726	13.0	14.1	88	2924	16.3	23.9	110
West Central	14343	6494	16.6	45.3	96	1395	17.7	9.7	102	2226	16.8	15.5	96	2873	16.1	20.0	92
South	22609	11171	28.6	49.4	104	2061	26.1	9.1	95	3852	29.0	17.0	106	5257	29.4	23.3	107
Pacific	13640	7057	18.1	51.7	109	1903	24.1	14.0	146	2190	16.5	16.1	100	2963	16.6	21.7	100
County size A	31836	16191	41.4	50.9	107	3441	43.6	10.8	113	5498	41.4	17.3	107	7252	40.5	22.8	105
County size B	23829	11532	29.5	48.4	102	2421	30.7	10.2	106	4007	30.2	16.8	105	5104	28.5	21.4	99
County size C	13911	5830	14.9	41.9	89	1230	15.6	8.8	92	2005	15.1	14.4	90	2596	14.5	18.7	86
County size D	12948	5516	14.1	42.6	90	802	10.2	6.2	65	1768	13.3	13.7	85	2947	16.5	22.8	105
Metro central city	26101	13419	34.3	51.4	109	2904	36.8	11.1	116	4427	33.3	17.0	105	6088	34.0	23.3	108
Metro suburban	34453	16174	41.4	46.9	99	3236	41.0	9.4	98	5797	43.7	16.8	105	7141	39.9	20.7	96
Non metro	21970	9477	24.3	43.1	91	1753	22.2	8.0	83	3054	23.0	13.9	86	4670	26.1	21.3	98
Hshld inc $35,000 or more	9814	4869	12.5	49.6	105	981	12.4	10.0	105	1722	13.0	17.5	109	2166	12.1	22.1	102
$25,000 or more	22954	11276	28.9	49.1	104	2103	26.6	9.2	96	3764	28.3	16.4	102	5409	30.2	23.6	109
$20,000–$24,999	9934	4875	12.5	49.1	104	1053	13.3	10.6	111	1637	12.3	16.5	102	2186	12.2	22.0	101
$15,000–$19,999	10705	5425	13.9	50.7	107	1207	15.3	11.3	118	1922	14.5	18.0	112	2296	12.8	21.4	99
$10,000–$14,999	16626	7922	20.3	47.6	101	1822	23.1	11.0	115	2731	20.6	16.4	102	3370	18.8	20.3	93
$5,000–$9,999	12615	5670	14.5	44.9	95	982	12.4	7.8	81	1802	13.6	14.3	89	2885	16.1	22.9	105
Under $5,000	9690	4012	10.0	40.3	85	726	9.2	7.5	78	1422	10.7	14.7	91	1753	9.8	18.1	83
Household of 1 person	11507	4256	10.9	37.0	78	780	9.9	6.8	71	1364	10.3	11.9	74	2112	11.8	18.4	85
2 people	26162	11598	29.7	44.3	94	2024	25.6	7.7	81	3993	30.1	15.3	95	5582	31.2	21.3	98
3 or 4 people	30393	15581	39.9	51.3	108	3261	41.3	10.7	112	5313	40.0	17.5	109	7007	39.1	23.1	106
5 or more people	14462	7634	19.5	52.8	111	1828	23.2	12.6	132	2608	19.6	18.0	112	3198	17.9	22.1	102
No child in hshld	46283	19600	50.2	42.3	89	3519	44.6	7.6	79	6553	49.4	14.2	88	9529	53.2	20.6	95
Child(ren) under 2 yrs	6515	3654	9.4	56.1	118	863	10.9	13.2	138	1132	8.5	17.4	108	1658	9.3	25.4	117
2–5 years	12221	6696	17.1	54.8	116	1386	17.6	11.3	119	2616	19.7	21.4	133	2693	15.0	22.0	102
6–11 years	16043	8713	22.3	54.3	115	1971	25.0	12.3	128	3056	23.0	19.0	118	3686	20.6	23.0	106
12–17 years	18397	9637	24.7	52.4	111	2199	27.9	12.0	125	3296	24.8	17.9	111	4142	23.1	22.5	104

Source: "Simmons Study of Media and Markets" (New York: Simmons Market Research Bureau, 1980), p. 312.

to marketing planning, whether the plan involves industrial goods or consumer goods, products or services. In the following discussion, we will focus primarily on ultimate consumers of tangible products because this group tends to be the most complex and enigmatic of the customer types. The parallel to industrial and service marketing should be apparent.

Who is the customer? Male or female? Rich or poor? Young or old? We describe customers demographically and psychographically, and these descriptors guide the marketing planner in several ways, the most important of which is the choice of a market segment. *What* does the customer buy? How is it used? We assume that what is bought and the volume in which it is consumed are rooted in the physical and psychological needs of the consumer. Utilizing this information, the marketing planner is able to make suggestions on product line and service offerings.

The most ambitious effort to profile the ultimate consumers of selected products or services is published annually by Simmons Market Research Bureau. A sample of its market report is shown in Exhibit 4.20. It provides an excellent summary of the customer information a marketing planner should have. Exhibit 4.21 displays selected descriptors for various usage segments of the personal care market. Notice that two segmentation distinctions have already been identified. The first is on the basis of sex. The second is on the basis of usage. That there are significant differences among these bases is evident from the exhibit, which shows the incidence of usage for the same four personal-care products between males and females and among heavy to light users. From this summary, it is evident that women constitute a far more important market for these products than do men. Accordingly, Exhibit 4.20 looks only at female users of hair conditioners.

Exhibit 4.21.   Comparison of percentages of male and female users of hair care products.

	Total Users	Heavy Users	Medium Users	Light Users	Non-Users
Female					
Hair conditioners	47.3	9.6	16.1	21.7	52.7
Shampoo	92.7	35.4	37.1	20.2	7.3
Hair coloring	25.5	8.9	8.1	8.5	74.5
Disposable shavers	43.6	16.3	16.2	11.0	56.4
Male					
Hair conditioners	23.3	7.4	8.6	7.4	76.7
Shampoo	90.1	25.7	34.2	30.2	9.9
Hair coloring	5.7	2.6	—	3.1	94.3
Disposable shavers	29.0	8.6	10.2	10.2	71.0

Note: Percentages may not add exactly, due to rounding.
Source: "Simmons Study of Media and Markets" (New York: Simmons Market Research Bureau, 1980).

But all female users are not alike in their patterns of consumption. There are heavy, medium, and light users—and, of course, a few nonusers as well. If the consumers in these usage segments also differ in demographic and psychographic dimensions, this information can help the marketing planner to target a program to whichever segment appears most attractive.

The Simmons figures represent an extrapolation from its sample to the overall market. Thus the figures actually show the number of females in each category. These numbers are useful in estimating actual consumption, but are cumbersome in trying to identify the highest potential segments. The index numbers are included to facilitate this. The index compares the extent of usage by any given category of customer to the market as a whole. Thus, if 25 percent of all female users of hair conditioners are heavy users, but 50 percent of all females between 18 and 35 are heavy users, this age segment's index would be 200—that is, twice the proportion of young females are heavy users as is found in the market as a whole.

When the time comes in the planning process to identify target markets, the marketing planner looks first at the high-index cells. In Exhibit 4.20, these would be:

18–24 years of age
attended college
employed full-time
probably single
blue-collar employment
located on Pacific coast
lives in a metropolitan area (center city, not suburb)
income $15,000 to $20,000
children, mostly older, in household

Of course it is always important to look at the absolute values as well as the index. It is possible for a high-index cell to have fewer occupants than a low-index one. For example, heavy female users of hair conditioners who are single show a higher index than do married users, but there are far fewer heavy users who are single (2.0 million) than married (4.2 million), simply because there are more married than single females.

Knowing the who and the what of consumer behavior leads directly to the *why* and the *how* of consumption. What motivates the customer? What attitudes and beliefs prevail? What process is employed in reaching decisions to buy or not to buy? One popular explanation lies in the theory of information processing; another is in the adoption process. These questions of why and how suggest that the marketing planner needs to be well schooled in the discipline of buyer behavior and thoroughly acquainted with the theories and concepts involved. And so you must be.[3]

When and *where* refer to the timing of purchase and use and to the locations where buying decisions are made and transactions are completed. Timing of consumption dictates the scheduling of promotional activities such as advertising and promotional events. Location affects trade channel selection, as well as the use of point-of-sale promotion and merchandising materials.

Company Capability Analysis

Successful marketing depends not only upon the existence of external opportunities, but upon the ability of a company to compete effectively. Here the marketing planner must deal objectively with the reality that his or her organization, in common with all others, possesses a mix of competencies and deficiencies. Some things it does with consummate skill; others it does not so well, perhaps even quite poorly. The company capability analysis focuses on the search for strengths and weaknesses that may affect the success of marketing efforts. These may be found in the marketing function as well as in other functions whose activities are closely tied to the effects of any marketing plan. Let us consider some of these factors.

Sales Performance

Ultimately, the most important consequences of a company's capability (including its marketing) is its impact upon sales and earnings. Past performance is a reflection of historical competence. The forecast is a statement which projects that competence into the future.

The starting point is an adequate data base. Company sales data should be displayed in exactly the same manner as industry sales, except in greater detail. Sales statistics by product, by price line or pricing point, by territory, by customer, by type of channel, and by time period are needed to pinpoint the effects that marketing is called upon to influence.

This information is needed for more than just the most recent past. The forward-planning time frame generally dictates how far back the sales data base should go. If the strategic planning process calls for a five-year planning horizon, then a sales history of at least five years is desirable. In any event, the history should be long enough to cover at least one full purchase cycle, one complete season, and (if possible) one complete business cycle. But if only one or two years' data are available, great care should be exercised in their use. Some businesses (agriculture, capital goods, and so on) are very cyclical. They swing dramatically from boom years to bust years. These swings have a great impact on sales, so you should be aware of the range in sales results between the two extremes.

An example of a sales analysis, using an electronic spreadsheet, is shown in Exhibit 4.22. The basic breakdown is by time period. The top part of the exhibit displays sales, cost, and margin information. The lower parts break down the sales figures by product line and by territory. With additional information, it would be possible to analyze the same information for trade channels and by customers. As long as the sales data base is properly coded, your information system should be able to report these figures in almost any way you feel helpful.

Once you have identified the sales categories you want to use and have these arranged chronologically, you can perform the same time series analyses that you used to study the industry sales data. In particular, you will want to isolate the seasonal, cyclical, and trend components. After you have a complete statistical picture of the

Exhibit 4.22. Sales analysis by territory and product—spreadsheet analysis.

	1980	1981	1982	1983	1984	1985
Sales in units	1,459,983	1,518,382	1,579,118	1,642,283	1,707,974	1,776,293
Price per unit	$19	$19	$20	$21	$22	$23
Sales in dollars	$27,018,165	$29,363,342	$31,912,080	$34,682,048	$37,692,450	$40,964,155
Cost per unit	$11	$11	$12	$13	$14	$15
Total cost of goods sold	$15,602,370	$17,281,185	$19,140,641	$21,200,174	$23,481,313	$26,007,902
Gross margin dollars	$11,415,795	$12,082,156	$12,771,439	$13,481,874	$14,211,137	$14,956,253
Gross margin percent	42.3	41.1	40.0	38.9	37.7	36.5
Sales by product line						
A	$145,998	$182,205	$252,659	$328,457	$426,994	$532,888
B	$291,997	$303,677	$315,824	$328,457	$341,595	$355,259
C	$583,993	$607,353	$615,856	$656,913	$683,190	$710,517
D	$437,995	$425,147	$394,780	$328,457	$256,196	$177,629
Total	$1,459,983	$1,518,382	$1,579,118	$1,642,283	$1,707,974	$1,776,293
Sales by territory						
NE	$291,997	$273,309	$252,659	$213,497	$170,797	$142,103
S	$145,998	$182,206	$221,077	$279,188	$358,675	$408,547
MW	$437,995	$409,963	$363,197	$312,034	$273,276	$248,681
SW	$145,998	$197,390	$252,659	$328,457	$375,754	$408,547
M	$218,998	$227,757	$252,659	$279,188	$307,435	$319,733
P	$218,998	$227,757	$236,868	$229,920	$222,037	$248,681
Total	$1,459,983	$1,518,382	$1,579,118	$1,642,283	$1,707,974	$1,776,293

company's sales history, you must put it into perspective. This is accomplished in two ways. First, you compare company sales to industry sales to determine your market share. Note any major differences between the manner in which your company's sales fluctuate and the ways in which industry sales vary. For example, if the trend factor for your company's sales is not as strong as for the industry, consider whether the product is losing share or has entered the decline stage of its product life cycle.

The second industry comparison involves an inspection of company sales versus market potential. Since estimates of potential usually can be generated even if actual industry sales are not known, this may be the only feasible comparison. But even if presumably accurate industry sales figures are available (and they may not be), they may not be as meaningful as an estimate of potential. For example, suppose an entire industry has failed to develop the potential market. Even if your company has a dominant share of the business, you may be able to increase business substantially by greater penetration without having to take sales away from competitors. For example, the marketing manager of a large metropolitan bank was able to obtain good increases in volume each year for quite some period of time. Management was pleased. Eventually, this person moved on to another position. A new marketing manager took over and was able to double the bank's business in a single year! The bank had been growing and had enjoyed increased market share, but it had not even begun to push the limit of its market potential. To avoid this kind of situation, compare company sales to industry potential to determine the effectiveness with which your company has developed its markets. This might involve the preparation of a brand development index, as described previously.

Another common way of looking at marketing is by monitoring market share. Market share is a simple concept, but it presents some serious measurement problems. It is the ratio of company sales to industry sales. That is simple enough, but what industry? Should a regional oil refiner in Wichita that primarily serves rural areas in the plains states calculate its share relative to all agribusiness, to those firms serving the same rural markets, or only to the volume of other regional refiners? What about a department store in a large city? Is its share figured by comparing its sales to those of all general merchandise stores in the city, to other department stores, or to only those carrying similar lines of merchandise and serving more or less the same group of households? In general, marketers prefer to relate their own sales to those in the served market—that market or area in which they actually compete.

The concept of the *served market* is helpful in selecting that part of a total industry which is relevant for the calculation of market share. See Exhibit 4.23. The total market can first be broken down to the portion that comes to your company as its share and the balance, which is called the *leaked market*. Your share of market is composed of two major sources of business: (1) those customers for which you have not had to compete (that is, volume that comes from other divisions of your company), and (2) those customers competed for and won in the open market. The leaked market—those customers your company has not gained—comprises four categories: (1) customers competed for and lost, (2) customers you have not been able to win because of merchandising and sales coverage deficiencies, and (3) customers that have been impossible to win because you have been unable to reach them, because of either channel deficiencies or a lack of geographical coverage. The final portion of the leaked market is made up of customers that have requirements which your firm cannot meet—in terms of technology, price, or both.

The served market is made up of portions of these categories. Only that portion of total sales made to outside customers is included in the served market. Of course, all outside business that your company has won in the open market, as well as those prospects whom you could satisfy with some modification of merchandising or sales strategy, are also part of the served market. Only those industry users whose needs your firm is not in a position to satisfy—that is, those who are outside of your market coverage or whose requirements in the way of technology or price you cannot meet—are considered outside your served market. A worksheet for estimating the served market, the leaked market, and the total market is found in Exhibit 4.24.

Exhibit 4.23.   Sources of market share and market leakage.

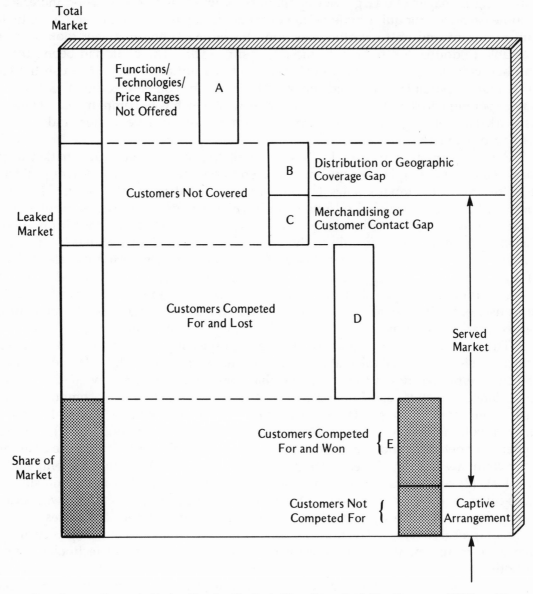

Source: Day, George. *Strategic Market Planning* (St. Paul, Minn.: West Publishing Company, 1984), p. 81.

Financial Performance

Sales is only one measure that marketing planners must track. At present, many companies are forced to limit the analysis of profit to an inspection of gross margin—that is, net sales minus cost of goods sold. Gross margin is expressed both in total dollars and as a percentage of net sales. Although gross margin fails to take into account any of the other costs, including marketing costs, it can be a very revealing figure. Consider the data in Exhibit 4.22. Gross margin percentage has steadily declined for five years. This is probably a serious problem, and its causes need to be identified. The data indicate that although volume in units and dollars has actually increased, cost of goods sold has increased faster. The fact that gross margin dollars have increased, owing to a substantial increase in unit volume, tends to hide the very serious problem that exists. Obviously, further fact-finding is required. What cost variances (raw material, labor, productivity) made cost of goods increase? Once the marketing planner gets a handle on these variables, actions can be planned to deal with them.

When managerial costing systems become more generally available, marketing managers will increasingly be held responsible for the planning, direction, and control of contribution margins (gross margin minus direct marketing costs). While marketing planners in many firms are not yet responsible for profit, they are sometimes held accountable for the profit consequences of the programs they propose. If you want your company to invest substantially in building awareness of a particular brand or to introduce a new product, you may well be asked how long the payout period will be, as well as the present value of the proposed strategy.[4]

Sales and profit information can prove invaluable in identifying the issues that must be addressed in the marketing plan. Declining sales, shrinking market share, and sagging profits often call for aggressive counter moves. But opportunities can also be

Exhibit 4.24. Worksheet for estimating market share and market leakage.

Record, as best you can measure or estimate, the following information.

Total Company Sales _____

Less:

1. Company sales to other divisions and departments _____

Equals:

2. Net sales to external customers _____

Add:

3. Sales lost to competitors competed for at parity _____
4. Lost sales owing to merchandising or customer contact gap _____
5. Lost sales owing to geographic or distribution coverage _____
6. Lost sales owing to technologies or prices not offered _____
7. Leaked market (Sum of 3–6) _____
8. Served market (Sum of 2, 3, and 4) _____
9. Total market (Sum of 2 and 7) _____

Exhibit 4.25.   Worksheet   for   recording   information   about   nonmarketing functions.

Function or department: _____

1. Briefly describe the activities of this function—notably the ways in which it affects the marketing planning process:

   _____

   _____

   _____

2. What abilities or competencies in this function can be utilized to achieve a competitive advantage?

   _____

   _____

   _____

3. What weaknesses does this function possess which could limit its ability to perform its marketing responsibilities? (Focus particularly on areas in which breakdowns have occurred in the past.)

   _____

   _____

   _____

4. Who is the principal decision maker?

   _____

   _____

   _____

5. Who are other important decision influencers?

   _____

   _____

   _____

6. Who is the initial contact person in the function?

   _____

   _____

Exhibit 4.25. Continued.

7. Any other useful information.

_____

_____

_____

detected, as when sales in certain markets or of particular products show signs of growth. In either case, the analyst needs a forecast to put these signals into perspective for the future.

Other Functions

As previously noted, marketing cannot function in isolation. Its ability to accomplish even its own specialized objectives often depends on the resources and skills provided by other functions and on the willingness of the managers of these other departments to get involved, even indirectly, in the marketing process. Exhibit 4.25 is a worksheet that can be used to record key information about the nonmarketing functions that affect your marketing plan. One of these sheets should be completed for each function.

Nonmarketing functions with which you will probably have to establish some rapport are:

Finance and Accounting. These functions affect marketing in many ways. Finance may or may not have the authority to approve or disapprove budget proposals, but it certainly assumes the responsibility for monitoring expenditures. It may have considerable power to approve payments to vendors, extend credit to customers, and allocate marketing costs to specific products or projects. The day is long past when marketing strategists were not expected to understand techniques of accounting and finance, or for financial managers not to get involved in marketing spending decisions. Of more particular concern to the financial executive are the availability of funds and the projection of cash flows. Budgeting decisions based on this information will vitally affect the level and timing of marketing expenditures.

Production and Materials Management. These functions, concerned as they are with manufacturing and inventory management, may seem far removed from the arena in which marketing decisions are made. The separation is more apparent than real. What production cannot provide or inventory managers cannot deliver, marketing cannot promote or sell. Close coordination is critical.

Moreover, circumstances in manufacturing create opportunities that marketing can address. Ideas for new or improved products often arise in the manufacturing department. Irregular production may stimulate a search for business opportunities to fill out the schedule. Cost of production always seriously influences the profitability of specific products. Marketing and manufacturing must be closely related in searching for ways to serve customers profitably.

Research and Development. It is here that ideas for new products are often born and developed. R&D drives the technology that eventually produces tomorrow's products. We have stressed continuously the importance of planning marketing strategies well into the future. R&D is often the basis for programs of this kind.

Management Information. Marketing is so dependent on a sufficient data base that the marketing planner must become thoroughly familiar with the information services that a company provides. Ideally, the management information system (MIS)—or, as it is coming to be called, the decision support system (DSS)—should be able to deliver the bulk of information sought for the marketing situation analysis. This is seldom the case, but each development in data processing brings the goal closer. Usually the internal data on sales and profits are available. Inventory levels and movement, production schedules, and budget status reports are equally accessible. External data bases can also be accessed. Decision models can be incorporated.

Marketing

The final and, in most respects, the most important internal factor is the marketing function itself. In general, what is important in the situation analysis is for the marketing planner to be up to date on the firm's marketing capabilities, on its present strategy and its results, and on any directions that management expects to take in the future. Of course, the marketing planner may have been personally involved in the development of these programs. But in some cases, as when the marketing responsibility is distributed among several functions and a number of product or brand managers, it is sometimes difficult for any one planner to be thoroughly familiar with the company's overall marketing strategy. The dimensions of capability and strategy are both conveniently described in terms of the company's marketing mix. A worksheet for summarizing the analysis of marketing mix is found in Exhibit 4.26.

The Product or Service Offering. What objectives have driven the development of the company's product or service offerings? What are these offerings? What are their unique and differentiating characteristics, if any? What benefits do they convey? Do they have any undesirable features? If so, what is being done to eliminate them? These and a number of equally important questions can be asked.

Distribution. What purposes have driven your distribution strategy? How and where is the offering made available to its final users? It is at this point that the marketing planner identifies any strengths and weaknesses of his or her company's distribution system. This assessment is second in importance only to that of the offering itself. Is the product in the right outlets? Is it in enough of them? Is it subject to out-of-stock problems? Is its shelf position optimal? Is it given point-of-sale promotional support? The answers to such questions inevitably paint a picture of distribution strength or weakness—factors that can easily make the difference between a successful and an unsuccessful program. Occasionally, distribution becomes the focal point of an entire marketing program.

(text continued on p. 98)

Exhibit 4.26.   Marketing mix analysis worksheet.

Product

Summarize the essential elements of the present product strategy.

1. What have been the recent product objectives?

    _____

    _____

    _____

    _____

2. How well have these been achieved?

    _____

    _____

    _____

    _____

3. List your major products and record the competitive strengths and weakness of each:

Product	Strengths	Weaknesses
_____	_____	_____
_____	_____	_____
_____	_____	_____
_____	_____	_____
_____	_____	_____
_____	_____	_____
_____	_____	_____
_____	_____	_____
_____	_____	_____

Exhibit 4.26.   Continued.

4. List the actions that might be taken to improve the competitive position of each major product:

Product   Actions to Improve Competitive Position

_____   _____

_____   _____

_____   _____

_____   _____

_____   _____

_____   _____

_____   _____

5. What services are offered to support the product strategy?

_____

_____

_____

6. What is the packaging program?

_____

_____

_____

7. What is the branding strategy?

_____

_____

_____

8. Summarize the strengths of the product strategy:

_____

_____

_____

Exhibit 4.26. Continued.

9. Summarize any weaknesses of the product strategy:

_____

_____

_____

Distribution

Diagram your distribution channels in the same manner as in Exhibit 4.18.

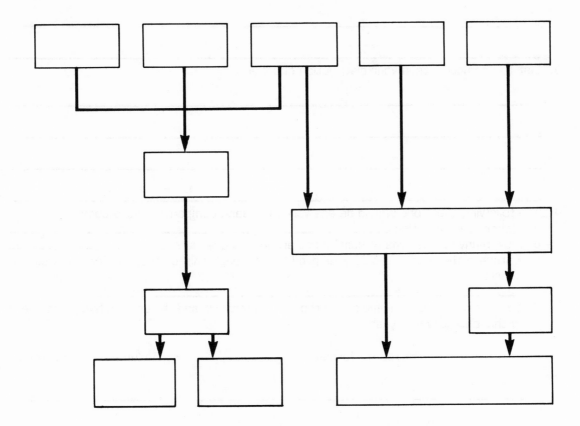

Exhibit 4.26.   Continued.

1. What have been the recent distribution objectives?

   _____

   _____

   _____

   _____

2. How well have these been achieved?

   _____

   _____

   _____

   _____

3. List the components in your distribution channel:

   _____

   _____

   _____

   _____

4. The following questions should be answered for each component listed above.
    a. Describe its function: _____
    b. How many of this type of component are in this channel? _____
    c. Estimate the total sales of your products through this component for the last five years:

    _____ _____ _____ _____ _____

    d. List the names and volume of the top five performers and the bottom five performers in this category last year:

5 Top Performers	Volume	% Total
_____	_____	_____
_____	_____	_____
_____	_____	_____
_____	_____	_____
_____	_____	_____

Exhibit 4.26.   Continued.

5 Bottom Performers	Volume	% Total
_____	_____	_____
_____	_____	_____
_____	_____	_____
_____	_____	_____
_____	_____	_____

e. What margin or cost is involved? _____

f. What problems arise when using this component?

    _____

    _____

g. What competitive capabilities does this component provide?

    _____

    _____

h. Other useful information:

    _____

    _____

    _____

Sales

Summarize the essential elements of the present sales strategy.

1. What have been the recent sales objectives?

    _____

    _____

    _____

Exhibit 4.26.   Continued.

2. How well have these been achieved?

   _____

   _____

   _____

3. Describe the manner in which the sales function is organized:

   _____

   _____

   _____

4. How is the sales effort distributed geographically?

   _____

   _____

   _____

   _____

   _____

5. Describe the method of sales compensation:

   _____

   _____

   _____

   _____

6. What incentives are employed (quota, contest, and so on)?

   _____

   _____

   _____

7. Summarize the strengths of the sales function:

   _____

   _____

   _____

Exhibit 4.26. Continued.

8. Summarize any weaknesses of the sales function:

_____

_____

_____

_____

Advertising

Summarize the essential elements of the present advertising strategy.

1. What have been the recent advertising objectives?

_____

_____

_____

2. How well have these been achieved?

_____

_____

_____

_____

3. List the advertising media used, together with expenditures last year:

Medium	Space Cost	CPM	Production
_____	_____	____	_____
_____	_____	____	_____
_____	_____	____	_____
_____	_____	____	_____
_____	_____	____	_____
_____	_____	____	_____
_____	_____	____	_____
_____	_____	____	_____

Exhibit 4.26. Continued.

Medium	Space Cost	CPM	Production
_____	_____	____	_____
_____	_____	____	_____
_____	_____	____	_____
_____	_____	____	_____
_____	_____	____	_____

Research

_____			_____
_____			_____

Total   _____

4. Describe the role of your advertising agency (if any):

_____

_____

_____

5. Identify the target audiences:

_____

_____

_____

_____

6. Describe the creative approach:

_____

_____

_____

7. Summarize the strengths of the advertising program:

_____

_____

_____

Exhibit 4.26. Continued.

8. Summarize any weaknesses of the advertising program:

_____

_____

_____

Sales Promotion

Summarize the essential elements of the present sales promotion strategy.

1. What have been the recent sales promotion objectives?

_____

_____

_____

2. How well have these been achieved?

_____

_____

_____

3. List the sales promotion media used, together with expenditures last year:

Medium	Cost
_____	_____
_____	_____
_____	_____
_____	_____
_____	_____
_____	_____

Research

_____	_____
_____	_____

Total   _____

Exhibit 4.26.   Continued.

4. Describe the role of your promotion agency (if any):

_____

_____

_____

5. Identify the target audiences:

_____

_____

_____

6. Summarize the strengths of the sales promotion program:

_____

_____

_____

7. Summarize any weaknesses of the sales promotion program:

_____

_____

_____

Pricing

Summarize the essential elements of the present pricing strategy.

1. What have been the recent pricing objectives?

_____

_____

_____

2. How well have these been achieved?

_____

_____

_____

Exhibit 4.26. Continued.

3. List major products and the average list price of each. In each case indicate whether this price is at, above, or below industry average:

Product	List Price	Compared to Industry		
		Par	Above	Below
_____	_____	___	___	___
_____	_____	___	___	___
_____	_____	___	___	___
_____	_____	___	___	___

4. Describe the discount strategy that is employed:

   a. Trade discounts: _____

   _____

   b. Quantity discounts: _____

   _____

   c. Promotional discounts: _____

   _____

5. Describe the way in which market and cost factors are balanced in setting your prices:

   _____

   _____

   _____

6. Summarize the strengths of the pricing program:

   _____

   _____

   _____

7. Summarize any weaknesses of the pricing program:

   _____

   _____

   _____

Sales. In many large companies, sales responsibility is not in the marketing department. Nonetheless, the interaction between sales and marketing is extensive. It is imperative that these two functions work in closest harmony, but often there is some conflict, some competition between the two.

It is at least partly the responsibility of the marketing planner to keep this friction from interfering with the achievement of the company's larger goal of satisfying customers. Specifically, the marketing planner must assess the effectiveness of the sales effort. This evaluation should start with a review of previous sales objectives and an examination of how well these have been accomplished. What type of sales organization has been used? How is the sales force assigned geographically? What compensation and motivation programs have been used? Viewed from the marketing planner's perspective, a sales organization can be strong or weak, cooperative or uncooperative. These assessments must be made, because they may well influence the kind of strategy that eventually is designed.

Advertising. Advertising is not a major force in the marketing programs of most industrial companies, whereas it is often the most important factor in the strategies of consumer packaged-goods firms. Regardless of the scope of your company's advertising program, it is important for the marketing planner to assess carefully the effectiveness of such advertising as is feasible for the company. What advertising objectives have been addressed? Is the target market correctly defined? Have message concepts and execution been "on strategy"? How well have they worked? Have the right media and spending levels been employed, and has the budget been allocated properly among products and markets?

Sales Promotion. Sales promotion straddles the sales and advertising functions. Sometimes the sales department is responsible, sometimes advertising is, and occasionally it is carried out by a separate department. Normally, sales promotion is a facilitating function and is dependent upon either, or both, of the other demand-creating forces for direction. Because of this intersection, sales promotion tends to be the specific area where coordination between advertising and sales is achieved and differences are resolved. The questions to be asked and answered for sales promotion are essentially the same as for advertising.

Price. Pricing is not so much a function, as a pervasive force that affects not only the rest of the marketing mix but the entire business. Price is the mechanism of revenue. It is the beginning of creating profit. It is, therefore, of prime concern to top management, to financial planners, and to marketing planners alike. Revenue must also cover costs, and so every function has a stake in the price. Marketing planners do not have the last say about what price is to be charged, but they have much to do with the consideration of what price might be charged. For these reasons, nonprice strategy decisions, such as product quality and advertising, should be made in concert with pricing decisions.

As you evaluate the pricing component of the marketing mix, it will be necessary to review the several decision areas that make up a pricing strategy. What have been your pricing objectives? What basic price has been employed? What discount structure? How well has this pricing strategy worked?

Summarizing the Data

At this point you have assembled the information you will need in preparing your marketing plan. You may think that you have far more information than you can possibly use. In the worksheet format, you probably do. Logically then, the next step in the situation analysis is to summarize the findings and isolate the most important ones. A procedure for doing this is presented in Chapter 5.

5

The Analytic Summaries

In the course of preparing the situation analysis, you have collected a great deal of information. It is well beyond the intellectual capacity of most human beings to store, recall, and process adequately this amount of information. To compress this into usable form, the marketing planner should prepare a set of analytic summaries. This is Step 5 in the planning process.

The planner has several options: SWOP analysis, product/market segment matrix, sales forecast, gap analysis, product life cycle analysis, directional matrix, and the financial summary. We will discuss each of these in this chapter.

SWOP Analysis

SWOP is an acronym for Strength-Weakness-Opportunity-Problem. Every circumstance you have identified in the situation analysis that will affect the success of your marketing program can be classified as a SWOP item. The SWOP summary is a prioritized list in which statements about each strength, weakness, problem, and opportunity are presented and explained.

A *strength* is any company capability that can be employed effectively in pursuit of an objective. It may lie in the firm's manufacturing ability or it could be in sales, advertising, or any number of other areas. In fact, a company should possess strengths in a number of functions—possibly in all key areas—to ensure success.

Think of a successful marketing company—perhaps IBM, Emerson Electric, or McDonald's. Each possesses many strengths, but it is not difficult to spot the capabilities that underlie their marketing successes. For IBM, it is its sales and service force, a well-disciplined army of highly trained customer-contact personnel. Emerson's strength is in its ability to be the low-cost producer in very large, mature industries. Strength at McDonald's is its skill in locating its restaurants and its ability to standardize service without sacrificing customer satisfaction.

A *weakness* is any important deficiency in a company that could detract from its ability to achieve its objectives. In a way, a weakness is simply the other end of the scale. A weakness could be in manufacturing, in marketing, in finance, and so on. Few firms can really expect to be exceptionally strong in all areas. Typically, a company will be less endowed in some aspects of its operations than in others. These areas of weakness represent liabilities, and to the extent feasible, they should be improved. At the very least, you should avoid strategies that require competence in an area of weakness until the deficiency is corrected.

Organizations with serious weaknesses do not survive. New products that possess serious deficiencies do not succeed. The marketing cemetery is full, but most of the graves are unmarked. Robert Hartley has published an interesting book on marketing failures.[1] Among those mistakes described are Nestlé's Infant Formula, Korvette, A. C. Gilbert, the World Football League, Burger Chef, W. T. Grant, Ford's Edsel, Corfam, Osborne Computer, and more. Sometimes the failure has been owing to a window that closed. Sometimes there was no opportunity to begin with. More often, however, a major weakness or deficiency in the company or its marketing program was to blame. Don't let this happen to you.

The term *competence* suggests another very instructive way in which to highlight a company's critical strengths. It has been suggested that every organization has, or should have, a distinctive competency: some function or capability in which it possesses an outright competitive advantage. It could be a unique product, a particular manufacturing process, low cost of production, or a highly desirable location. Strategies, in general, should be based upon distinctive competencies, for these are the unique strengths on which the company can capitalize. From the perspective of marketing management, it is highly desirable for a company to possess a distinctive competency that bears directly on the marketing opportunity. It could be a unique selling proposition—a benefit that the competition cannot claim to match. It could be in the funds available, or in many other areas.

On the other hand, there may be business weaknesses that are serious enough to impose an absolute obstacle to the company's ability to capitalize on a marketing opportunity. We call such serious disabilities *distinctive deficiencies*. The marketing planner must be as willing to recognize a deficiency as to rejoice in the discovery of a business competency. A distinctive deficiency heralds a serious situation that must be corrected before hope of achieving an objective can be justified. In marketing terms, the most serious deficiencies usually are in a lack of differentiated products, inadequate distribution, high costs, and insufficient funds.

An *opportunity* is a statement about an external circumstance which, if promptly and vigorously seized, may make it possible to achieve an objective. Note that an opportunity offers only the chance to succeed. There are no sure bets in the business of marketing. And timing is important. Many marketing opportunities are what Derek Abell calls "strategic windows."[2] They emerge, stay open for a brief period, and then close again. Like a rocket launch, there are limited fortuitous combinations of circumstances that present excellent marketing opportunities. When these strategic windows open, they should be pursued vigorously. A prolonged strike or a major fire that closes a company's plant is an opportunity for its competitor. An unexpected favorable shift in demand, a dramatic improvement in the economy, and a technological breakthrough are other examples of circumstances that usually produce marketing opportunities.

A *problem* is a statement about an external circumstance which, if not properly addressed, will make it difficult—if not impossible—to achieve an objective. An example would be the threat posed by a competitor's new price or aggressive advertising campaign. An unfavorable court ruling, a decline in the economy, a protracted period of inclement weather—these are all events that create problems which must be addressed in the marketing plan.

In preparing the SWOP summary, the marketing planner reviews every statement of fact about the marketing situation and classifies it as either a strength, a weakness, an opportunity, or a problem. *No fact can be classified in more than one way.* A given situation cannot be both problem and opportunity at the same time.

Exhibit 5.1 is a series of worksheets to be used in preparing the SWOP summary. In a way, each worksheet can be thought of as a log or diary. The marketing planner might well set up these worksheets at the beginning of the situation analysis. As information is assembled, important SWOP issues can immediately be recorded on the appropriate worksheet. An alternative method is to complete the worksheets as soon as the information-gathering phase of the situation analysis has been completed. It is a good idea to do this as the review of each analytic perspective is completed.

Note that each worksheet has four columns. Column 1 is for an identification number. These numbers are assigned sequentially as the issues are recorded. A prefix letter—S, W, O, or P—followed by a series of consecutive numbers is used to identify each issue recorded on the worksheet. Thus, the first listed strength is S–1, the fifth is S–5, and so on. Column 2 is for a succinct and clear statement of the circumstance. Column 3 is used to identify the information source, such as "Quarterly Sales Summary, January–March 1987" or "*Wall Street Journal*, 1/6/87, p. 22." If two or more sources have been found, cite the most reliable and comprehensive.

A final step in SWOP analysis involves scoring each statement in terms of its importance to strategic thinking. Column 4 is used to score each statement, with a score from 0 (low) to 10 (high) assigned to each item. Eventually, a rule can be adopted as to the level of score that will be selected for inclusion in the final SWOP summary. If there are more than ten items (or whatever reasonable number you elect to employ) on any of the SWOP lists, prepare an abbreviated list containing only the ten most important items; see Exhibit 5.2. List the items in descending order of importance. Record the original identification number so you preserve a clear audit trail back to your data base.

Product/Market Segment Matrix

This is an exhibit that shows exactly which products are (or could be) sold in each market segment, as well as the growth rate and the future potential of each. This matrix is used to assist in selecting the market focus of the marketing plan. The determination could have been made in Step 3, prior to the situation analysis, but as was pointed out

(text continued on p. 111)

Exhibit 5.1. SWOP worksheet.

	Strengths		
I.D. No.	Circumstance or Issue	Source	Score
——	————————————	——————————	——
——	————————————	——————————	——
——	————————————	——————————	——
——	————————————	——————————	——
——	————————————	——————————	——
——	————————————	——————————	——
——	————————————	——————————	——
——	————————————	——————————	——
——	————————————	——————————	——
——	————————————	——————————	——
——	————————————	——————————	——
——	————————————	——————————	——
——	————————————	——————————	——
——	————————————	——————————	——
——	————————————	——————————	——
——	————————————	——————————	——
——	————————————	——————————	——
——	————————————	——————————	——
——	————————————	——————————	——
——	————————————	——————————	——

Exhibit 5.1. Continued.

I.D. No.	Circumstance or Issue	Source	Score
Weaknesses			
____	_____	_____	____
____	_____	_____	____
____	_____	_____	____
____	_____	_____	____
____	_____	_____	____
____	_____	_____	____
____	_____	_____	____
____	_____	_____	____
____	_____	_____	____
____	_____	_____	____
____	_____	_____	____
____	_____	_____	____
____	_____	_____	____
____	_____	_____	____
____	_____	_____	____
____	_____	_____	____
____	_____	_____	____
____	_____	_____	____
____	_____	_____	____
____	_____	_____	____

Exhibit 5.1.   Continued.

Opportunities

I.D. No.	Circumstance or Issue	Source	Score
___	_____	_____	___
___	_____	_____	___
___	_____	_____	___
___	_____	_____	___
___	_____	_____	___
___	_____	_____	___
___	_____	_____	___
___	_____	_____	___
___	_____	_____	___
___	_____	_____	___
___	_____	_____	___
___	_____	_____	___
___	_____	_____	___
___	_____	_____	___
___	_____	_____	___
___	_____	_____	___
___	_____	_____	___
___	_____	_____	___
___	_____	_____	___
___	_____	_____	___

Exhibit 5.1.   Continued.

	Problems		
I.D. No.	Circumstance or Issue	Source	Score
___	_____	_____	___
___	_____	_____	___
___	_____	_____	___
___	_____	_____	___
___	_____	_____	___
___	_____	_____	___
___	_____	_____	___
___	_____	_____	___
___	_____	_____	___
___	_____	_____	___
___	_____	_____	___
___	_____	_____	___
___	_____	_____	___
___	_____	_____	___
___	_____	_____	___
___	_____	_____	___
___	_____	_____	___
___	_____	_____	___
___	_____	_____	___

Exhibit 5.2. SWOP summaries.

Company Strengths

Summarize in descending order of importance.

	Circumstance or Event	I.D. No.
1.	_____	____
	_____	____
2.	_____	____
	_____	____
3.	_____	____
	_____	____
4.	_____	____
	_____	____
5.	_____	____
	_____	____
6.	_____	____
	_____	____
7.	_____	____
	_____	____
8.	_____	____
	_____	____
9.	_____	____
	_____	____
10.	_____	____
	_____	____

Exhibit 5.2.   Continued.

Company Weaknesses

Summarize in descending order of importance.

Circumstance or Event

I.D.
No.

1. _____ ____

_____ ____

2. _____ ____

_____ ____

3. _____ ____

_____ ____

4. _____ ____

_____ ____

5. _____ ____

_____ ____

6. _____ ____

_____ ____

7. _____ ____

_____ ____

8. _____ ____

_____ ____

9. _____ ____

_____ ____

10. _____ ____

_____ ____

Exhibit 5.2.   Continued.

External Opportunities

Summarize in descending order of importance.

Circumstance or Event	I.D. No.
1. _____	____
_____	____
2. _____	____
_____	____
3. _____	____
_____	____
4. _____	____
_____	____
5. _____	____
_____	____
6. _____	____
_____	____
7. _____	____
_____	____
8. _____	____
_____	____
9. _____	____
_____	____
10. _____	____
_____	____

Exhibit 5.2.   Continued.

External Problems

Summarize in descending order of importance.

	Circumstance or Event	I.D. No.
1.	_____	___
	_____	___
2.	_____	___
	_____	___
3.	_____	___
	_____	___
4.	_____	___
	_____	___
5.	_____	___
	_____	___
6.	_____	___
	_____	___
7.	_____	___
	_____	___
8.	_____	___
	_____	___
9.	_____	___
	_____	___
10.	_____	___
	_____	___

previously, this step may have been postponed if there was not sufficient information to make a proper identification of the target market.

Exhibit 5.3 illustrates one way in which target market information might be summarized. The vertical columns in the matrix represent different customer market segments—for example, different geographic regions or different buyer types. The horizontal rows in the matrix represent different products or services. Each cell in the matrix marks the intersection of a column and a row and it indicates a potential product/market.

Each product/market should be analyzed further and data important in selecting target markets should be shown. In the exhibit, the upper left-hand cell has been divided into four sections, labeled *A, B, C,* and *D*. Part A contains an estimate of the sales potential in the product/market. Part B shows the growth rate in the segment. Part C indicates the company's present share position in the product/market. Part D contains an estimate of the potential profitability of the segment. The matrix is now used to finalize the choice of a focus for the marketing plan.

Exhibit 5.4 is a worksheet to use in preparing the product/market matrix. The designations P1/M1, P1/M2, and so on refer to the cells in the matrix. For each product/ market you are asked to estimate its sales potential, its growth rate, your firm's market share, and its potential profitability. This information can be recorded in the cells of the matrix in the bottom half of Exhibit 5.4.

Sales Forecast

There may be no more important outcome of the situation analysis than the forecast of future sales. Not only does it become the basis for developing marketing plans, but it provides information for planning in other parts of the company. Among the uses to which the sales forecast is put are:

> scheduling of production
> planning inventory, both raw materials and finished goods
> making procurement decisions
> establishing sales goals
> determining advertising budgets
> establishing financial needs, such as working capital and capital spending
> setting prices
> expanding or contracting manufacturing or distribution facilities
> determining organizational and human resource requirements
> planning and scheduling research and development

Some of these are short-run applications. They require immediate decisions that affect current operations. Scheduling production, planning inventory, setting sales goals, estimating working capital needs, and setting advertising budgets are short-run considerations, for example. Ordinarily, a projection of sales for a period of between 3 and 12 months is adequate for these operational decisions. Projections of sales covering

(text continued on p. 114)

Exhibit 5.3.   Product/market segment matrix.

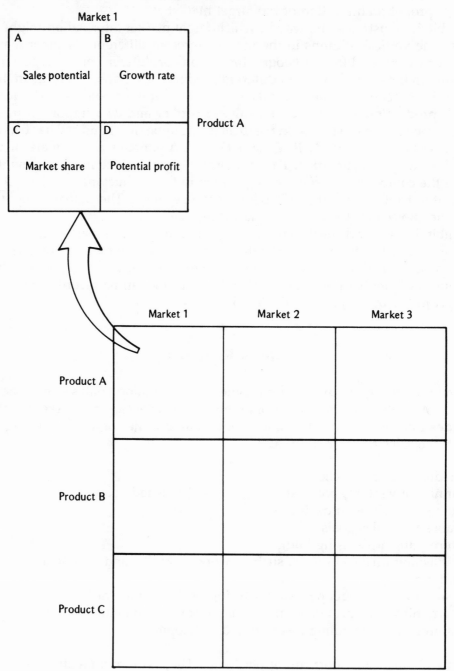

Exhibit 5.4. Product/market matrix worksheet.

1. For each of the cells in the matrix, provide the following information:

	Potential	Growth Rate	Company Share	Profit
P1/M1	_____	_____	_____	_____
P1/M2	_____	_____	_____	_____
P1/M3	_____	_____	_____	_____
P2/M1	_____	_____	_____	_____
P2/M2	_____	_____	_____	_____
P2/M3	_____	_____	_____	_____
P3/M1	_____	_____	_____	_____
P3/M2	_____	_____	_____	_____
P3/M3	_____	_____	_____	_____

2. Note the cells on the matrix below that appear to offer the best opportunities for the company:

Product/Market Matrix

	Market 1	Market 2	Market 3
Product 1			
Product 2			
Product 3			

periods longer than one year, although seldom more than five years, are classified as long-run forecasts. The balance of the applications on the list are of this nature. They are still of importance in the marketing plan, for they cover the same time span as does your marketing strategy.

There are a number of steps which are followed in forecasting sales.[3]

1. Determine the purposes for which forecasts are to be used. These are essentially the same as the list just presented.

2. Divide company products into homogeneous groups. If the company's marketing programs are to be specialized according to the needs of different product/markets, this step has already been accomplished. Even if the firm sells to a fairly homogeneous market segment but its line of offerings is composed of products at different stages of their product life cycles, it is still wise to forecast each of the major product groups separately.

3. Determine the factors affecting the sales of each product and their relative importance. This information results from an understanding of the nature of product demand. The industry and competitive phases of the situation analysis should provide the information needed to complete this step in forecasting.

4. Choose a forecasting method. There are numerous forecasting techniques available, some of which are described in the next section. Usually a choice must be made among these techniques, because it is uneconomical and too time-consuming to use all of them. The choice of technique is generally determined by the purposes of the forecast, the kinds of information available, and the statistical competencies of the marketing planner.

5. Gather the needed data. The need for a forecast and a general idea of the type of forecast to be made should have been kept in mind as the situation analysis was prepared. For example, in analyzing industry and company sales data, the obvious use of these data in preparing the forecast would have been recognized.

6. Analyze the data. This step has also been taken. The basic tools of time series analysis have been mentioned. In addition, other statistical analyses can be made. Of particular use is regression analysis, which can lead to the development of a forecasting model.

7. Check and cross-check findings. The future is always uncertain, and forecasting always involves some error. To reduce the risk arising from an incorrect forecast, it is wise to recheck the work carefully. This should probably be done at least twice, preferably by a different individual each time.

8. Make assumptions regarding other factors. The ability to forecast accurately depends on the ability of the marketing planner to make valid assumptions about factors that cannot be measured. Sometimes, factors that are known to be important are omitted altogether. For example, the character and intensity of its competitors' future programs can be the single most important element affecting a company's sales. Obviously, some assumption regarding competitors' actions and reactions must be made in order to forecast future sales with any degree of reality. As we have seen, when more than one possible state of an external factor could occur, it may be wise to prepare one or more contingency plans.

9. Convert findings and assumptions into specific forecasts. The statistical projec-

tions and assumptions about nonmeasureable factors must be translated into specific sales estimates. As noted previously, a single overall forecast is not very useful in marketing planning. The forecast should be broken down (or built up) by product lines, market segments, territorial coverage, or some combination of the three. Both a long-range forecast (more than one year) and short-run forecasts (three months to a year) should be prepared.

10. Apply the forecast. This step takes the forecaster directly into the decision making involved in preparing the marketing plan. The long-range forecast is used principally in the development of strategy. The short-run forecast is employed in setting goals and standards for short-run performance.

Forecasting Methods

If every minor variation that can be introduced into forecasting were classified as a separate method, the number would be astronomical. Yet, for important reasons, every forecasting assignment tends to be different. Each forecast is made from a slightly different vantage point. The factors that influence sales are constantly changing. The forecaster grows in experience and confidence. The amount of time available for forecasting frequently changes. However, in spite of these factors, there are four general methods that are typically employed.

Naive Methods

Naive methods are unsophisticated and nonscientific mechanical extrapolations of historical data. There are two naive methods that are often used. One is *factor listing*. Factor listing as a forecasting method takes us no further than the third step in the forecasting process. The marketing planner identifies those factors expected to influence sales and attempts subjectively to estimate the extent of their influence. The approach is quick and easy. It can always be used on an interim basis, such as when you must determine if a forecast made some months previously is still valid. The great weakness of the method, however, is that its very simplicity may cause the forecaster to miss a subtle sign of an important impending change.

A second naive method is the *extrapolation of historical data*. The most common approach is to assume that future sales will reflect an increase over the current period that is in proportion to the increase in the current period compared to the preceding one. This is not the same method as the careful use of trend and cycle analysis, which takes into consideration the basic forces of demand that have affected sales over a considerable period of time. Even so, the future is always uncertain; to a degree, even those forecasts based on time series analysis are rooted in the assumption that the basic determinants of demand in the future will not change. This may simply not be true.

Another method of extrapolation employs much more recent sales data. For example, sales figures for the past three to six months are analyzed and extrapolated for a similar short-run period by one of several methods. By far the easiest is that of moving averages. A series of data—say, the past three months of sales—is averaged to produce a forecast for the fourth month. At the end of the fourth month, the average is recalculated, substituting actual sales for the fourth month and eliminating the oldest month's sales. Obviously, the monthly sales data should first be adjusted for seasonal variations, using a seasonal index.

More sophisticated statistical techniques for short-term forecasting are referred to generally as methods of *exponential smoothing*. In general, this type of forecast places the most weight on the most recent sales figures and progressively less weight on sales in prior periods. A smoothing constant is employed in the equation. By selecting the proper value of this constant, the forecaster can influence the degree to which recent or prior sales experience is to be reflected in the moving average.

Correlation Methods

Regression analysis is not in itself a forecast. It is a way of looking at the marketing situation; it is a tool for making the forecast. Regression analysis involves the comparison of two (or more) series of data to discover the relationships between them. We speak generally of independent and dependent variables. A regression analysis permits the identification of these variables. Typically, sales volume is the dependent variable; any number of other factors that influence the level of sales are the independent variables. The correlative relationships may be either linear or nonlinear. As the analysis moves from single to multiple factors and from linear to nonlinear relationships, correlation studies become increasingly complex. However, standardized computer programs that are part of all statistical analysis packages are available.

The use of multiple regression analysis is illustrated by the Conference Board in its description of how a major engine manufacturer estimated demand for its products.[4] The company combines externally produced economic forecasts, internal marketing research information, and previous demand data in a multiple regression model with an extremely good fit. Notice that one of the independent variables for this forecasting method was general economic indicators. This means that forecasts of the independent variables are typically available before the job of forecasting sales begins. So, while it may be difficult to predict your own company's sales, you can do so with this approach as long as there are reliable predictions for the independent variables. Many industrial and consumer-products companies make use of this method of sales forecasting.

Survey Methods

With the exception of factor listing, the forecasting techniques described up to this point are based principally on statistical analysis. In many forecasting situations, however, lack of data, insufficient time, and the inability of the average marketing planner to use sophisticated statistical techniques combine to make such methods unworkable. But the need for forecasting is no less imperative. In such cases, survey methods of forecasting are often utilized. They are superior to purely naive methods because they employ controlled techniques of information gathering. There are three important survey techniques that the marketing planner can utilize.

The Jury of Executive Opinion. Some companies use the opinions of key executives in creating the forecast. These executives, of course, do not venture opinions about future sales without adequate study. In some cases they back up their opinions with the statistical analyses already described.

The jury of executive opinion produces a forecast quickly and often minimizes the effort involved. One of its greatest advantages is that it brings a diversity of viewpoints and experience to the forecasting assignment. The result, however, is usually very subjective and tends to be based on the barest of facts, even in situations in which data are available. But when opinion and data can be combined, a good forecast often results.

Sales Force Composite. In contrast to the jury of executive opinion, this method makes use of the judgments of salespeople, who are in a position to know the market well. The forecast is built up from grassroots estimates of future sales. The PQ Corporation has utilized such an approach for a number of years. Specific estimates are made of the expected volume of products to be sold to each major account, including current customers, old customers who are expected to return, and new customers to be added in the planning period.[5] This type of sales forecast is employed by almost all industrial firms, as well as by consumer-products companies that have access to retail store movement.

Customer Intentions. Closely related to the sales force composite method is the technique of obtaining estimates of future business directly from customers. This method is used principally by direct-selling industrial firms, and it is especially valuable when lack of data concerning the demand determinants precludes the preparation of forecasts in any other way. User-expectation surveys are of critical importance when a firm relies on a limited number of large customers. Marketers of electrical generating equipment, such as General Electric and Westinghouse, rely on the expansion and modernization plans of public utilities as the basis for estimating future sales. Some research sources, such as McGraw-Hill's department of research, periodically publish summaries of user expectations. Similarly, capital spending plans are reported quarterly for most industrial sectors. Process machinery manufacturers, construction firms, machine tool builders, and the like make use of this kind of analysis.

Do not restrict your forecasting to the use of a single method. You should perform two or more simultaneously and then compare the results. It is preferable if these forecasts are prepared by different individuals or departments. One approach might be to ask the marketing research department to prepare an overall economic forecast using correlation techniques and time series analysis. At the same time, a jury of executives can be polled; and, of course, a grassroots sales force composite or a customer intentions survey could be conducted. Whether you decide to undertake such an elaborate approach will depend on the tradeoff you make between the uncertainty you face about the future and the cost and effort required to make more than one independent forecast.

Gap Analysis

This is a chart that portrays the "gap," or difference, between an objective that has been set and the forecast of what the company can expect to achieve *without a change in its present strategy.* Exhibit 5.5 presents an example of gap analysis. The jagged line represents the company's sales between 1980 and 1984. A trend line has been drawn through this sales history and extrapolated to 1989 (point *F* on the chart). This forecast might be modified if the marketing planner chooses to incorporate assumptions about changes in the external environment. For example, the forecast might be adjusted down to *F'* if poor economic or industry demand conditions are expected to prevail for the planning period. Or, it might be adjusted upward to *F"* if the opposite economic climate is expected to prevail. In any event, a forecast (*F*, *F'*, or *F"*) will be made. Note again that this forecast assumes no change in the company's marketing strategy. Therefore, any difference between the objective (shown as *O* on the chart) and the forecast represents a "planning gap" that must be filled (or closed) by an appropriate marketing strategy.

A worksheet for preparing the gap analysis is provided in Exhibit 5.6. In the upper part of the worksheet, record the data you will need to prepare the chart below. The past sales figures can be taken directly from the analysis performed previously. Space is provided to insert forecast figures for each of the next five years, using at least three different forecasting methods. A final, or composite, forecast is entered on line 4. The

Exhibit 5.5.   Gap analysis.

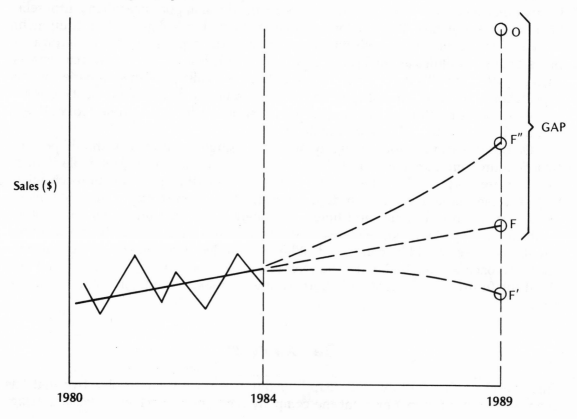

Exhibit 5.6.   Gap analysis worksheet.

	198__	198__	198__	198__	198__
Historical Sales	_____	_____	_____	_____	_____
Forecasting Method	19__	19__	19__	19__	19__
1. _____	_____	_____	_____	_____	_____
2. _____	_____	_____	_____	_____	_____
3. _____	_____	_____	_____	_____	_____
Composite Forecast	_____	_____	_____	_____	_____
Objectives	_____	_____	_____	_____	_____
Planning Gap	_____	_____	_____	_____	_____

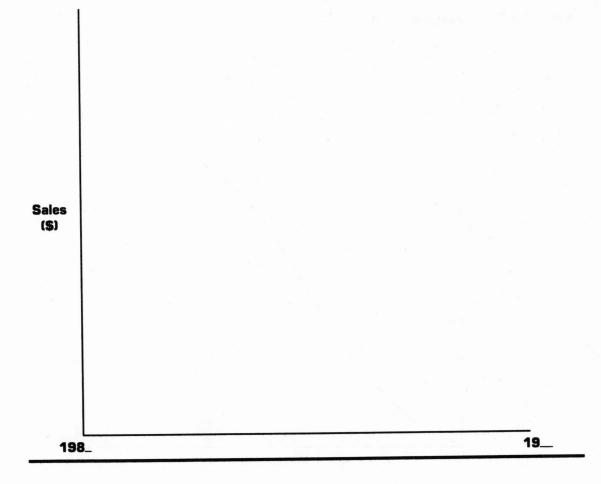

Gap Analysis Chart

objectives for each year come from upper management and were recorded on worksheets that you prepared previously.

The chart provides for plotting the historical sales for the past five years, the forecast for the next five years, and the objectives for the next year, for five years out, and for intermediate periods, if this information is available.

The planning gap establishes the magnitude of the planning assignment. How is this gap to be filled? By developing a marketing strategy that will impel the business beyond the level of the forecast and, it is hoped, to achieve the objective.

A second type of marketing forecast is employed in the search for a strategy to fill the gap. It is called *conditional forecasting* and often is informally employed, although most managers do not realize they are doing so or call it by this name. A conditional forecast is an estimate of the outcome of a strategy. It takes the form of an "if, then" statement. For example:

- If we decrease price by 10 percent, sales volume will increase by 20 percent.

Exhibit 5.7.   A response function.

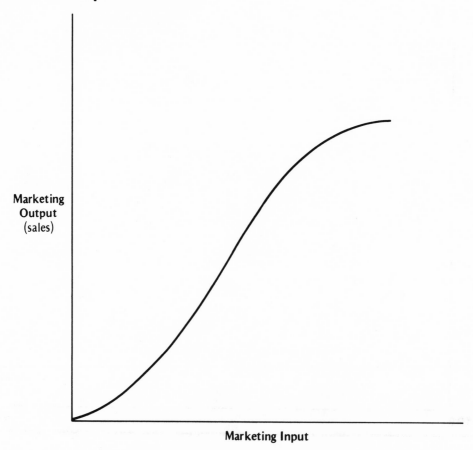

- If we introduce this product improvement, market share will increase to 18 percent.

The relationship of such statements to gap filling should be apparent. We simply reverse the conditional forecast, as in the following:

- If we need to increase sales by 20 percent, we must reduce price by 10 percent.
- If our objective is an 18 percent share of market, then we should introduce this product improvement.

How can the marketing executive make these kinds of forecasts? First, you should accept the fact that the ability comes naturally to those with sufficient experience. The experienced manager cannot usually tell *how* he or she estimates the outcome of a proposed strategy. That manager just does it, naturally—and often with uncanny accuracy.

The inexperienced marketing planner can rely on another diagnostic tool in preparing the conditional forecast. It is called a *response function,* and an example is shown in Exhibit 5.7. The exhibit shows the relationship between marketing input and output. What is shown is a sales (output) curve that continually increases with increased input, but at a declining rate of increase. This is called *diminishing returns,* and it applies without exception in marketing management.

This is not simply theory; it is a practical, everyday phenomenon. Consider these two situations.

1. A sales manager assigned five salespersons to a new district, one added each six months over a period of three years. This is what the effect of gradually increasing the level of sales input has been:

Period	Number of Salespersons	Sales
1	1	100
2	2	180
3	3	250
4	4	310
5	5	350
6	6	370

Based upon the notion that every salesperson should be as productive as the first one to be assigned, the manager might have expected total sales at the end of three years to have been 600 units. But he knows better. He knows the law of diminishing returns, and realizes that each additional salesperson will contribute less to total sales than the one hired just previously. An interesting aspect of this analysis is that it leads to the optimum allocation of salespeople across all districts. In this case, the manager may find that the last salesperson, who added only 20 units to total sales in the district where there were already five representatives, might be expected to bring in substantially more incremental volume in a less well-developed territory.

2. An advertising manager is selecting magazines to include in the schedule. Using available information on audience duplication (from Simmons Market Research Bureau, for example), she discovers that adding additional magazines has these results on cumulative net reach:

Number of Magazines	Cumulative Net Reach (Million)
1	4
2	6
3	7
4	7.5

Suppose it costs $50,000 to add each magazine to the schedule. The total cost of the schedule is $200,000 and the cost per thousand customers reached is $12.5—very reasonable. But consider now the incremental cost per thousand as each magazine is added:

Number of Magazines	Incremental Cost Per Thousand
1	$12.50
2	25.00
3	50.00
4	100.00

Clearly, the cost of the fourth magazine in terms of additional readership is unwarranted. Either the money should not be spent, or the advertising manager should consider other media that reach other segments of the overall market.

Graphs showing these relationships are found in Exhibit 5.8. These are response functions. A marketing planner could use such charts as follows. Suppose the sales goal assigned to a district is 300 units. The graph shows that at least four salespeople will be needed. To achieve a net reach of 5 million, the graph shows that ads will have to appear in at least two magazines, and the cost per thousand would be $16.67—still a fairly reasonable figure.

The best way to produce the kinds of response functions that the marketing planner would like to have in preparing a conditional forecast is to conduct controlled exper-

Exhibit 5.8. Sales and advertising response functions.

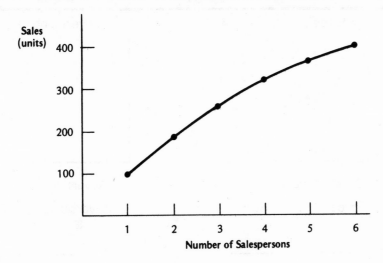

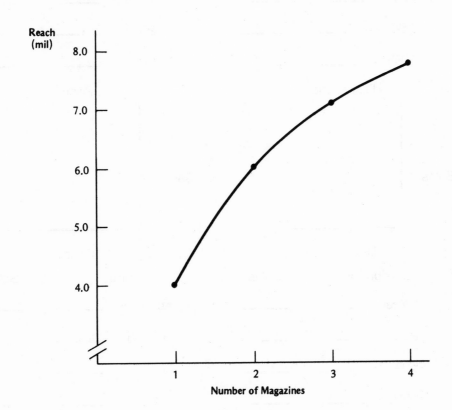

Exhibit 5.9.   Worksheet for estimating response functions.

Sales graph — y-axis: Sales, x-axis: Sales Force

Advertising graph — y-axis: Sales, x-axis: Advertising $

Sales Force	Sales
Last Year	
+25%	
+50%	
−25%	
−50%	

Advertising $	Sales
Last Year	
+25%	
+50%	
−25%	
−50%	

Distribution graph — y-axis: Sales, x-axis: Distribution

Price graph — y-axis: Sales, x-axis: Price

Distribution	Sales
Last Year	
+25%	
+50%	
−25%	
−50%	

Price	Sales
Last Year	
+25%	
+50%	
−25%	
−50%	

iments in which the input variable is manipulated and actual measurements of the corresponding marketing output are measured. A few companies have been willing to spend the research dollars to do this. For example, a number of years ago Anheuser-Busch conducted a massive test of its advertising expenditures by manipulating the amounts of money spent in various markets.

A shortcut to estimating the response function is found in a procedure that Professor John Little calls a *decision calculus*.[6] The planner should prepare a worksheet as shown in Exhibit 5.9 for each of the major marketing decision areas that involve variable inputs: sales, advertising, distribution, and price. The output will ordinarily be sales volume, and the inputs for each variable should be measurable in some appropriate way. We will use sales force size as an example. The steps are as follows:

1. Plot a point on the chart for last year's sales volume and the average size of the sales force for the year.
2. With the assistance of the sales manager, estimate what the sales figure would have been if: (1) the sales force had been 25 percent larger; (2) the sales force had been 50 percent larger; (3) the sales force had been 25 percent smaller; (4) the sales force had been 50 percent smaller.
3. Plot these points on the chart and connect them.

Barring the presence of some other variables, the curve you have drawn will approximate the response function. In almost every case, with the possible exception of the growth stage of the product life cycle, the curve will reflect the law of diminishing returns. In fact, if it does not, you should probably go back and review your estimates.

For the marketing planner who has not formally considered such relationships previously, the response charts can be very useful in looking for ways to fill the planning gap. However, the limitations of the method should be recognized. First, these graphs reflect subjective viewpoints, not actual data. Second, each is developed with the assumption that all the other marketing variables will hold constant. This is not going to be the case very often. Moreover, most of the marketing decision variables are more productive when used in concert with others than when employed alone. Finally, response charts make no provision for the impact of uncontrolled external factors, such as competitor actions or changes in economic conditions. All of these can be addressed by refining the method, but doing so limits its value as a shortcut analytic summary.

Product Life-Cycle Analysis

The stage in the growth history of a product or service has considerable impact on the type of marketing strategy employed. A product life-cycle analysis is a chart showing a product's sales and profit performance over its entire life. An example of a product life-cycle chart is shown in Exhibit 5.10.

The principal stages of the product life cycle (PLC) are indicated in the exhibit. The *introduction* period is a critical stage in the life cycle. A great deal of uncertainty prevails.

Exhibit 5.10. Product life cycle.

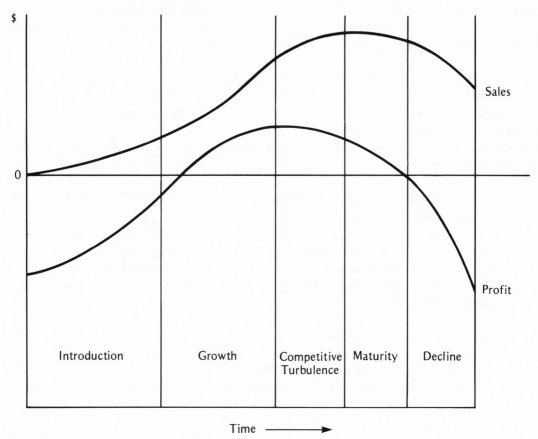

Is the product right? Is the marketing program feasible? Will consumers buy it? What will be the competitive response? Two out of three new products never make it out of the introduction stage, and those that do succeed are seldom profitable until well into the growth stage. Is it any wonder that marketing managers want to push through the introduction period as quickly as possible?

The *growth* stage is a period during which sales grow at an increasing rate. The natural process of new product adoption provides the basic force for growth, accelerated by marketing programs intended to increase the company's share of the growth market. Because unit costs fall with rapidly increasing volume, and price competition has not yet appeared, the product reaches its maximum profitability in this stage.

The *competitive turbulence* stage occurs as the growth rate declines. Several forces are at work. Late entrants into the market can avoid the heavy development expenses that the innovator incurred. Their costs are lower. They make fewer mistakes in positioning because there is less uncertainty. Simultaneously, the distinctiveness of the innovator's product has started to wane, and its competitive superiority begins to falter.

Sales continue to increase, but at a much slower pace and only because costly share-preserving marketing tools are employed. By the end of this period, maximum sales will have been achieved. Profits that were at a maximum at the beginning of the maturity stage fall steadily throughout the period.

In the *maturity* period, sales volume falls off only slightly, but profits continue to fall significantly. Forced to lower prices as well as continue heavy levels of advertising and sales promotions, the marketing manager finds profit margins shrinking rapidly.

In the *decline* stage, sales volume drops at an increasing rate. The product is out of touch with the times. It has few, if any, meaningful differentiating properties. The sales volume it does enjoy comes from brand-loyal diehards who refuse to switch to other, newer products. The product may contribute margin, but overall is unprofitable in this stage.

It was at this point that classic product life-cycle theory suggested the product become a prime candidate for deletion. True, many older products should be abandoned. But not all of them. There are a number of mature-product strategies that can be employed to extend a mature product's life expectancy. Take-off strategies based on the discovery of new uses or new users; repositioning, or adapting the product to the new needs of the market; and recycling (using several short-term injections of marketing support) can all help to extend the product life cycle. But this seldom goes on indefinitely. Eventually, the product cannot cover even its own variable costs. A strategy of deletion must be employed.

You should construct a life-cycle chart for each major brand or project for which a marketing plan is to be prepared. The data range you select will depend upon the product. If it is a consumer packaged-good, it may only be necessary to record about five years of data, since the life cycle of these products is relatively short. You may even want to record quarterly sales data. For a longer-lived product, you may need to go back a good many years, in which case you might be limited by the availability of data. For extremely long product life cycles it may be sufficient to record data in five-year intervals.

Once you have the data, plot this information. An example of a worksheet for this purpose is found in Exhibit 5.11. But don't be alarmed if your sales data do not plot out very nicely. The period of time covered may be too short to show more than one stage of a very protracted life cycle. Or you may have combined the sales of two or more products with offsetting life cycles. Exhibit 5.12 shows the life-cycle curves of two different forms of the same product category. Combine them, as shown in Part B of the exhibit, and you have a sales curve that is flat, without any apparent life-cycle characteristics at all. However, if you were responsible for developing a marketing plan for one of these product forms, you would want to be very sure about the product life cycle it faces. Be careful that these kinds of mistakes do not prevent you from detecting evidence of the product life cycle for your products or services.

When it is fairly certain that a given product or service is in a specific stage of its product life cycle, it is possible to apply some generalizations about the kinds of marketing strategies appropriate for it. One such presentation of alternative product life-cycle strategies is shown in Exhibit 5.13.

Exhibit 5.11.   Product life-cycle worksheet.

1. Record the historical sales of the product or brand. If you need more room, attach a supplementary sheet:

Period	Sales	Period	Sales	Period	Sales
_____	_____	_____	_____	_____	_____
_____	_____	_____	_____	_____	_____
_____	_____	_____	_____	_____	_____
_____	_____	_____	_____	_____	_____
_____	_____	_____	_____	_____	_____
_____	_____	_____	_____	_____	_____
_____	_____	_____	_____	_____	_____
_____	_____	_____	_____	_____	_____

2. Record the historical profit of the product or brand. If you need more room, attach a supplementary sheet:

Period	Profit	Period	Profit	Period	Profit
_____	_____	_____	_____	_____	_____
_____	_____	_____	_____	_____	_____
_____	_____	_____	_____	_____	_____
_____	_____	_____	_____	_____	_____
_____	_____	_____	_____	_____	_____
_____	_____	_____	_____	_____	_____
_____	_____	_____	_____	_____	_____
_____	_____	_____	_____	_____	_____
_____	_____	_____	_____	_____	_____

Exhibit 5.11. Continued.

3. Plot the sales and profit histories on the chart below:

$

Time

4. Based on the inflection points on the sales curve, draw vertical lines to identify the various stages of the product life cycle.

You will note that there are only four product life-cycle stages shown in this exhibit, compared to the earlier Exhibit 5.10. This is how they can be combined:

Exhibit 5.10	Exhibit 5.13
1. Introduction	1. Introduction
2. Growth	2. Growth
3. Competitive Turbulence	3. Maturity
4. Maturity	4. Decline
5. Decline	

The characteristics of the marketing situation that prevail in each of the four stages of the product life cycle are shown in the second section of Exhibit 5.13. The customer classification comes from the widely accepted concept of the adoption process. (This

(text continued on p. 132)

Exhibit 5.12.   Comparison and combination of two product life cycles.

A. Life cycles for filter and nonfilter cigarettes

Filter   Nonfilter

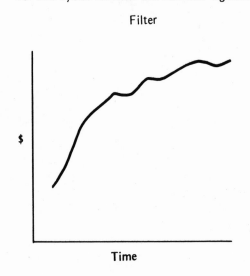 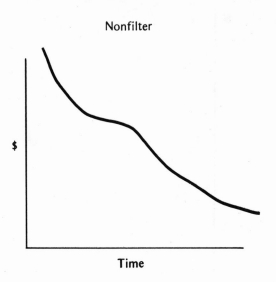

B. Combined sales of filter and nonfilter cigarettes

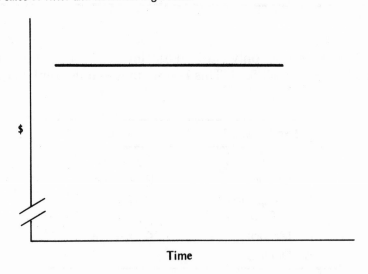

Exhibit 5.13.   Product life-cycle strategies.

	Introduction	Growth	Maturity	Decline
Characteristics				
Sales	Low sales	Rapidly rising sales	Peak sales	Declining sales
Costs	High cost per customer	Average cost per customer	Low cost per customer	Low cost per customer
Profits	Negative	Rising profits	High profits	Declining profits
Customers	Innovators	Early adopters	Middle majority	Laggards
Competitors	Few	Growing number	Stable number beginning to decline	Declining number
Marketing Objectives				
	Create product awareness and trial	Maximize market share	Maximize profit while defending market share	Reduce expenditure and milk the brand
Strategies				
Product	Offer a basic product	Offer product extensions, service, warranty	Diversity brands and models	Phase out weak items
Price	Use cost-plus	Price to penetrate market	Price to match or beat competitors	Cut price
Distribution	Build selective distribution	Build intensive distribution	Build more intensive distribution	Go selective: phase out unprofitable outlets
Advertising	Build product awareness among early adopters and dealers	Build awareness and interest in the mass market	Stress brand differences and benefits	Reduce to level needed to retain hardcore loyals
Sales Promotion	Use heavy sales promotion to entice trial	Reduce to take advantage of heavy consumer demand	Increase to encourage brand switching	Reduce to minimal level

Source: Kotler, Philip. *Marketing Management*, 5th Edition (Englewood Cliffs, N.J.: Prentice-Hall, 1984), p. 373.

theory of how consumers respond to new products has been adapted from work by E. M. Rogers.[7]) The first people to buy a new product are called *innovators* because they are willing to risk the uncertainties involved. The innovators are opinion leaders and trendsetters whose buying behavior is carefully watched by others. The next to follow suit are called *early adopters*. There are somewhat more early adopters than there are innovators, so when they enter the market, sales that were very modest to begin with start to increase sharply. The *middle majority* constitutes the bulk of the total market, and it is about evenly divided between the early majority and the late majority. The ultimate size of the market really depends on how many of these middle majority customers there are. Customers in the final category are called *laggards*. Interestingly, they become buyers only after almost everyone else has already tried the product. Total sales may already have started to decline before these customers appear.

A chart that shows the relationships of both the adoption and "disadoption" (product abandonment) processes of the product life cycle is found in Exhibit 5.14. Disadoption is the exact reverse of adoption. The first customers to abandon a product in favor of something newer are the former innovators. Next, the early adopters switch to some other product, followed by the early and late majority. Last to leave, of course, are the laggards, who may become its only customers by the time it is withdrawn.

Competitive activity is principally a function of the number of competitors, although the proportions in which these firms share the market and the ways in which they choose to preserve or increase their share also shape the character of the com-

Exhibit 5.14.   Adoption, disadoption, and the product life cycle.

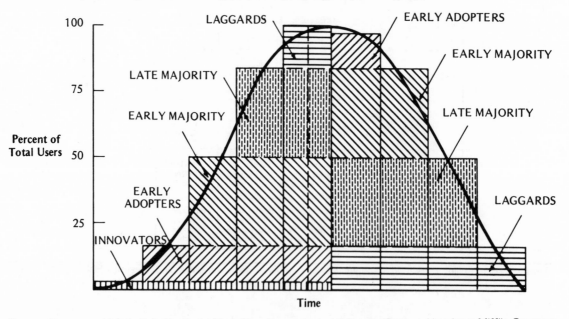

Source: From an exhibit in Bell, Martin L. *Marketing: Concepts and Strategy* (Boston: Houghton Mifflin Company, 1979), p. 254.

petitive environment. Exhibit 5.13 indicates the changes in the number of competitors that generally occur throughout the stages of the product life cycle.

The third section of Exhibit 5.13 indicates the kind of marketing objectives that are appropriate in each stage of the cycle. The important objective during the introductory period is to get the product established—to build awareness and encourage innovators to try the new product. The growth period is of tremendous importance in achieving a successful share position. It is critical to build share while the market is growing; there is no more opportune time in which to increase market share. The market is responsive. Competitors, satisfied with absolute increases in volume, may not be watching their share positions carefully. The product achieves peak sales and share in this PLC stage. It is also the period in the life cycle in which a product's profit contribution is highest.

By the time the product has entered the maturity stage, it has reached its maximum level of sales and earnings. Competition is becoming keener, and it will increase as the pressure is on all firms to maintain volume in the face of declining demand. The objectives, then, are to protect market position and at the same time generate cash flow—goals that may be somewhat inconsistent. A tradeoff is often required.

In the decline stage, the objective is to produce as much positive cash flow as possible, even by withholding share support. The reason is to produce the funds needed to build other new and growing products. Of course, objectives that are derived in this way must be consistent with other objectives in the business unit and in the corporate hierarchy.

The fourth section of Exhibit 5.13 deals with the marketing strategies appropriate at each stage of the product life cycle. A row is provided for each of the elements in the marketing mix. The general pertinence of the recommendations in each cell should be obvious.

It must be understood, however, that this matrix does not provide a prescription for your marketing plan. The strategies are only statements of what you *might* do—not what you *should* do. Some marketing people are very much opposed to this kind of "cookbook" marketing mix. Largely because of their disagreement with the promotion strategies suggested for mature and declining products, Nariman Dhalla and Sonia Yuspeh wrote a compelling article, "Forget the Product Life Cycle."[8] You may well take exception to other strategy suggestions—for example, using cost-plus pricing for new products. Consider this: Charging a high, skimming, very much above cost may actually be the best approach. On the other hand, a low price—even below cost—may be what is needed. It is because of this that we stress that the product life cycle is a *diagnostic* tool, not a *prescriptive* tool.

To prepare your own diagnosis using the product life cycle, start with the worksheet provided in Exhibit 5.15. Note that it is virtually a blank page, except for the labels of the various sections and rows. Reproduce the product life-cycle curve you have already created on the Exhibit 5.11 worksheet. For only those stages you have already been able to identify, fill in the various cells in the market characteristics section with actual descriptions of sales, costs, and so on. In the marketing objectives cells, record what your objectives are and have been. In the strategies section for stages already passed (if any), record the mix strategies you actually employed. For the stage in which your

Exhibit 5.15.   PLC strategy worksheet.

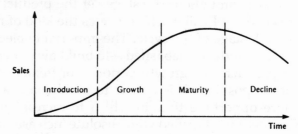

Characteristics

	Introduction	Growth	Maturity	Decline
Sales				
Costs				
Profits				
Customers				
Competitors				

Marketing Objectives

Strategies

Product				
Price				
Distribution				
Advertising				
Sales Promotion				

Source: Adapted from an exhibit in Kotler, Philip. *Marketing Management*, 5th Edition (Englewood Cliffs, N.J.: Prentice-Hall, 1984), p. 373.

product is currently positioned, list all the strategy options that are available for consideration. You will find this the most useful part of the exercise because it directly affects the thinking that goes into your marketing plan. While the exercise will seldom tell you what you should do, it will help set the agenda for considering your various strategy options. It is from analyses of this kind that you will later develop your list of strategy alternatives.

Directional Matrix

A directional matrix depicts the position of a given product or portfolio of products in terms of both the market and the company. It can take several forms. For example, the Boston Consulting Group's growth/share model positions a product according to the rate of market growth and the company's relative market share. This format is shown in Exhibit 5.16. Market growth rate is essentially the same phenomenon as is presented

Exhibit 5.16. Growth/share matrix.

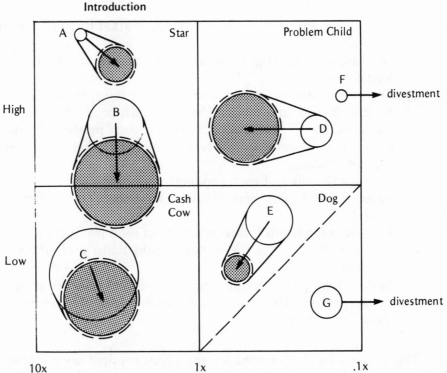

Source: Day, George. "Diagnosing the Product Portfolio," *Journal of Marketing* (April 1977), p. 29.

in the product life-cycle curve. The demarcation line between low and high growth depends somewhat upon the industry being studied, but in general any growth rate in excess of 10 percent is judged to be high. Relative market share is the ratio of the company's sales to those of the holder of the largest share. The vertical demarcation line on this dimension is drawn at 1.0 relative market share. The four cells of the matrix are often given labels, as shown in the exhibit. The names describe the circumstances faced by a product located in the cell.

It is interesting to note the "directional" aspects of the positions, as indicated by the differences between the present and future positions of the various products, or business units. One exception is for new products, which have important differentiating characteristics that enable them to capture a high relative share at introduction. However, as other firms introduce their versions, the relative market share of the innovator declines, even though overall sales are increasing. Another exception is found for certain low-share, low-growth products that have been successfully niched against a particular market segment and have been able to increase relative market share as competitors leave the industry.

Exhibit 5.17 is a worksheet for positioning each product on the growth/share matrix. Prepare this worksheet for each market in which you have positioned products. Nine steps are involved.

1. Record the annual growth rate of the market for the current period for each product.
2. Forecast the annual growth rate of the market for the period of time selected for the analysis.
3. Record the sales (in dollars and units) for the current period for each product.
4. Record the absolute market share for each product.
5. Calculate the relative market share for each product. To do this, divide each company's market share percentage by the market share percentage of its largest competitor.
6. Forecast the sales of each product.
7. Forecast the absolute and relative market shares for each product for the future period.
8. Plot the current and future positions of each product on the growth/share matrix. The diameter of the circles should be in proportion to the actual sales volume.
9. Since it may prove useful, you can also plot the current and future positions of competitors. This provides interesting insights on what your competitors' strategies may be.

The strategies to be pursued for any given product are suggested by the position it occupies on the matrix. A *problem child* is a relatively low-share product in a high-growth market. The proper strategy is one that will grow the product *and* increase its relative market share. Large marketing budgets and capital spending authorizations are usually required. Product *D* is in this situation. Not all such products can be successfully

Exhibit 5.17. Worksheet for preparing growth/share matrix.

Part A—Calculations

Market Share:

			Current Period				Future Period		
Company	MGR	Sales	MS	RMS	MGR	Sales	MS	RMS
1. _____	____	____	____	____	____	____	____	____
2. _____	____	____	____	____	____	____	____	____
3. _____	____	____	____	____	____	____	____	____
4. _____	____	____	____	____	____	____	____	____
5. _____	____	____	____	____	____	____	____	____
6. _____	____	____	____	____	____	____	____	____
7. _____	____	____	____	____	____	____	____	____

MGR = Market Growth Rate
MS = Market Share
RMS = Relative Market Share

Part B—Matrix

Market Growth Rate

	Star	Problem Child
High		
Low	Cash Cow	Dog

10x   1x   .1x

Relative Market Share

Diameters of circles are in proportion to volume
1/2 inch = $_____

Source: Day, George. "Diagnosing the Product Portfolio," *Journal of Marketing* (April 1977), p. 29.

marketed. Possibly it does not possess sufficient differentiation. Probably it gets inadequate support. Like Product *F* in Exhibit 5.16, it is divested.

The successful problem child should become a *star*—a product with a dominant share position and that continues to enjoy the benefits of a high market growth rate. Two stars are shown in Exhibit 5.16.

Product *A* is a new product. In the current period, it enjoys 100 percent market share, but the market is small, albeit growing. Competitive entry is anticipated. Some share loss will occur, but the high growth rate will result in substantially increased company sales. As the innovator, it can hope to retain the dominant share position.

Product *B* is a high-share, high-growth, high-volume product for which only even higher levels of attainment are expected. This product is marketed much like a problem child, except that the marketing is from a position of strength rather than hope. Invest to stimulate both market growth and share improvement. Don't slack off. Hitch you wagon to this rising star.

Product *C* is a cash cow, a fallen star. Market growth rate has declined. Share should not change. As a cash cow, it is expected to contribute funds to support problem children and stars, while simultaneously attempting to retain its high relative market share. But this cannot go on indefinitely. Eventually, it will lose both relative share and volume. It may become the victim of the superior competition of another firm, or it may have been milked dry of the funds with which to preserve its market position.

There are two kinds of *dogs*. There are products like *G*, which are in very low or no-growth markets and have lost (or never gained) much market share. As a marketing manager from Atlanta once said, "We shoot dem dawgs." Product *E* is in a quite different situation. True, market growth is low and falling. But relative market share is actually increasing. Obviously, some (maybe eventually all) competitors have deserted the market. Product *E* has niched itself in a declining market, but because of its commitment to serving that customer segment, it finds both sales and profits increasing. How long this situation lasts will depend on how long lived is the remaining customer base. It could possibly survive indefinitely.

Another version of the directional matrix is known as the GE screen, reflecting its origin as part of the strategic planning procedures at General Electric Company. Partly because of General Electric's traditional care and depth of analysis in strategic planning, a somewhat more comprehensive analytical directional matrix was developed. In a number of instances, the simpler growth/share analysis produced some rather absurd results. For example, one large, successful company that used the growth/share matrix approach discovered to its dismay that all of its products fell into the dog category. All were low-share products in low-growth markets. But a good case against deletion could be made for most of them. A subsequent analysis, using the GE screen, provided much more appropriate conclusions. The GE screen is illustrated in Exhibit 5.18.

This is a nine-cell matrix that has as its two dimensions somewhat broader variables than does the growth/share matrix. One variable is called *market attractiveness*. It includes a number of factors external to the business that make a particular market either attractive or unattractive. Market growth rate is one of them, as is correct; but there are others that can be of equal or greater importance. The matrix also incorporates a number of factors that determine a company's capability, or its business strengths. Obviously,

Exhibit 5.18. GE screen.

	Market Attractiveness High	Market Attractiveness	Market Attractiveness Low
Business Strengths High	Invest for Growth	Invest Selectively for Growth	Develop Selectively for Earnings
Business Strengths	Invest Selectively and Build	Develop Selectively for Earnings	Harvest or Divest
Business Strengths Low	Develop Selectively and Build Strengths	Harvest	Divest

Business Strength Factors:

Relative market share
Company image
Production capacity
Cost of manufacture
Financial resources
Extent of integration
R&D capability
Patent protection
Product quality
Distribution system
Sales/customer service
Advertising
Sales promotion
Pricing

Market Attractiveness Factors:

Market size
Market growth rate
Demand segmentability
Demand stability
Competitive climate
Ease of entry
Industry capacity
Industry capacity use
Industry profitability
Investment intensity
Regulatory climate
Environmental climate
Market quality
Accessibility

Source: Adapted from several sources, including La Rue, T. Hormer. *Strategic Management* (Englewood Cliffs, N.J.: Prentice-Hall, 1982), p. 310; and Hofer, Charles W., and Dan Schendel. *Strategy Formulation: Analytical Concepts* (St. Paul, Minn.: West Publishing Company, 1978), p. 32.

Exhibit 5.19. Worksheet for GE screen.

Market Attractiveness Factors	Weight	Score	Weighted Score
1. _____	_____	_____	_____
2. _____	_____	_____	_____
3. _____	_____	_____	_____
4. _____	_____	_____	_____
Total	1.0		_____

Company Capability Factors	Weight	Score	Weighted Score
1. _____	_____	_____	_____
2. _____	_____	_____	_____
3. _____	_____	_____	_____
4. _____	_____	_____	_____
Total	1.0		_____

Position the products on the matrix:

relative market share is one, but only one, of these. The exhibit lists a number of factors for both market attractiveness and company capability. However, these are only examples. Your analysis may produce more or different factors.

The procedure for using such a matrix is as follows. Exhibit 5.19 is a worksheet for assembling the information. First, select a particular product/market for analysis. Second, identify the factors which make that market either attractive or unattractive to the company; list these factors on the worksheet in descending order of importance. Third, determine what capabilities are required to compete effectively in that product/market. Make sure that you do not simply list the things your company does well. The purpose of this analysis is to evaluate how well equipped the company is to address its customers. Fourth, assign weights to the factors in each list; this is because the various factors are seldom of equal importance. Decimal fractions are utilized (for example, 0.3, 0.2, and so on). The weights assigned for each list must add up to exactly 1.00. Fifth, score the particular product/market on both dimensions—market attractiveness and company capability. These scores can be in any range, but a scale from 0 to 6 is quite satisfactory.

There are two things about proper scoring that are important. First, you must be able to assign scores from 0 to 6 to other values, both objective and subjective. For instance, take an objective factor such as overall market size. You might list the market potentials for all of the markets your company serves. List these markets in descending order of magnitude. Your list might look like this:

Market	Potential	Score*
A	100,000	6
B	90,000	6
C	60,000	4
D	35,000	2
E	20,000	1
F	10,000	0
G	5,000	0

* These scores are employed to adjust the potential figures to a scale of 0 to 6.

Consider a qualitative market attractiveness factor such as competitive climate. Describe the various degrees of competitive intensity that might be found in a market which you are evaluating, and assign score values to each. One analyst used the following:

Competitive Condition	Score
There is virtually no competitive activity.	6
Occasionally there is a moderate amount of restrained competition.	5
There is a fairly consistent but low level of competitive pressure.	4
The competitive climate is neutral.	3
There is a fairly consistent level of quite strong competitive pressure.	2
From time to time, outbreaks of intense competition occur.	1
There is a consistently high level of aggressive attack from several strong competitors.	0

Your task is to match the kind of competitive circumstances you observe in the market with the descriptions and assign the corresponding score.

This example also illustrates the other scoring consideration. Notice that a high level of competition gets a low score, and a low level of competition in the market gets a high score. Why is this? Because an intensely competitive market is usually unattractive; it must get a low score. A market with little or no competition is attractive; it deserves a high score.

In the sixth step, the scores are multiplied by the weights previously assigned to each factor. These are totaled for both market attractiveness and company capability. Finally, in step seven, the total weighted scores for each dimension can be plotted on the GE screen, and the position of the product or service can be determined. General strategies for each of the nine cell positions are indicated in Exhibit 5.18.

Again, these strategy descriptions are not prescriptive. They are simply suggestions of approaches that might be considered. Other factors besides those indicated in the analysis will affect the ultimate choice of a strategy. But the GE screen is a powerful analytic tool to sort out your strategy options.

Financial Summary

The final analytic summaries are the financial forms and documents. During the situation analysis, you will have analyzed historical sales performance, cost behavior, profit contribution, cash flow, return on investment, and previous payback of marketing investments. Summary exhibits of these findings should be prepared and included in this section of your planning materials.

In addition, it is a good idea to set up worksheets and layouts of exhibits and tables that will be included in the final planning document. In general, these will be similar to the financial reports that have been analyzed. Some may differ, such as when you consider other ways in which to display the data. For example, if you plan to show the results of a "what if" or sensitivity analysis, you may want to plan how you can display this most effectively.

Financial aspects of the marketing planning process will be covered in some detail in Chapter 7.

The analysis is complete. Facts have been assembled. Analytic summaries have been prepared. In Chapter 6, which follows, we continue the marketing planning process by looking at the way in which strategy alternatives are identified and a choice is made among them.

6
Developing
a Marketing Strategy

Your are now ready to begin the process of developing a marketing strategy. Many of the steps in the situation analysis have provided preliminary ideas on possible directions for your marketing plan. However, your strategy should not be just a collection of ideas gleaned while reviewing the business situation. Strategy is a carefully thought-out approach to the achievement of marketing objectives, given the nature of the particular business situation.

This chapter covers Steps 6 through 9 of the marketing planning process. As you recall, these are:

6. Finalize marketing objectives
7. Identify marketing strategy alternatives
8. Develop the marketing mix
9. Select a strategy option

Step 6:
Finalizing the Marketing Objectives

A strategy is a statement of how a company intends to go about accomplishing its objectives. The objectives provide the purposes of the marketing plan. They define what you want to have happen as the result of preparing and implementing that plan. Finalizing these objectives is the first step in the preparation of the strategy. Therefore, we begin this chapter with a review of the nature and importance of marketing objectives.

As we have already seen, business objectives and the broad strategies for achieving them are determined by upper levels of management. Recall that higher-order objectives and strategies are two of the planning prerequisites that top management should contribute to the marketing planning process.

You may well ask, "Why, then, can't we just proceed with a consideration of our marketing strategy options? Why do we have to go over the objectives again?" The answer lies in the importance of having the correct objectives to ensure the final success of the plan. The objectives drive everything else that happens. If the objectives are misdirected or misunderstood, the planning and the plan will have been for naught.

Remember that the objectives, as they were first stated, were framed before the situation analysis had been conducted. These objectives came from top management and undoubtedly reflected what senior managers believed to be the situation and what they hoped could be accomplished. But these preliminary objectives may not meet the requirements for marketing planning. We noted these planning requirements previously, but they are so crucial to the effective performance of the plan that they should be reviewed again before proceeding further.

1. Objectives should be stated *quantitatively*. This requirement makes it possible at the end of the program to measure how well the objectives were achieved. A quantitative objective eliminates the ambiguity inherent in imprecise statements.

2. An objective must be *realistic*. It should be attainable (with some stretch, of course) using the company's existing capabilities and resources. An important role of the company capability assessment is in determining the realism of the objectives. Gap analysis is especially useful in determining if a particular objective is realistic. If the planning gap can be filled with a marketing strategy that is within the ability of the company to implement, then the objective is realistic. If no such strategy can be identified, it is very probable that the objective has been overstated. (Of course, gap analysis can also identify the situation in which the objective understates the capability of the firm. In this case, management may well want to raise its sights.)

3. Objectives should be *consistent*. Marketing objectives must be consistent with financial, manufacturing, and other objectives in the organization. Marketing objectives should be internally consistent. For example, it is not generally consistent to set objectives that call simultaneously for an increase in market share and a short-term improvement in earnings. Objectives also should be reasonably consistent over time. If you failed to meet the objective last year, don't just add the difference to the next year's objective.

4. Objectives should be *hierarchical*. That is, marketing objectives must be properly related to divisional and corporate objectives. For example, a company's advertising campaign must be well suited to its overall marketing strategy; the marketing strategy must be equally well linked to the overall business strategy of the company. This linkage is achieved through a hierarchy of objectives—a concept that was discussed in connection with the prerequisites for marketing planning.

A worksheet is provided in Exhibit 6.1 that can be used at this juncture in your planning. It is identical to Exhibit 3.5. Your task at this point is to modify as necessary the objectives that were stated initially. Now, with the completion of the situation

Exhibit 6.1. Worksheet for identifying the hierarchy of objectives.

			Requirements Met?			
			Obj. "a"		Obj. "b"	
			Yes	No	Yes	No

Top level (corporate): _____ (name)
    1. Objectives:

	Yes	No	Yes	No
Quantitative	___	___	___	___

      a. _____

	Yes	No	Yes	No
Realistic	___	___	___	___
Consistent	___	___	___	___

      b. _____ Hierarchical ___ ___   ___ ___

    2. Strategies (as they involve the next
      lower level planning units):

      a. _____

      b. _____

Second level (SBU) _____ (name)

  1. Objectives:

	Yes	No	Yes	No
Quantitative	___	___	___	___

      a. _____

	Yes	No	Yes	No
Realistic	___	___	___	___
Consistent	___	___	___	___

      b. _____ Hierarchical ___ ___   ___ ___

    2. Strategies (as they involve the next
      lower level planning units):

      a. _____

      b. _____

Third level (marketing) _____ (name)

  1. Objectives:

	Yes	No	Yes	No
Quantitative	___	___	___	___

      a. _____

	Yes	No	Yes	No
Realistic	___	___	___	___
Consistent	___	___	___	___

      b. _____ Hierarchical ___ ___   ___ ___

analysis, you should be able to identify a set of objectives that meets the four requirements just mentioned.

Because of the great value that understanding these relationships can add to your own planning efforts, this worksheet should be prepared as soon as the situation analysis has been completed.

Exhibit 6.1. Continued.

	Requirements Met?			
	Obj. "a"		Obj. "b"	
	Yes	No	Yes	No

2. Strategies (as they involve the next
   lower level planning units):

   a. _____

   b. _____

Fourth level (product/market) _____
                                (name)

1. Objectives:

	Yes	No	Yes	No
Quantitative	—	—	—	—
Realistic	—	—	—	—
Consistent	—	—	—	—
Hierarchical	—	—	—	—

   a. _____

   b. _____

2. Strategies (as they involve the next
   lower level planning units):

   a. _____

   b. _____

Fifth level (marketing function) _____
                                 (name)

1. Objectives:

	Yes	No	Yes	No
Quantitative	—	—	—	—
Realistic	—	—	—	—
Consistent	—	—	—	—
Hierarchical	—	—	—	—

   a. _____

   b. _____

2. Strategies (as they involve the next
   lower level planning units):

   a. _____

   b. _____

Step 7:
Identifying the Marketing Strategy Alternatives

As the final outcome of the steps described in this chapter, you will produce a marketing
strategy statement that will be used to direct the development of action programs.

The development of a marketing strategy involves two basic steps: (1) the identification of a set of alternatives, and (2) the selection of the best alternative. We will approach this two-step process by first exploring how one strategy option is developed, then considering why and how the alternatives are to be identified. We will conclude with a discussion of how to choose the most appropriate strategy.

Exhibit 6.2 is a worksheet for preparing the strategy statement. Remember, if in determining the focus of your plan you selected more than one product/market, you will be preparing alternative strategies for each. For the present, we focus attention on only one strategy alternative for a single product/market. Eventually, of course, you will produce as many strategy statements as there are product/markets multiplied by the number of alternatives. The simplest situation would be one product/market with only two alternatives; you would prepare two strategy statements. If you have identified three product/markets and have been able to produce an average of three alternatives for each, you will have to prepare about nine strategy statements.

With this many strategy statements to prepare, it is helpful to assign brief identification symbols to each. Label the product/markets by letters and the alternatives by number. For three markets, each with three strategy alternatives, you would have:

Product/ Market	Strategy Option	Identification Number
A	1	A-1
	2	A-2
	3	A-3
B	1	B-1
	2	B-2
	3	B-3
C	1	C-1
	2	C-2
	3	C-3

This identification number heads the strategy statement. It should also be placed on all supporting exhibits, documents, and so forth.

The first major section of the strategy statement is a brief description of the customers in the target segment. This profile was produced during the situation analysis. Consumer markets are described geographically, demographically, and psychologically. Industrial customers are described by location, size, SIC classification, product application, and so on.

The next section of the strategy statement is a restatement of the marketing objective(s) for the product/market. These are taken directly from the worksheets prepared previously. (See Exhibit 6.1.) Obviously, objectives may differ somewhat from one prod-

Exhibit 6.2. Marketing strategy statement worksheet.

Product/market: _____ ID. No. _____

Alternative: _____ ID. No. _____

1. Target Marketing Description:

   _____

   _____

   _____

2. Objectives:

   a. _____

   b. _____

3. Marketing Mix:

   a. Product strategy:

      _____

      _____

      _____

   b. Distribution strategy:

      _____

      _____

      _____

   c. Promotion strategy:

      _____

      _____

      _____

   d. Price strategy:

      _____

      _____

      _____

uct/market to another. However, the objectives do *not* change across alternatives for any given product/market. This would change the rules, and the whole point of considering alternatives would be lost.

The last part of the strategy worksheet is a general description of the marketing mix. *Marketing mix* is the term employed to describe the components of a marketing strategy. According to the literature of marketing management, there are four basic mix elements. These have been mentioned previously, and were the object of the marketing capability analysis in Step 4 of the planning process. These elements are frequently referred to as the four *P*s of marketing: product, place (distribution), promotion, and price. Actually, each of these Ps needs to be broken down into its own set of components. One source suggests that there are about 40 such subcomponents; another indicates that the number is closer to 400.[1] In this book, we concentrate on the subcomponents listed in Exhibit 6.3.

Before turning to each of the basic elements of marketing mix and their planning components, it is desirable to consider the overall thrust or basic character of the strat-

Exhibit 6.3.   Marketing mix subcomponents.

Product
1. Specifications, additions, deletions
2. Length of line
3. Depth of assortments
4. Product/service augmentation
5. Packaging
6. Brand/trademark

Distribution
1. Wholesale distribution
2. Retail distribution
3. Facilitating agencies
4. Warehousing
5. Transportation

Promotion
1. Advertising
2. Personal selling
3. Sales promotion
4. Publicity
5. Message
6. Media

Price
1. Basic (list) price
2. Discounts
3. Extras
4. Price maintenance
5. Price discrimination
6. Psychological pricing

egy. In spite of the convenience of looking at a marketing strategy as composed of four distinct elements, this view somewhat distorts the real nature of a marketing plan. The marketing planner does not develop separate strategies for each element of the mix. The basic components seldom stand alone, although as we shall see, detailed action programs are usually developed in each area. But the mix elements must always be closely related. Their task elements have to be carefully integrated and coordinated. After screening the alternatives, the marketing planner will have only one overall marketing strategy for each product/market. It is this strategy that appears on the strategy statement worksheet.

The strategy statement should be written. The worksheet itself may suffice. However to present it to others, you may need to structure it somewhat differently or to include some elaboration. Try to limit the length. Generally, a single page is all that is required. After all, Winston Churchill is said to have required his military commanders to summarize their major strategies on a single sheet of paper. Your overall strategy statement should never exceed two or three pages.

The Marketing Mix

The marketing mix is simply a convenient way of looking at an overall strategy. Remember that there is only one marketing strategy, and keep this in mind as the process unfolds. There will be times when you will get so deeply involved in one of the mix areas that you may lose sight of the overall strategy. Try not to let this happen. Nevertheless, there is really no option other than looking at the components one at a time. It would be virtually impossible to try and juggle dozens of subcomponents simultaneously. Besides, this is not necessary. There is a logical, systematic way to look at the mix elements separately and yet keep the overall strategy at the forefront.

It is logical to ask, "With which marketing component should I begin to develop my strategy?" There are two concepts about the marketing mix that help answer this question. The first has to do with the logical sequence in which the mix elements should be considered; the second is concerned with the concept of a core strategy.

A Logical Sequence in Market Mixing

It is next to impossible to defend arbitrarily any given sequence in developing the components of the marketing mix. However, a good case can be made that some components depend to a considerable degree on prior consideration of other elements. For example, consider the mix elements in their reverse order: price, promotion, distribution, and product. It should be fairly obvious that setting the pricing strategy depends a good deal upon the development beforehand of the other elements. The weakest argument, although a very practical reason, is that the other three elements in the mix are all cost impacting—something that the market strategist needs to know before making a final pricing decision. A stronger line of reasoning is that the other mix elements all have a bearing on demand, and therefore on what the company should be able to charge for its product. The product defines the value of the offering. The distribution determines where the product will be available, and when, and with what kinds of service. The promotion establishes the strength of demand and its relative responsiveness to various pricing options. So, in developing a marketing mix, it is usually correct to begin with the product, then to deal with distribution, move next to promotion, and conclude with a consideration of the price.

The Core Strategy

Another useful concept, when considering the order in which to develop a strategy statement, is that of the core strategy component. One might think of marketing mixing not so much as a series of decisions, but rather as a set of decisions in the form of three concentric bands around a core, or central, mix element. The core is the central thrust of the strategy. It is based either on the firm's distinctive competency (for example, a superior business strength, such as a new product) or on a compelling marketing opportunity (for example, the rising demand for personal computers)—or, it is hoped, on both!

When it is possible to identify a core strategy component, the marketing planner should build the mix around it. Once the core is determined, it is possible to identify the relationship of the other mix elements to it. Suppose a new product is at the core of the strategy. Promotion, distribution, and price are likely to be considered in that order. If, on the other hand, distribution or price is at the core, the order in which the other mix components would be considered might be different. The approach is always situationally determined.

In the discussion of the next four steps in the marketing planning process, the order is the traditional one: product, distribution, promotion, and price. As each component is discussed, four topics will be considered. Each topic represents a step in the planning process through which the marketing planner must move in the development of a complete and integrated marketing mix. First, since each component of the mix is a key results area, a subobjective for it needs to be established. This subobjective is determined largely by the role the mix component is expected to play in the overall marketing strategy. (This is simply an extension of the hierarchical requirement.) Second, the specific issues in each area of the mix must be identified. Third, market-oriented resolutions to the various issues need to be established. Fourth, the planner must consider the manner in which the evolving component interacts with the other mix elements in the overall strategy.

Exhibit 6.4 illustrates this market mixing process. The four Ps are shown in the overlapping boxes. The four steps in the mixing process are indicated in the four boxes to the left. The planner begins by selecting the first strategy component (product) and then moves through the four steps. When this first phase is completed, the process is repeated for the next component (distribution). This continues until all four components have been processed. The mixing process is then complete, and the planner can proceed to develop the formal strategy statement.

Exhibit 6.4.   The market mixing process.

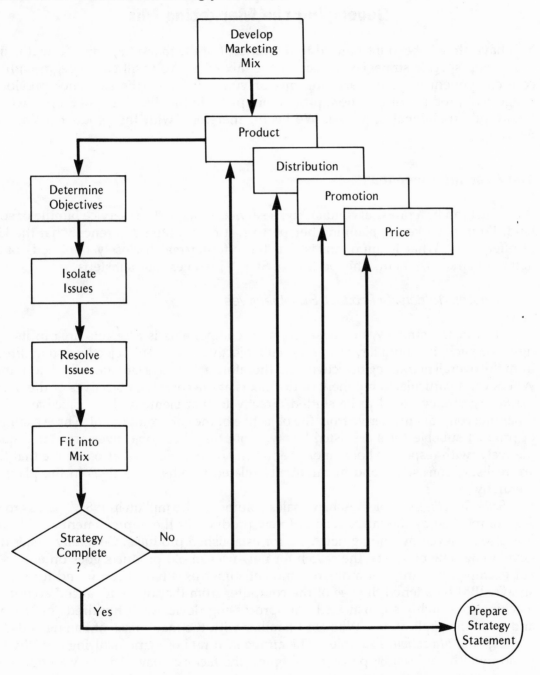

Source: Adapted from an exhibit in Bell, Martin L. *Marketing: Concepts and Strategy* (Boston: Houghton Mifflin Company, 1979), p. 438.

Step 8:
Developing the Marketing Mix

You have already been introduced to the concept of the marketing mix. Now it is time to develop specific strategies in each of the mix areas. You will either begin with the core component in your marketing mix or you will follow the sequence previously suggested: product, distribution, promotion, price. In the discussion of Step 8, we will follow this traditional sequence. We begin, therefore, with the product (or service) offering.

The Product Component

A product can be a physical commodity, a service, or a goods or service bundle of some kind. From a marketing planning perspective, it makes little difference what the kind of offering is. What is important is that the offering match closely the needs of the defined market segment. This portion of Step 8 involves four substeps.

Substep 1: Identify Product Subobjectives

Each of the strategy, or marketing mix, components is a results area in its own right. As such, it should have a specific subobjective. These subobjectives stem directly from the overall marketing objective, and therefore are always situationally determined. Whenever a particular component of the mix is at the core, the objectives of the overall marketing strategy tend to be shifted directly to that element. The objectives of the other mix components derive from the objective of the core component. Three examples of product subobjectives are listed below. Note that these objectives are stated quantitatively, with respect to both amount and time frame. We must also assume that they are realistic, consistent, and hierarchically related to other objectives in the planning hierarchy.

Sales Growth. Example: "Achieve sales volume of $1.5 million in 1987." Sales growth is accomplished by the introduction of new products or the improvement of old ones. It is also achieved by finding new uses for established products. Generally easier than developing new products, the search for new uses of old products goes on endlessly. For example, hundreds of industrial and consumer uses have been found for silicone sprays. IBM broadened the use of the computer from that of an advanced accounting machine to a highly sophisticated data processing device with hundreds of business and scientific applications. Who isn't familiar with the many uses of baking soda?

Capacity utilization. Example: "The annualized rate of manufacturing capacity utilization will be at least 80 percent." Keeping the factory busy and the warehouse full may place considerable stress on the development of new products or on finding new uses for old ones. In a way, this objective is not very different from the first, except that the pressure is not for growth but for product-related programs that enable the company to better utilize the investments it has already made.

Improve market share. Example: "Improve market share from 10.2 to 12.3 percent."

This objective usually has a direct bearing on the company's product decisions, because one of the most basic ways to achieve a competitive advantage is through product differentiation. Several aspects of product strategy relate directly to competition for market share. Product design, packaging, and branding are three important ways to differentiate an offering.

Substep 2: Identify the Issues in Product Strategy

There is no easy path to the development of product strategy. A considerable number of elements are involved. By breaking down the general task of product planning into a list of individual component decisions, the planner can concentrate on each of several important considerations. The specific product issues or problems to be resolved in this stage of the marketing planning process are as follows:

What products or services should we offer? This is the basic question of product strategy. Remembering that the purpose of a business is to satisfy its customers, the question might be rephrased, "What satisfactions, or benefits, should we offer?" However, in most firms the form in which satisfactions are delivered is that of a product, a service, or a product-service combination. Hence the vital importance of this issue.

What new products, if any, should we add? This question is really an extension of the first, except the focus is on the future. A few decades ago, a company might well have considered whether or not to introduce new products. One well-known pasta company entered the 1980s without having introduced a new product in over 100 years. Today, there is little choice. The rapid technological obsolescence of most products forces every marketer to consider the inevitable necessity of introducing new products in order to survive and grow.

What should be the breadth and depth of the product line? Your product line must be broad enough and deep enough to meet the needs of the segments you serve. It must also take into consideration the needs of your wholesalers and dealers.

What products, if any, should be dropped or phased out? Candidates for deletion should be spotted well in advance of the time they are to be dropped. The detection of "sick" products, the timing of their abandonment, and the method of their withdrawal from the line are all important aspects of this particular issue.

When should product additions and/or deletions be made? Timing changes in the product line are always troublesome issues. New products are seldom available at the exact moment the marketing planner would like to introduce them. The timing of product deletions is also a thorny problem. Sales departments are always reluctant to abandon products that are producing any sales at all. Moreover, if no replacement is available, it may be better to continue selling the unprofitable item than to leave a glaring void in the product line.

How should products be packaged? Today almost all consumer goods are packaged in some way. Many industrial products are also packaged, especially shelf items that are sold through warehouse distributors and dealers. Certain commodities, such as fluids, cannot be marketed unpackaged. Others can be marketed efficiently only when attention has been given to packaging from both a functional and a promotional point of view.

How should products be branded or otherwise identified? Products can be identified, other than by uniqueness of appearance, performance, and package, by *branding* and by *trademarks.* A brand name is a copyrighted word used to identify a company's product or product group. A trademark is a registered symbol that distinguishes the products or services of one company from those of others.

Brand names, whether national (branded by a manufacturer) or private (branded by a reseller), are extremely important in the identification of products. They are mandatory if manufacturers or distributors intend to promote their products through advertising. Branding makes word-of-mouth advertising effective. Without such identification, repeat purchases of a particular product would be virtually impossible. Only the most generic of commodities are marketed without brands, and even sellers of cement, celery, and computer software use brand names.

What kinds of pre- and post-sales servicing will be required? Since a firm is in business to satisfy its customers, a transaction is not complete until the satisfaction has been delivered. When products are not consumed at the time of purchase, there is often a need for post-sales servicing. The longer the consumption period, the more likely some type of warranty and service must be included in the marketing mix. Sears has found it effective to remind its customers that "Sears Services What it Sells." GM has emphasized its "Guardian Maintenance" program and its skilled mechanic, Mr. Goodwrench. Chrysler Corporation, followed or bested now by most other auto makers, promotes a seven-year, 70,000-mile warranty. It is possible to purchase a service contract for almost any type of household appliance.

The marketing of almost all industrial products involves post-sales servicing. The marketing of machinery and equipment often requires that the vendor supply technical service for installation, maintenance, and repair. A large chemical company found that it had to work very closely with its customers to make sure its products were used properly and safely in the customers' plants. This type of activity is critical in keeping a customer "sold" and in encouraging repeat business.

What costs will be involved in implementing the product strategy? The costs of product planning seldom come to the surface of a profit-and-loss statement as dramatically as, for example, do the costs of advertising and selling. Product costs are accumulated in manufacturing and engineering areas, as well as in the marketing department. But they are usually indirect, or overhead, costs. These may or may not be allocated to the product planning and development function. But the fact is that these are real costs of marketing that should be anticipated and planned. They will have to be covered in someone's budget. The preferred way is to have these costs funded through the marketing budget, thereby enabling the marketing planner to retain financial responsibility and control.

Substep 3: Resolve the Product Issues and Problems

The resolution of the various product issues identified in the previous substep is accomplished by working from the data base that was assembled in the situation analysis. Begin this process by looking at the target market and working back to the specific issues that must be resolved at the marketing planning level. The steps that might logically be followed are:

Identify the ultimate users—the target market segment. The first important step in developing product strategy is properly identifying the product's ultimate consumer or user. Your strategy statement already contains this information. In the situation analysis, you have explored the "six honest serving men" of who, what, where, how, why, and when.

Determine the use (satisfaction) specifications of the target market. The engineer, the computer programmer, the dress designer—they need to know *exactly* what the product is supposed to do. They need to know how the product will be used, how often, and with what efficiency it is supposed to function. It is not nearly so important to know what a product is capable of doing as it is to understand what its buyers expect it to do. A well-designed product is one that provides exactly the satisfactions desired—neither more nor less.

Determine the resale specifications of wholesalers and dealers. A product must provide satisfaction for wholesalers and retailers as well as for its ultimate users. For a product to "fit" into a wholesale or retail assortment, it must match the reseller's expectations in terms of inventory requirements, stock turnover, margin, packaging, and so forth. These expectations are important considerations in designing the product, its package, and its brand identification.

Match the user expectations and reseller requirements with the design, performance, and cost specifications of the product. Generally, product design involves developing three important product elements: (1) appearance specifications, (2) performance specifications, and (3) cost specifications. These specifications affect both the product and its package. No point we make in this book is more important. We bend the offering to the needs of the market; we do not try to bend the customer to what it is we have to sell.

Determine product identification requirements. Users generally prefer and resellers require that products be identified. Without a brand identification of some kind, resale of products that have proved satisfactory is extremely difficult.

The manufacturer may have product identification requirements that are only indirectly related to the needs of users and resellers. A company may desire to differentiate among various items in its product line. For example, if the general marketing approach calls for an aggressive promotion of a low-priced product, the manufacturer may wish to disassociate this promotion from its regular marketing activities. This can be accomplished by using a *fighting*, or *secondary*, brand. For example, when Bullova decided to compete directly with Timex, it introduced its low-priced watches with the name Caravelle. In contrast, Pulsar and Seiko used the same name on both high-priced and low-priced watches. This latter move may well have been triggered by a desire to take advantage of favorable user acceptance of an established product by using a family brand for both products. This favorable brand-name carryover may be an important product identification requirement.

Match product identification requirements with brand name and trademark options. This step involves the creation of a brand name and the design of a trademark. This creative activity is often assigned to the advertising department or advertising agency. Various techniques are used in developing a brand name. For example, DuPont follows a set of fairly tight requirements in coining a name for a new product. These are their *musts:*

It must be coined.
It must be nondescriptive.
It must be readily pronounceable.
It must be easily spelled.
It must be capable of being registered and protected.

In addition, it should be:

romantic
dramatic
spectacular
promotional
lyrical

On the basis of these requirements, these DuPont brands came into being: Dacron, Corfam, Delrin, Lucite, Lycra.

Fit immediate product decisions into a long-run product line program. This program should involve future products, products to be deleted, and timing of product line changes. The number of products to be offered is generally determined by other requirements of the marketing program. It is a function of new product decisions, as well as decisions on the deletion of older ones. If the company's products are complementary, the line will be longer than if those products tend to compete with each other. Most companies offer products for more than one market segment. This very fact tends to multiply the number of products offered. Resellers like to have more than one product in a category so they can "trade up" or "trade down" as necessary to make a sale.

Estimate the cost of this product strategy and prepare a preliminary budget. Estimating the cost of product strategy presents some serious problems. First, because the tasks of product design, development, and improvement are often carried out in several different departments, there arises the thorny question of who is going to pay. As noted earlier, one effective approach is to have all these activities funded through the marketing budget. This has the added advantage of your being able to track and control these costs more easily. A second problem is that the cost of introducing a new product or making major changes in an old one may involve the purchase of equipment and facilities. These are capital budget items, involving such considerations as discounted rates of return, cost of capital, payback periods, and the like. Marketing managers do not frequently get into the capital budgeting arena, and may have to learn an entirely new set of techniques. The third complication is that the task of new product development corresponds more to a project than it does to an ongoing activity. Project costing involves different procedures and reporting than typically are involved in marketing administration. This is because the project period may overlap two or more accounting periods.

Ultimately, of course, the marketing planner must sort through these budgeting aspects, evaluate alternatives in the light of their financial implications, make a decision about the financial commitment required, submit it to the proper approval levels, and incorporate the final approved figures into the marketing plan.

Test new or improved products by engineering, manufacturing, and marketing criteria. The testing of a new product in its embryonic stage is extremely difficult. Three aspects of pretesting are suggested. First, the product concept can be tested. This should be done long before much time and money are spent on design and development. A second test is done internally. The product plan is reviewed carefully by the engineering, product design, and manufacturing departments. The purpose of this review is to reaffirm that the company has the capability to develop and make the item. Finally, the product should be subjected to some type of formal market testing. When a prototype is available, the actual product should be placed in the hands of prospective users for their evaluation. Turbine automobiles, automatic washers, and synthetic fibers have been tested in this way. Obviously, any necessary modifications that these tests bring to light should be taken care of before much more work is done on the introductory marketing plans.

Substep 4: Evaluate the Product Strategy Component

The product strategy component, which has evolved out of this process, must be evaluated as it relates to the overall marketing plan. Specifically, you must consider the effects of product decisions on channel, promotion, and pricing issues that are yet to be considered. For example, if the overall marketing strategy did not anticipate the need for a major advertising effort, but the product strategy as it has been developed appears to make such a program necessary, it may be wise to reconsider the overall strategy that has been selected. Generally, however, such a major change in overall approach would not be necessary.

Rather, product decisions simply raise certain warning signals that must be heeded as you move through the rest of the planning process. A checklist is useful at this stage, and Exhibit 6.5 provides such a worksheet. First fill out the form, listing the various decisions that have been made under each of the categories. Then review each decision to determine if it is consistent with the overall marketing strategy. Check the appropriate response. If not consistent, correct the discrepancy before proceeding.

The Distribution Component

The second major component in the marketing mix is distribution. In marketing terms, distribution refers to the arrangements required to maintain and move physical products, to the resale structure that is employed, and to any facilitating agency services required. The first aspect is sometimes referred to as *marketing logistics;* the others as *marketing channels.* Actually, there is a good deal of overlap, since resellers are often physical handlers of the product—storing, breaking bulk, delivering, and so on. In spite of this, marketing planners are seldom deeply involved in the strategic use of

(text continued on p. 162)

Exhibit 6.5. Product strategy worksheet.

Product/market: _____ ID. No. _____

Alternative: _____ ID. No. _____

	Check Consistency	
	Yes	No

Product Objectives:

1. _____ ___ ___

2. _____ ___ ___

3. _____ ___ ___

Product Strategy Issues:

1. Product Offering:
    a. List products now in the line:

    (1) _____ ___ ___

    (2) _____ ___ ___

    (3) _____ ___ ___

    (4) _____ ___ ___

    b. List new products to be added:

    (1) _____ when: _____ ___ ___

    (2) _____ when: _____ ___ ___

    (3) _____ when: _____ ___ ___

    (4) _____ when: _____ ___ ___

    c. List products to be dropped:

    (1) _____ when: _____ ___ ___

    (2) _____ when: _____ ___ ___

    (3) _____ when: _____ ___ ___

    (4) _____ when: _____ ___ ___

Exhibit 6.5. Continued.

Check
Consistency

Yes   No

d. List products in line at end of planning period:

(1) _____   ___   ___

(2) _____   ___   ___

(3) _____   ___   ___

(4) _____   ___   ___

2. Packaging: How will each product be packaged?

Product   Package

a. _____   _____   ___   ___

b. _____   _____   ___   ___

c. _____   _____   ___   ___

d. _____   _____   ___   ___

3. Product Identification: How will each product be branded or trademarked?

Product   Brand or Trademark

a. _____   _____   ___   ___

b. _____   _____   ___   ___

c. _____   _____   ___   ___

d. _____   _____   ___   ___

4. Service: What kinds of services will be provided?

a. _____   ___   ___

b. _____   ___   ___

c. _____   ___   ___

d. _____   ___   ___

Exhibit 6.5.　Continued.

	Capital	Expense	Check Consistency	
			Yes	No
5. Budget: What costs will be incurred?				
a. New product development	_____	_____	____	____
b. Product improvement	_____	_____	____	____
c. Packaging	_____	_____	____	____
d. Brand/trademark development	_____	_____	____	____
e. Service program	_____	_____	____	____

physical distribution. One reason for this is that responsibility for logistics is seldom assigned directly to the marketing function. Another reason is that logistic arrangements tend to be relatively fixed and only infrequently have a critical bearing on a company's competitive position. (There are, of course, important impacts of logistics on a marketing operation, as when market penetration is determined by the availability and/or the cost of transport.)

The development of a distribution strategy is approached in the same general manner as is the development of the product strategy. Subobjectives are determined, key issues are identified, a market-focused approach to resolving the issues is pursued, and the distribution strategy is evaluated in terms of the overall marketing plan as well as the other components in the marketing mix.

Substep 1: Identify Distribution Subobjectives

Here are some examples of strategic marketing that may give rise to distribution subobjectives:

Obtaining distribution in new markets. Example: "By the end of Fiscal 1988, product distribution will be attained in no less than 85 percent of all retail outlets." The ultimate purpose behind this objective is to increase sales.

Maintain or improve share of market in existing channels. Example: "Increase share of market in existing channels from 15 percent to 18 percent." The pressure here is, again, to increase sales. Indeed, this is probably the first place any company should look for additional business. What the objective requires is greater output through the entire channel.

Achieve a predetermined pattern of distribution. Example: "By the end of 1990, achieve the following distribution sales by retail outlet:

department stores	25%
mass merchandisers	40
specialty outlets	15
private label	20

Quite aside from its effect on sales or market share, a specific pattern of distribution might be useful. This might be a critical objective for a new company or one introducing a new product. On the other hand, an established firm may find it necessary to change its basic channel arrangements to better focus on a given market segment. For example, as the do-it-yourself hardware market grew, companies which had traditionally sold through channels reaching professional carpenters now had to find ways to reach ultimate consumers.

Improve channel performance. Example: "Increase turnover of dealer stocks from 3.2 to 4.5." In particular, channel efficiency is usually sought by improving the flow of goods and information. Bottlenecks of materials or the loss, delay, or distortion of information are critical handicaps in any marketing effort. A principal objective may be to eliminate these bottlenecks and information traps to improve channel performance.

Substep 2: Identify Channel Issues and Problems

Channel issues and problems are discovered in the marketing data base, as are problems for each area of the marketing mix. In general, these kinds of channel issues typically arise:

Should a company sell direct? This question arises sooner or later in the design of most marketing programs. There is no easy answer. In general, it would be yes, if the following conditions prevail:

1. End users insist, or prefer, to do business with the manufacturer.
2. Existing channels are already filled.
3. There are no important logistic or distributive barriers to direct sale.
4. It is critical to maintain close supervision and control over installation and use of the product.

That these circumstances occur quite frequently is evidenced by the fact that a substantial number of firms have either integrated vertically or have simply taken over the functions of both wholesaler and retailer. Direct marketing is on the increase.

This issue should be resolved as early as possible in the marketing planning process. If a firm does decide to sell direct to its user-customers, all the other channel questions tend to merge with those of company organization and sales management.

What type(s) of channel components should be utilized? This is almost as important as the issue of what products to sell. It is also difficult to answer. Consider, for example, the many types of retail establishments in which a camera might be purchased: camera stores, department stores, sporting-goods stores, discount houses, mail-order establishments, variety stores, drug stores, audiovisual stores, and so on. Which of these types of retailers should a company like Kodak use? The answer to this question will determine the company's ability to put its products into the hands of its target customers.

The problem is repeated at the wholesaler level. There are several kinds of wholesalers that handle this type of product. For example, cameras might be handled by photo supply distributors, jewelry wholesalers, drug wholesalers, and general merchandise distributors. Although the list is not as long as that of possible retailers, the problem of choice among wholesalers is still serious.

How many components of each type should be employed? There are several possibilities, ranging from distribution through a single outlet to distribution through every store of selected types in the market. The use of a single retail outlet is referred to as *exclusive distribution.* Exclusiveness carries important advantages, although not without commensurate costs. Strong dealer loyalty and solid sales support are usually exchanged for exclusive distribution rights. Control over retail marketing is usually easier. Better forecasting, more efficient inventory allocation, and greater merchandising efficiency are all possible with exclusive distribution. The principal sacrifice is the loss of the greater sales volume that might be obtained through wider distribution. Moreover, the manufacturer tends to become very dependent upon a single outlet, a dependency that is not always justified by performance.

At the other extreme is *broadcast* or *extensive distribution.* With this type of strategy, the manufacturer attempts to get as many retailers as possible to carry the product. The advantages are generally in increased sales volume, wider consumer recognition, and considerable impulse buying. Problems associated with extensive distribution include high inventory and slow turnover. Low price, low margin, and small orders often result, tending to depress profits. It is also very hard to exercise much control over resale if a large number of retailers are involved.

Between the two extremes is a compromise that meets the requirements of both manufacturer and resellers. We call it *limited distribution.* A special aspect of limited distribution is the selection of particular resellers through whom the manufacturer can sell most profitably. The manufacturer elects to distribute only through those outlets whose sales volume, rate of turnover, order size, and so forth create profitable business. This is known as *selective distribution.*

Should a company use multiple channels? Many companies have to deal with the reality of using more than one channel of distribution. These channels can be either *complementary* or *competitive.* Companies selling differentiated product lines to two or more market segments often develop separate channel systems. The most obvious example is a company that sells both consumer and industrial products. For example, IBM uses its own sales force to sell its large mainframe and minicomputers direct to businesses. Its personal computers are sold through dealers, including computer stores and Sears. A manufacturer of hydraulic brake fluid, on the other hand, sells through four different channels.

These channels are basically noncompetitive because they reach quite different customers. However, this is not always the case. Sometimes, competitive channels are purposely arranged. For years, General Motors used separate dealer arrangements for its major lines of cars, although in smaller markets it sometimes combined them. Sometimes, too, multiple channels are accidentally created. Bussman, the fuse company, attempted to keep separate the channels for its two main lines of fuses: one channel to serve customers in the traditional electrical industry; the other to reach the electronics market. Different pricing and discount structures existed. However, electrical wholesalers had customers who also wanted fuses for electronics applications, and electronics distributors had some demand for conventional electrical fuses. The company's products were eventually sold in two channels that were directly competitive. Sometimes a company prefers to use one channel, but its customers shop in another. Mead Johnson, the ethical pharmaceutical manufacturer, faced this dilemma with its food products. Mead was strongly entrenched in drugstore distribution; however, consumers expected to find Mead Johnson's products in grocery stores. The company had to open a new distribution channel for its non-drug products.

What special assistance or monitoring will be needed to maintain an effective distribution system? The need for channel supervision and control arises because most channel members are independent. This independence gives rise to problems that must be anticipated in planning a distribution strategy. In rare instances, real conflict may arise.

Lack of interest and support on the part of resellers is a common cause of manufacturers' discontent. Distributors and dealers handle the products of hundreds, sometimes thousands, of suppliers. The retailer's efforts must be spread among these many vendors. Very little attention can be devoted to a single manufacturer.

There are four ways in which channel assistance and control can be exercised. Where the problem exists, these tools should be included in the channel strategy:

    direct financial incentives
    direct personal supervision
    management services
    dealer stimulation

What improvements or changes are needed in the logistic support system? This issue arises primarily when the manufacturer sells direct to its users. However, there are circumstances when physical distribution problems arise in indirect channels. For example, when sales agents or brokers handle the sales task, they do not typically take physical possession. Warehousing and delivery must be arranged by the manufacturer. When entering new markets and the channel system has not yet been fully developed, it may be necessary—at least temporarily—to arrange for warehouse stocks to be located locally.

How much should be budgeted for channel development and administration? This question is seldom considered a part of the budgeting process, because the costs of channel development and control are usually submerged in other categories of marketing expenses. The work of the sales force in dealing with resellers falls within the sales budget. The cost of special deals, discounts, advertising allowances, and contests usually are covered by the advertising and sales promotion budgets. Ideally, if the need for channel development is critical and there is resistance from sales, advertising, and promotion managers to absorb these costs, a separate allocation of funds to channel development ought to be considered.

Substep 3: Resolve the Channel Issues and Problems

Each of the channel issues needs to be resolved. As in the case of product strategy, the starting point is again the marketplace; channel strategy, no less than any other part of the marketing mix, needs to be developed with customers' needs foremost in mind. These actions are useful in resolving channel issues:

Identify ultimate users and purchasers (if not the same). Remember, in the context of distribution strategy, you are not trying to sell something to a buyer. Rather, you are planning how you will get the product into the hands of its ultimate user. These are exactly the same users you identified when developing the product offering. The homework has been done; you need now to use the information in a different way.

However, in contrast to the development of product strategy, now you are also very much concerned with the *buyers* or *purchasers* of the product. These may or may not be the users. If not, then the purchasing needs and behavior of these buyers must also be considered. This is notably true in industrial procurement. To a less formal extent, the same situation is found in the consumer market. There is usually a principal shopper who does most of the buying. But every member of the household influences the purchasing activity.

Determine the buying specifications of these users and purchasers. This is fundamentally a matter of discovering where, when, and how these persons prefer to make selections and to purchase goods and services.

Match the buying specifications with location and performance characteristics of resellers. It has already been suggested how this is accomplished. We have determined the buying specifications of our target customers. We need now only locate those specific types of resellers whose operations most closely match the needs of the customers.

Determine the number of dealers (retailers) in each market that is required to serve purchasers. Set the number in the light of the company's distribution objectives and by the retailers' needs for share protection. If the channel strategy calls for exclusive distribution, there will be no problem. It is when the manufacturer is interested in extensive coverage that resellers begin to object. Here, the marketing strategist must be empathetic and see the situation through the dealers' eyes. The thinking should be long run. Short-term profit maximization might result in pitting one dealer against another; in the long term, the approach could be fatal. If, after careful consideration, the number of dealers is considerably greater than the resellers judge reasonable, the manufacturer must stand ready to help its dealers improve their operations so they can survive in the face of increased competition.

Determine the buying specifications of dealers (retailers). In much the same way that buying specifications of end-use buyers were determined in the first step, the manufacturer must discover how resellers prefer to buy. Of particular importance is the question, "From whom do our retail outlets prefer to buy?" The answer to this question identifies the type of wholesalers (if any) that the manufacturer should use.

One might assume that all retailers prefer to buy directly from the manufacturer, but this is not true. Retailers are inclined to buy from local vendors who can offer a wider assortment of merchandise than do most manufacturers. A retailer doesn't want to take time away from customers to talk to an endless stream of manufacturers' salespeople. He or she economizes on buying time by concentrating purchases with one or two suppliers—usually a full-service or specialty wholesaler best meets this need.

Of course, most large retail organizations do buy direct from manufacturers. In this case, a wholesaler is not necessary; it is not because the manufacturer would rather sell direct, but because the retailer chooses to buy direct. The driving force is always backward—or upstream—in the channel. Eventually, if you follow this procedure back up the channel, you will come to a level at which the reseller prefers to buy direct from the manufacturer. Then, and only then, is the vertical linkage to the end user actually completed.

Match buying specifications of retailers and wholesalers with location and performance characteristics of vendors, including other wholesalers, as needed in the channel. This is exactly the same procedure as is employed in locating the right types of retail outlets. Once you know what retailers need in the way of vendor services, you can look for types of middlemen in a position to satisfy those needs. Of course if dealers prefer to buy direct from the manufacturer, this should be evident from their buying specifications and the manufacturer's channel will have been defined. If an intermediate middleman is required, the marketing planner will know exactly what type of wholesaler to approach.

Match the buying specifications of distributors or other wholesalers with sales, service, and logistics offerings of the company. In most cases, this will be the last step in the channel-building process. In 99 cases out of 100, distributors buy from manufacturers. The exception appears to be with very small wholesalers who may actually prefer to buy from larger wholesalers—for about the same reason that retailers prefer to do so.

Determine the special problems of training, motivation, and control expected to arise within the channel. The source of this information is the marketing situation analysis. The industry and trade analysis should highlight general problems in the distributive trades. The internal marketing analysis will indicate areas in the company's existing channels of distribution that need to be improved.

It is possible that the need for channel development may not be evident until specific strategy changes have been identified. For example, if a major channel change has been decided, there may be very little in the data bank to suggest the specific kinds of problems that may be encountered. Here, a knowledge of general industry trade practices and behavior can be helpful.

Estimate the cost of implementing the channel strategy and prepare a preliminary budget. It has already been pointed out that few costs can be traced directly to channel issues. This is particularly true of operating expenses incurred as a firm puts its marketing plan into action. However, the expenses incurred in setting up a new channel, training resellers, and providing management assistance can be anticipated with considerable accuracy. The biggest issue likely to arise is when salespersons, especially those on commission, are asked to perform duties in connection with channel development. To get them to do these tasks at all, and certainly if they must forego sales activities which would produce income for them, it may be necessary to compensate them or the sales department for services. If this is the case, the cost involved will have to be included in the marketing budget.

Substep 4: Evaluate the Channel Strategy Component

It is important to evaluate the proposed channel plan according to the channel subobjectives that were set forth earlier. If the issues have been properly dealt with, these subobjectives should have been addressed. It is a little less certain that the other two aspects of coordination in market mixing will have been observed. First, it is vital that the channel plan be absolutely "on strategy"—that it be completely consistent with the overall marketing plan for which it is being developed. In addition, it is important that the channel plan be consistent with the product strategy that has already been developed. At the same time, it is important to look ahead in the planning process to consider any implications that the combined product and distribution strategies may have on those parts of the marketing mix yet to be determined—namely, promotion and price.

Exhibit 6.6 is a worksheet for summarizing and checking the channel strategy.

The Promotion Component

The third component of the marketing mix is promotion. The term *promotion* is employed to describe all types of marketing activities designed to stimulate demand. The overall function can be divided into four basic subcategories: personal selling (sales), advertising, sales promotion, and publicity. Responsibility for each is often assigned to separate departments within the marketing organization. These are not really separate functions, however. They are integral parts of the overall marketing program. In this regard, it is helpful to think of these various promotional elements as composing a *promotion mix*, just as the four Ps constitute the marketing mix. These four elements must work together to reach the same overall promotion objectives. The proper coordination of advertising, sales, publicity, and sales promotion produces a far more efficient program than considering them separately does. In the discussion that follows, we will deal with promotion generally, as is appropriate in developing an overall marketing plan.

The process of developing a promotion strategy is identical to that used in preparing product and distribution strategies. Subobjectives need to be determined, decision issues and problems must be stated, a market-focused approach to resolving these issues is employed, and finally an evaluation is made to ensure that the promotion strategy coordinates with all other parts of the marketing mix.

Substep 1: Identify Promotion Subobjectives

Promotion objectives originate in the marketing strategy statement, which defines the role promotion is to play in the effort to achieve overall marketing objectives. This

Exhibit 6.6.   Distribution strategy worksheet.

Product/market: _____   ID. No. _____

Alternative: _____   ID. No. _____

	Check Consistency	
	Yes	No

Distribution Objectives:

1. _____   ___   ___

2. _____   ___   ___

3. _____   ___   ___

Direct Marketing: Will we sell direct to end users? [　] Yes　[　] No   ___   ___

> If yes, do not complete the rest of the worksheet. Go immediately to promotion strategy. If no, continue.

Distribution Strategy:
1. List the types of channel components to be used:

   a. _____   ___   ___

   b. _____   ___   ___

   c. _____   ___   ___

   d. _____   ___   ___

2. Which type of distribution coverage will be used?

   [　] Exclusive   ___   ___

   [　] Limited   ___   ___

   [　] Selective   ___   ___

   [　] Extensive   ___   ___

3. Will multiple channels be used? [　] Yes　[　] No   ___   ___

> If yes, continue. If no, go to next channel issue.

Exhibit 6.6.   Continued.

		Check Consistency	
		Yes	No
[ ] Complementary?		____	____
[ ] Competitive?		____	____

4. List the channel assistance and monitoring programs that will be needed:

a. _____		____	____
b. _____		____	____
c. _____		____	____
d. _____		____	____

5. Budget: What costs will be incurred?

	Capital	Expense		
a. Channel development	_____	_____	____	____
b. Channel supervision	_____	_____	____	____
c. Channel assistance	_____	_____	____	____

general description of what promotion is expected to accomplish is actually a statement of the subobjectives for the promotion component of the marketing mix. This is consistent with the hierarchical requirement. The statement of promotion subobjectives should also meet the other tests of realism, consistency, and quantification. You will find that the situation analysis, particularly the SWOP summary, should provide insights into possible communications objectives. These could include exploiting a differential advantage of some kind or, perhaps, addressing a threat from an important competitor. Following are some examples of typical promotion objectives.

Increase sales. Example: "We will increase total sales from $1.5 million in the current year to $1.85 million in Fiscal '88." This promotion objective is most often and most closely related to the company's overall business objectives and, therefore, to its marketing objectives as well. The achievement of a specific sales goal is usually the direct responsibility of the personal selling component of the promotion mix.

The sales objective frequently is broken down in great detail. Promotion objectives can be set for specific products, for given customer types, for particular territories, or during given periods of time. And combinations of these objectives are also possible—

for example, sales of a given product to a particular class of customer during a set period of time.

Promotion objectives are also set as a means of achieving a given profit goal. Since contribution margins often differ from one product to another, promotion objectives may be set in such a way as to achieve a given mix of product sales. This, in turn, will determine the contribution margin that is realized.

Maintain or improve market share. Example: "Increase share from 12.5 percent in 1987 to 14.5 percent in 1988." This promotion objective takes direct cognizance of competition. It is derived from insight provided in the directional matrix, especially the Boston Consulting Group's growth/share matrix, which specifically focuses on existing and expected relative share position. The responsibility for achieving a share goal is usually shared by all four elements in the promotion mix. It is widely accepted that a company's share of market is more or less directly related to its share of industry promotional effort.

Create a favorable climate for future sales. Example: "By year end 1988, nine out of every ten prospects will know the name of our company and the products it sells." This objective recognizes that it often takes considerable time and effort to win over a new customer. Sometimes it takes years to do so, as well as many thousands of sales and advertising dollars. This effort is made consciously, not on a random basis, with the hope that one day the company will "hit a hot button" and make a sale. Each contact builds on past ones and lays the groundwork for the future.

This type of promotion objective is commonly encountered in industrial marketing or in other areas where there is long-term development of customers. It can be addressed either through direct sales contact or other forms of marketing communications.

Increase awareness. Example: "By December 31, 1988, 75 percent of the target market will have top-of-mind (unaided recall) awareness of our brand." Awareness is only one of several cognitive levels that can be used to direct promotion strategy. Known as the *hierarchy of effects,* cognitive states include: (1) awareness, (2) comprehension, (3) preference, and (4) intention to buy. All of these conditions precede an actual sale and present viable objectives for promotion strategy.

Improve promotional efficiency. Example: "Decrease promotion cost as a percent of sales by 1.5 points in 1988 without reducing promotional effectiveness." Because of the rather widely held belief that promotional efforts are inherently wasteful, there is always an opportunity (perhaps even a mandate) to address the ways in which the promotion mix can be involved in the improvement of efficiency. Previously, we explored the response function and discovered that it is sometimes more efficient to use a given promotion tool less intensively and use the released resources in some other way.

Substep 2: Identify Promotional Issues and Problems

There are a number of promotional issues that will arise as you develop your marketing strategy. While some promotional decisions are quite specialized and need to be handled as such, many of them are general and apply to all aspects of the promotion mix. It should be recognized that issues—like objectives—can be situationally determined; the suggestions provided here are intended to serve primarily as examples.

Is there a promotional opportunity? Not all companies can make effective use of promotion, especially not all the time. Whether a marketing program should make heavy use of promotion depends primarily on the nature and extent of the promotional opportunity. The following are some of the conditions that generally create a good opportunity to use promotion:

1. There should be favorable movement in demand (trend, cycle, season). Marketing always works best when overall demand conditions are favorable; and it works far less well, if at all, when demand conditions are poor. This is why it is so important to press aggressively when a product is in the growth stage of its product life cycle.

2. There should be strong product or service differentiation. The purpose of promotion is to influence demand, and demand can be created or stimulated best when the offering possesses clear-cut differences that set it apart in meaningful ways from the offerings of competitors. A differentiated offering should be the marketing-oriented company's most important, distinctive competency. The late Rosser Reeves, an advertising pioneer with the Ted Bates advertising agency, coined the powerful expression "the unique selling proposition." Every offering should have its own special USP. Without it, the promotional opportunity is weak, indeed.

3. There should be some subtle qualities in the product or service that warrant communications efforts. With less objective attributes—such as flavor in foods, style in ready-to-wear, purity in drugs, and cleansing power in detergents—consumers often rely upon advertising to explain the values in the product.

4. Emotional buying motives should be important factors in affecting buyer behavior. A good deal of interest has been shown recently in the opposite nature of human response to stimuli. The concept of brain hemispheres suggests that each individual is impelled by both emotional and rational thought processes. Promotional tools appear to work best when emotional forces dominate the buying decision. This does not imply that emotionally inspired promotion is necessarily uninformative or misleading. Rather, it simply suggests that, as a marketing planner, you will always give special attention to the promotional content of your program when strong emotional buying motives appear to exist.

5. Adequate funds must be available. This is really not so much an opportunity as a prerequisite. There is no point even in contemplating an expensive advertising campaign if the company cannot afford it. We will see later that sometimes there are ways to deal with this problem in budgeting. However, there is an underlying belief among managers that promotion must pay its own way. If you can't afford it, you shouldn't do it.

To whom should we promote? The answer to this question requires a definition of the target audience. You have already done this as you developed both product and distribution strategies. But there is more to the issue. Many individuals affect the buying process, and the promotional program must be designed to reach all of them. Consumers and end users are, of course, vital. The actual buyers or purchasing agents provide inputs that affect the final purchase. Communicating with these people is important. In addition, there are likely to be any number of purchase influencers who, directly or indirectly, affect the buying process. Friends and relatives, acquaintances and neighbors, pharmacists and physicians all may be potential influencers of a new mother's choice of an infant formula. The counterparts of these influencers in industrial marketing include engineers, plant managers, accountants, and even production workers, who can influence the decision to replace a piece of machinery.

There is another whole set of targets for the promotional effort. These are the managers and merchandisers in the distribution channel. What they decide to buy and offer to their customers is often the key to a successful program. Promote to these people just as consciously and carefully as you do to the end market and its influencers. In addition, explore every means available to have these channel members assist in the promotional effort. We speak of advertising *through the trade;* this means that a company expects wholesalers and retailers to promote its products. It may assist them in preparing their campaigns, and may even help pay for their efforts through advertising allowances or cooperative advertising programs.

What should be the promotional message? At the heart of promotion is the communication of a persuasive message to the target audience. Whether the message is received and perceived depends in large part on the skill with which the promotion strategy is devised.

The promotion strategy must state clearly what it is that the planner wants to have the target audience understand as a result of the promotion. Thus, determining *what* the creative content of the promotion should be is the responsibility of the marketing planner. *How* the creative content should be executed to accomplish its assignment is up to specialists, such as copy writers, sales promotion managers, and salespersons.

What promotional media should be employed? A medium is a means of communicating with a target audience. Person-to-person communications is the medium employed almost exclusively by the sales department. Advertising utilizes a number of different nonpersonal media, including television, radio, magazines, outdoor advertising, newspapers, direct mail, and a number of lesser specialty forms. Publicity can use these media, but does not involve payment for time or space. Sales promotion may utilize both personal and nonpersonal media as a way of reaching potential customers and purchase influencers.

How much should be spent on promotion? Promotion can involve very large sums of money. This is the aspect of your plan that is most likely to meet resistance from top management and peer managers in other departments and divisions. Funds are almost always scarce relative to the demands for them. Top management must always use funds wisely, in ways that promote the best interests of the business.

There are two very important aspects of budgeting for promotion. First, the marketing planner must determine the total amount to be spent on promotion. Second, the planner must decide how this total is to be allocated to the various elements in the promotion mix. Since the overall budget may be determined independently of the programs it will fund, there is often a conflict between what the desired program should cost and the amount available. Tradeoffs will be required, and the choice among promotional tools may ultimately rest on their relative cost effectiveness.

Substep 3: Resolve the Promotional Issues and Problems

A pattern of looking to the market to resolve the issues and problems that arise in marketing planning has been set. This pattern holds for the design of promotion strategy, too. The answers to the issues and questions that face the promotion planner are found in information about customers, purchasers, and purchase influencers. The specific steps in resolving the promotional issues are as follows:

Identify ultimate users, purchasers, and purchase influencers. As we have seen, the list of target audiences also includes members of the distribution channel. In general, you need to know exactly the same things about these prospects as you have to know to develop other parts of the marketing mix. The "six honest serving men" still serve well. In particular, at this point, you are interested in the "how" and "why" of buyer behavior. How people make buying decisions and the motives that impel their choices are important inputs to planning the promotional program.

Determine the kind and amount of assistance, information, or persuasion that will alter knowledge, attitudes, recognition, and motivation of users, purchasers, and purchase influencers. If this were an easy task, there would be no need for marketing planners. It is probably the most difficult aspect of the marketing planning assignment. But it is a double assignment. You have studied your consumer carefully. You have identified those barriers of habit, ignorance, attitude, influence, and so on that inhibit the sale of your product. The task of promotion is to encounter directly one or more of these barriers, remove it, and thus improve the chances of winning the individual as a new customer.

Identify the sources of information or personal influence from which users, purchasers, and purchase influencers obtain their information and develop their attitudes. This information may have been assembled during the situation analysis. Fortunately, a relatively modest amount of qualitative research can probably generate the information you need. A few focus-group interviews with consumers should help identify the characteristics of the people to whom shoppers turn for advice. Once you are able to describe these influencers, you have a fairly good chance of finding a communications vehicle to reach them. The task is even easier for members of the target audience. You already know what kinds of people these are. From data sources such as Simmons Market Research Bureau you can discover their media exposure patterns—even obtain some information on the specific magazines they read and television shows they watch.

Develop a promotional message. A useful way for the marketing planner to resolve what the message content should be and to communicate this to the specialists who will determine how it will be expressed is to prepare a *message platform*. This is very commonly done in the development of an advertising campaign, and the concept is equally appropriate when applied to the entire promotion mix. Exhibit 6.7 is a worksheet for preparing a message platform. It closely resembles a strategy statement, which, in fact, it actually is. The message platform is a statement of message strategy, an important component in the overall promotion strategy.

The message platform first describes the target audience, which must, of course, be the same target audience as identified for both product and distribution strategies. Remember, besides the product and channel target markets, the promotional audience also includes purchase influencers. It should be equally apparent that, if different message contents must be directed at different promotional audiences, separate message platforms have to be produced for each.

The next section of the message platform states the communications objective to which the promotion is addressed. Ask yourself what you expect the target audience

Exhibit 6.7. Message platform worksheet.

1. The target audience (Whom do you want to reach?):

_____

_____

_____

2. The message objective (What is it that you want the target audience to do or think?):

_____

_____

_____

3. The message (What is central idea of the message?):
    a. What is the need of the target audience?

_____

_____

    b. What is your promise to the target audience?

_____

_____

4. Evidence (What facts can you present to support the promise?):

_____

_____

_____

5. Media (What methods of communicating with the target audience will be used?):

_____

_____

_____

6. Mandatory content (What must you include by law or company policy?):

_____

_____

_____

to do or think as a result of exposure to the message. For example, if the purpose of the promotion is to broaden the awareness base, the properly stated objective might be "By January 1, 1988, 50 percent of the target audience will be aware of this product."

The next section deals with the message itself. It has two parts. In Part A, you state the principal need that the target audience seeks to satisfy. Part B requires that you describe, briefly, the promise or benefit that the promotion is to communicate.

Section 4 contains the key facts to be used in developing the promotional message. These facts are limited to information that can support the claim or promise made.

Section 5 reviews the promotional media that will be employed. Your comments will be general in character, since specific advertising vehicles and sales promotion techniques will be known only as the tactics are developed.

The last section of the message platform contains a list of mandatory material that must be included in any communications. For instance, any requirements concerning the use of the company logotype or trademark, any disclaimers which must be made, or any policies which may affect the development of the promotional materials should be included.

Determine the magnitude and frequency of exposure necessary to transmit the selected promotional message. The exposure impact of a promotional campaign is measured in two ways: (1) by the unduplicated reach of the program, and (2) by the frequency of exposure. These dimensions are thought of primarily in terms of advertising, but they apply equally well to every component in the promotion strategy.

Net (unduplicated) reach is the number of people, or percent of a total audience, that is exposed to a promotional message one or more times during a given period, usually four weeks.

Frequency is the average number of times a commercial message is received by its target audience. Frequency is estimated by dividing gross reach by net reach. For example, suppose you place a commercial in the same television time slot six times. The reach (percent of the television audience) is 20; the gross reach (gross rating points) is 120. If the net reach is 40, the frequency is 3.

Which is most important—reach or frequency? This depends upon the promotional strategy. If you are trying to establish awareness, you will probably want to maximize reach. If your program involves a fairly complicated message, you may feel that frequency is more critical. Generally, a frequency of at least 3 is recommended. Any exposure past 10 is thought to be wasteful.

Select a promotion mix, defining the exact contribution and cost of each element. The development of the promotion mix is, in many ways, similar to the development of the overall marketing mix. Remember that the components of the promotion mix are personal sales, advertising, sales promotion, and publicity. The basic ingredients are not difficult to identify, but the exact amounts of each element and the order in which they are combined represent the artistry of promotion mixing. The final effect and effectiveness may depend more upon the manner in which they are *combined* than on the selection of the elements themselves. The mix elements must be integrated carefully. They must work together toward the same promotional objectives. For example, it is well established that it is easier to complete a sales transaction if the prospect has been preconditioned, or even presold, by advertising. The deal may be more quickly closed if there is a promotional incentive involved.

Estimate the total cost of the promotion strategy and prepare a preliminary budget. Determine the cost of the various elements in the promotion mix. There are various methods for determining the size of the appropriation. These include:

1. Available funds approach. In contrast to what this label might imply, the commitment of available funds to promotion is a *conservative* appropriation approach. Sometimes it takes the form of committing dollars to *all other* manufacturing and marketing activities; then, if any money remains, the balance is spent on promotion.

2. Competitive parity approach. In this method, an amount is budgeted which is equal to that budgeted by competitors, using either an average of the industry or of some specific competitor or set of competitors. The rationale for this approach is that it is necessary to spend at this level to preserve market share.

3. Percentage of sales approach. The traditional means of setting the promotional budget is to appropriate a fixed percentage of forecasted sales. A major criticism of this approach is that it assumes a linear relationship between promotional expenditures and sales. We already know that this is a poor assumption, because it fails to recognize the presence of decreasing returns.

4. Fixed sum per unit approach. This is similar to the percentage of sales method except that a specific amount per unit is appropriated, rather than a percentage of the dollar value of sales. The advantage of using a fixed sum per unit is that the promotional budget is not affected by changes in pricing strategy. The method is often used in determining the budgets for industrial products and consumer durables.

5. Task method approach. The task method of setting the budget involves three steps: (1) determine promotion objectives, (2) identify the promotion task, and (3) "cost out" the promotional task. You have already completed the first two steps. Once the promotion mix has been determined, it is possible to estimate the specific kinds of activities that will be necessary to carry it out. For example, in personal selling, the fixed expense of the sales organization or the variable expense of sales commissions can be readily determined. If the cost per sales call is known and the number of sales calls required in the planning period have been estimated, the selling budget can be determined by multiplying the number of planned calls by the cost per call. In advertising, the cost of the media schedule is easily obtained, as can be estimates of production costs. The sales promotion component is based on estimates of the cost of producing and distributing the materials.

Establish standards of promotional effectiveness and pretest proposed promotional materials. The only productivity measure of promotion that we have discussed so far involves the cost factor. There are, of course, other ways to evaluate the effectiveness of advertising, personal selling, and sales promotion. You will want to establish these prior to implementing the program. Since these standards will be the basis on which the productivity of the implementation will be evaluated, it is important that the marketing organization know exactly how performance will be appraised. The standards, thus, become the starting point of marketing control.

Substep 4: Evaluate the Promotion Strategy Component

Having formulated a promotion strategy, you are in the home stretch in developing the total marketing mix. Unfortunately, in the course of developing a promotion strat-

Exhibit 6.8.   Promotion strategy worksheet.

Product/market: _____   ID. No. _____

Alternative: _____   ID. No. _____

                                                                        Check
                                                                    Consistency

Promotion Objectives: Yes   No

    1. _____   ____   ____

    2. _____   ____   ____

    3. _____   ____   ____

Promotion Opportunity: Is there a promotion opportunity?
[ ] Yes   [ ] No   ____   ____

If no, explain briefly and go on to pricing strategy. If yes, continue below.

Promotion Strategy:

    1. Describe the target audience: ____   ____

       _____

       _____

       _____

       _____

       _____

    2. Message: Attach a copy of message platform.   ____   ____
    3. Media:
       a. List major sales media to be used: Cost

       (1) _____   ____   ____   ____

       (2) _____   ____   ____   ____

       (3) _____   ____   ____   ____

       (4) _____   ____   ____   ____

Exhibit 6.8. Continued.

Check
Consistency

b. List major advertising media to be used:

                                                           Yes   No

(1) _____ ____ ____ ____

(2) _____ ____ ____ ____

(3) _____ ____ ____ ____

(4) _____ ____ ____ ____

(5) _____ ____ ____ ____

(6) _____ ____ ____ ____

c. List major sales promotion media to be used:

(1) _____ ____ ____ ____

(2) _____ ____ ____ ____

(3) _____ ____ ____ ____

(4) _____ ____ ____ ____

4. Budget:
  a. Describe the method used to determine the
     promotion budget: ____ ____

     _____

     _____

     _____

     _____

b. What costs will be incurred?	Capital	Expense		
(1) Sales	____	____	____	____
(2) Advertising	____	____	____	____
(3) Sales promotion	____	____	____	____
(4) Organization	____	____	____	____

egy, often there is substantial drift away from the overall marketing strategy. This is understandable because of the many diverse elements that go into promotional planning and because of the numbers of people in different areas who are almost always involved.

As a marketing planner, you should carefully review the promotion component to make sure it fits not only the overall strategy but the other parts of the marketing mix. A worksheet for this purpose is found in Exhibit 6.8. Remember, the product and distribution components have already been determined. The mix is flexible in a forward, but not backward, sequence. If the promotion plan is somehow inconsistent with either the product or distribution components, then the promotion component will have to be modified to make it fit the mix. It is hoped, however, that these kinds of changes will not be major ones. And they should not be so if the promotion planners have carefully utilized the information base, the established hierarchy of objectives, and the approved marketing strategy statement.

The Pricing Component

Pricing is the last of the mix elements to be considered in developing an overall marketing plan. By this stage in the planning process it should be fairly evident why the pricing decisions should follow the others. Not until the product or service offering has been defined is there anything to price. Not before a distribution channel has been determined is there any way to decide what trade discounts will be required. Only after the promotion strategy has identified the role of nonprice activities in creating demand can a decision be reached on the price to be charged. It is also true that there is no practical way of estimating costs until the expense-incurring elements in the marketing plan have been determined.

The approach is exactly the same as for the other elements of the marketing mix. The planner begins by identifying those marketing subobjectives that can be addressed through the pricing strategy. Next, the various pricing issues and problems are defined. Third, these issues are addressed, presumably in a market-directed fashion. Finally, with the pricing strategy completed, it is possible to review the entire set of component strategies to make sure all four elements are properly integrated and that the entire program is consistent with the marketing strategy statement from which each component was individually derived.

Substep 1: Identify Pricing Subobjectives

Pricing subobjectives emanate from various sources within the business. Obviously, there will be pricing objectives that are closely related to the overall marketing program. Others may stem from needs in other parts of the organization. Some typical pricing subobjectives are described here:

Growth in sales. Example: "Increase sales from the 1987 level by 50 percent by the end of Fiscal 1988." Price is probably the single most powerful marketing tool. When used wisely, a strategic price can move more merchandise faster than almost any other marketing instrument. If plans call for an increase in sales of particular products, to particular customers, or at particular times, pricing can be used to accomplish these short-term sales goals.

Maintain or improve market share. Example: "Maintain market share of 15% in the automotive market." Sales increases *per se* do not necessarily result in an improved market position. For this reason, rather than direct pricing strategy toward sales objectives alone, it is the practice in some companies to use pricing as a means of attaining a specific share position. This is likely to call forth a strategy that is aimed at particular competitors rather than one that aims at improving sales generally. Price is used both as a method of differentiation and as a means of penetrating a competitor's customer base. Thus, it is overall strategy that dictates how price is used.

Achieve a predetermined profit or contribution margin. Example: "Produce profit before taxes of $1.5 million for Fiscal 1988." Pricing for profit would appear to be a simple matter of making sure that the price of each product covers its full cost plus profit. Actually, this is not a feasible approach. Pricing for profit requires planning of the entire business process, including the management of investment capital, manufacturing costs, marketing expenses, research and development—in short, any activity necessary to serve the established customer base. The best approach is to work backward from the optimum market price and develop a product or service offering that can be sold profitably at that level. But there is no doubt that when there is a squeeze on profits, one of the first solutions managers consider is pricing—generally an increase in price. This may, however, be self-defeating. A housewares manufacturer, faced with increased competition from lower-priced offerings, kept dropping the lower-priced items in its line because they were the principal victims of the low-priced entrants into the market. At the same time, prices were raised on the more expensive items in the line. Gradually, the company was pushed to higher and higher price points and, as a result, lost a substantial share of market. Profits improved for a short period, but then took a permanent downward trend.

Stabilize prices and margins. Example: "Maintain gross margin of 30 percent for the planning period." In heavily concentrated industries—that is, where a few firms account for a substantial portion of industry sales—the stabilization of price levels or of operating margins may be more critical than the maximization of short-run profits. This stability is necessary for efficient financial management of the business.

Manage cash flow. Example: "Produce a cash flow of $1.7 million for the period January 1, 1987–December 31, 1988." Because of the high cost of capital—both within and outside of a business—more attention is being paid in marketing planning to the cash flow consequences of a company's marketing programs. It is quite common for the marketing plan to include a pro forma cash flow statement so that top management can obtain a clear picture of what the implications of the proposed marketing program will be.

Substep 2: Identify Pricing Issues and Problems

For several reasons, the design of a pricing strategy is especially challenging. First, more uncertainty surrounds pricing than any other part of the marketing mix. Consumer response is unknown; competitive pricing behavior is uncertain. Pricing decisions are complicated. Pricing, because it comes last in the sequence of strategy decisions, is very dependent upon the other parts of the marketing mix. To a degree at least, pricing strategy is constrained by decisions that have already been made. Finally, pricing is difficult because there are so many nonmarketing decision makers with a stake in the outcome of pricing decisions. Pricing decisions have to be "signed off" by more non-marketing people than any other part of the marketing mix. General management, accounting and finance, legal, manufacturing—all have a stake in the price, and they all tend to get into the pricing act somewhere along the line.

There are a number of pricing issues and problems that are common to most pricing strategy situations.

What should be the basic price? A "basic" price is a reference price for a product or service. Your pricing strategy will be made up of two elements: the basic price and the pricing structure. The first issue has to do with setting the basic price; the second issue deals with the discount structure.

Sometimes the notion of a basic price is hard to grasp. It is not usually an actual price, although it could be. It is simply a point of reference for calculating each and every variation in price that will be charged. If your company sold only one product to a single customer and if the selling conditions never varied (for example, if the customer always purchased the same amount with no variation in the terms of sale), then the basic price might be the same as the actual price. But such pricing situations are highly unlikely. At least to a degree, every transaction differs from every other one; and the price paid is likely to differ accordingly. These "actual" prices are determined by the discounts or extras that are offered in connection with each transaction.

What discounts (or extras) should be allowed? The set of discounts offered to adjust for variations in product offerings, customer requirements, and competition constitutes the pricing structure. Although pricing discounts and extras can be designed to fit almost any pricing situation, there are a number of typical pricing situations for which traditional forms of discounts have been developed.

1. Trade discounts. Over the years, marketers have adopted the general practice of granting discounts based on a customer's position in the channel of distribution. These discounts are usually justified on the basis that they cover the services performed by the customer on behalf of the seller. You have already identified your channel of distribution. You know what kinds of middlemen are involved. You know, or can easily discover, the trade discounts that are typical.

2. Quantity discounts. It is quite common, indeed almost expected, for sellers to accept a lower unit price for items sold in large quantities than for the same products sold individually or in smaller lots. Quantity discounts can be either cumulative (based on a number of orders over a period of time) or noncumulative (based on the size of a single order.) There are important legal requirements to satisfy when using quantity discounts, as there are on all preferential prices that may be discriminatory.

3. Promotional discounts. One of the most important uses of discounts is to stimulate sales to and through the channel. Some of these discounts—for example, a co-operative advertising allowance—are built more or less permanently into the pricing structure. Other discounts are quite temporary, as when a special allowance of free goods is offered at the time a new product is introduced.

4. Transaction discounts. The best known of these is the cash discount—an allowance offered for prompt payment. Occasionally, a manufacturer will offer a discount for taking early delivery, especially for highly seasonal merchandise. Quite obviously, a seller can offer a discount to a customer whenever it desires to do so to close a sale or to meet a competitor's price. The seller is limited in this only by its relations with its other customers and by legal restrictions against price discrimination.

How should prices relate to cost? Almost everyone agrees that prices should cover costs. However, it would be quite wrong to insist that every product be priced to cover its own individual costs each time it is sold. Since there are many different concepts of cost, there must be many ways of pricing in relation to costs.

How should prices relate to promotion? This raises some particularly interesting questions in marketing planning. Here we are talking about the direct integration of two parts of the marketing mix. It is especially important that these be carefully coordinated. To begin with, consumers must be aware of prices they influence. Accordingly, pricing information is one of the most important elements in the message platform. In advertising, for instance, we talk about "price copy."

Price is of extreme importance in selling, too. More objections are raised about price than any other single aspect of the offering. Almost everybody would rather pay less than more (prestige goods excepted). A lower price, then, becomes a powerful tool to stimulate interest, to get ahead of the competition, and to close a particular sale.

This whole discussion can be reversed, also. Promotion can be a powerful tool in making pricing strategy work. If the pricing strategy is to be above the competition, then the rest of the marketing mix must support this approach. The product must be better and different, the distribution channel must be willing and able to sell quality, and, most vital of all, the promotion strategy must be capable of convincing the customer that the value exceeds the price. We call these other marketing forces "nonprice" competition, and it is absolutely mandatory that they work well when a high-price strategy is at the core of the marketing mix.

When and under what conditions should a price be changed? This is a key concern in marketing strategy. The best tool in addressing it is the product life-cycle model. You will employ a different pricing strategy for each stage of the cycle. Anticipating the need to make such changes as the competitive situation evolves is the mark of an astute marketing planner.

There is probably never a really good time to raise prices, however certain circumstances are better than others. In periods of economic prosperity, buyers typically expect prices to rise. It is easier to raise prices when everybody else is doing the same thing. But in the absence of a general rise in price level, price increases are best accomplished in connection with a major change in marketing strategy. The introduction of a new product or a dramatic change in distribution may make it possible to put a higher price into effect without serious repercussions. If you have an opportunity to lower price and this appears to be the right strategy, go for it!

Should a company engage in legal price discrimination—that is, charge different prices to different customers? The practice is widespread. The trade discount is a good example. Additionally, the very existence of market segments suggests that it is no less useful to charge different prices than it is to advertise differently to separate market segments.

The law becomes a factor in pricing to business customers. The Robinson–Patman Act prohibits charging different prices to customers who are in competition with each other. There are exceptions to this broad generalization, but the safest course is to make sure that there are documented cost savings or evidence of a competitor's comparable price before you offer a lower price to one customer than to another.

Substep 3: Resolve Pricing Component Issues and Problems

As marketing planner you should understand that, while cost constitutes an important consideration in pricing, it is not the sole or most important factor. In no case should a price be determined simply by adding up costs. Pricing strategy begins with the customer, as does every other part of the marketing mix. Follow what might be called a *market-minus* approach instead of the traditional "cost-plus" method. This marketing-oriented approach is embedded in the following planning steps.[2]

Identify ultimate users and purchasers. Purchasers must pay the final price for a product or service; they are, therefore, the focal point in creating a pricing strategy. It is clearly impossible to design an appropriate pricing plan without first identifying those whom the pricing strategy is supposed to affect.

For each market segment, determine the relationship of price to demand. This usually requires a schedule of the various volumes that could be sold in the segment at different prices. If possible, empirical studies of demand should be undertaken in the situation analysis in order to produce these demand schedules. Since these data are usually hard to get on an industry-wide basis, the most fruitful approach is a controlled experiment of some kind. Such a project, however, is costly and time consuming. It is sometimes possible to substitute opinion research for statistical analysis. Although it is dangerous to place too much reliance on what users say they will pay for a product, this may be the only feasible approach for exploring the dimensions of the demand curve. The task in industrial marketing is somewhat easier. By using engineering estimates, it is possible to anticipate with some accuracy the cost advantages of a given product to a particular industrial customer. When these cost advantages are known, it is possible to forecast the maximum price a prospective industrial buyer will be willing to pay.

Exhibit 6.9 is a worksheet for recording your estimate of the demand schedule. You should record the volumes you expect could be sold at each of seven prices—three above and three below your existing price. Then plot the curve of this schedule on the graph below.

Determine the prices actually charged by competitors. This is information you previously assembled during the situation analysis stage. You prepared a worksheet (Exhibit 4.19) for each competitor, which summarized its marketing mix. Each competitor's pricing strategy should be there; use it to plot their prices on the same demand curve you prepared for Exhibit 6.9. Adjust your estimate of the quantity you expect to sell at any given price in the light of prices charged by competitors. Record these in the two columns to the right at the top of the Exhibit 6.9 worksheet. You should now have a schedule of prices and their corresponding quantities.

You will want to use this information in a price-cost-volume analysis as a guide to selecting the best price among the options you face. Exhibit 6.10 is an example of such an analysis.

(text continued on p. 186)

Exhibit 6.9.   Demand analysis worksheet.

	Without Considering Competition			Considering Competition	
	Price	Quantity		Price	Quantity
Higher	_____	_____	Higher	_____	_____
	_____	_____		_____	_____
	_____	_____		_____	_____
Present	_____	_____	Present	_____	_____
	_____	_____		_____	_____
	_____	_____		_____	_____
Lower	_____	_____	Lower	_____	_____

Plot the figures on the chart below:

**Price
($)**

Quantity

Exhibit 6.10.   Price-cost-volume analysis.

Basic price	300	250	200	150	100
Volume (units)	25,000	40,000	60,000	75,000	100,000
Discounts*	122.25	101.87	81.5	61.12	40.75
Net price	177.75	148.13	118.5	88.88	59.25
Revenue	4,443,750	5,925,200	7,110,000	6,666,000	5,925,000
Fixed cost/unit	120	75	50	40	30
Variable cost					
Material	20	20	20	20	20
Labor	20	20	20	20	20
Total unit cost	160	115	90	80	70
Total variable cost	1,000,000	1,600,000	2,400,000	3,000,000	4,000,000
Total fixed cost	3,000,000	3,000,000	3,000,000	3,000,000	3,000,000
Total cost	4,000,000	4,600,000	5,400,000	6,000,000	7,000,000
Profit	443,750	1,325,200	1,710,000	666,000	−1,075,000

*In this example, list less 30–10–5, 1/10 net 90.

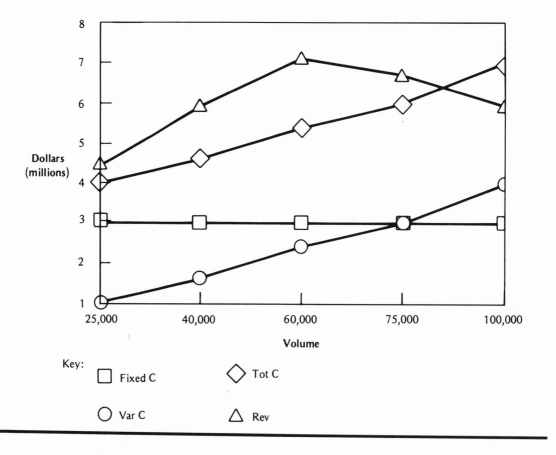

The time has come to transfer the information you developed in Exhibit 6.9 to your own price-cost-volume worksheet, preferably a computer spreadsheet similar to the one in Exhibit 6.10. A worksheet for doing this is found in Exhibit 6.11. Use this worksheet as you complete the next several steps.

Exhibit 6.11.   Pricing worksheet.

Basic price	——	——	——	——	——	——	——
Discounts	——	——	——	——	——	——	——
Manufacturer's net	——	——	——	——	——	——	——
Volume (units)	——	——	——	——	——	——	——
Revenue	——	——	——	——	——	——	——
Costs	——	——	——	——	——	——	——
Fixed cost	——	——	——	——	——	——	——
Variable cost	——	——	——	——	——	——	——
Total cost	——	——	——	——	——	——	——
Profit	——	——	——	——	——	——	——

Plot the information on the chart below:

$

Volume

Deduct margins and discounts of channel components to determine the manufacturer's net sales price. You should have this information on the trade channel worksheet you prepared during the situation analysis (Exhibit 4.27B). You have determined your channel strategy, so you know which of the various kinds of middlemen are going to be used. Consolidating their respective discounts, you can determine the amount to deduct from your basic price to calculate the net factory price. (Remember, you cannot simply add up these discounts because they are figured on a constantly decreasing base. They must be calculated in succession.) The next row of the worksheet contains the estimated volumes at each of the alternative prices. Multiply the net prices by the volumes and insert the total in the proper cells of row 5. This is your estimate of total revenue. Plot these total revenue figures on the chart in Exhibit 6.11.

Estimate the total fixed and variable costs of each price-volume alternative. Fixed costs, by their very nature, remain constant regardless of volume. Typical fixed costs are such things as depreciation of plant and equipment, rent, interest, insurance, and most administrative salaries. Variable costs are fixed per unit of output. Raw material, direct labor, and sales commissions are examples of variable expenses. There are always a number of semivariable costs. These costs increase with output, but not directly. They are found in both manufacturing and marketing. For example, as output and sales increase, additional supervisors are usually needed. When output falls, fewer are needed. In the example in Exhibit 6.10, no semivariable costs were included. You should now plot the fixed cost, variable cost, and total costs on the chart in Exhibit 6.11. This will create a form of breakeven chart that differs from the classic type only in that total revenue is not shown as a straight line.

Deduct total costs from total revenue for each price-volume alternative to obtain profit estimates of the various pricing options. At this point it should be apparent which is the most profitable basic price; and under most circumstances, that price would be selected. You can see this in the table in Exhibit 6.10 and on the breakeven chart as well. Ordinarily, you would try to price the product or service at about this point.

Remember, of course, that this is really only a reference price. It has been selected on the basis of normal trade-channel discounts. The actual prices will always vary somewhat from the basic price because of special discounts and extras that may be charged. Given this analytic approach, it is always possible to go back subsequently and inspect the consequences on profits of any changes in the discount structure. Since these changes would ordinarily also involve some change in expected volume (after all, that is why the discount is being awarded), an entirely different cost-price-volume worksheet would be prepared. At this point, you are exactly where you need to be. You have discovered the price that is most profitable, given the demand and the cost structure.

Substep 4: Evaluate the Pricing Strategy Component

You have now completed what might be called a "rough draft" of the entire marketing mix. It is "rough" in the sense that the preliminary decisions for the pricing component may not be consistent with the overall plan. Unfortunately, pricing decisions are likely to stray off course, in part because a good many different people in a number of different areas (and some outside of marketing) have played a role in formulating the pricing plan. It is the marketing planner's responsibility to bring these diverse elements together and to develop a pricing strategy in harmony with the overall marketing plan. It is important, also, to make sure that there has been no slip up in integrating the various elements of the mix as the pricing strategy has been developed. If necessary, some adjustment in the pricing strategy may be required to achieve maximum consistency among the four components of the marketing mix.

Step 9:
Selecting a Strategy Option

To this point, we have not stressed the importance of considering alternative marketing strategies. But this is a very important part of the overall marketing planning process. For many years the president of an advertising agency had on his desk a sign, directed to his account service people, that read, "Do not bring me your strategy recommendations until you are ready to discuss alternatives." This marketing-oriented CEO understood how important it is to explore options before selecting a course of action.

The Value of Alternatives

The marketing manager should not just explore one way of achieving the marketing objectives. There should be as many alternatives as necessary to provide a reasonable choice. There are several reasons why you should consider alternatives. First, alternatives provide the opportunity to select among two or more different ways of achieving the same objectives. Only by looking at alternatives can you be sure that you have found the best.

Another reason for considering alternatives is to make sure that the need for a contingency plan has been adequately studied. A contingency plan is a strategy designed for use under a set of environmental circumstances that could have an important impact on the company but do not, at the time, have a high probability of actually taking place. The need for contingency plans is often recognized at the stage at which strategy options are considered.

A third reason to have alternatives is to avoid the temptation to engage in "tunnel planning"—that is, to come up with a single strategy time and time again. This predictability of strategic response is just what the competition likes to see, because it enables a competitor to forecast your future strategy with great accuracy. Remember, the light at the end of the tunnel is a freight train coming in the opposite direction. The hand on the throttle of that locomotive belongs to your competitor's marketing director. If you plunge carelessly into the darkness, your marketing program is very likely to be wrecked by your competitor's superior strategy.

Finally, you may be asked to present alternatives for top management's consideration. More frequently, these alternatives are viewed as *management options.* An example of such options might be:

Strategy Option	Expected Results	Cost
A	Sales = $1,000,000	$100,000
B	Sales = $ 750,000	$ 80,000
C	Sales = $ 500,000	$ 65,000

The marketing planner thus promises to deliver one of three different levels of result, each at a different cost to the company. Of course, a number of other marketing planners are presenting their lists of options at the same time. Top management must select a set of strategies from among all the lists. This will be done by "cherry picking" from the various lists, selecting those which top management feels it can afford and which will offer the best prospects for achieving overall company objectives. Obviously, the marketing planner cannot provide a list of options until a set of alternatives has been developed. This was the procedure followed at a large telephone company. Every division of the company (for example, residence telephone service) was required to present a set of alternative strategies, each utilizing a different level of budget support and each with a unique objective. For example, one such set of options might have been:

Option A. Employ a high level of advertising promotion throughout the year.
  Objective: Generate 25% increase in new orders for extension telephones.
  Budget: $2.8 million.
Option B. Employ two flights of advertising—one in March, the other in October.
  Objective: Generate 10% increase in new orders for extension telephones.
  Budget: $1.5 million.
Option C. Distribute a coupon worth $10 off on the purchase of an extension telephone.
  Objective: Generate 50,000 new orders for extension telephones.
  Budget: Lost revenue of $500,000 due to $10 coupon. Nominal printing cost. Mailed with monthly statements.

Making the Choice

Having identified two or more strategy alternatives, it is necessary to choose among them. How is this done? Very carefully, because much hangs on the choice. There are often many things to consider, and the risk may be considerable.

Several decision models have been developed to help in such situations, and one of them is illustrated in Exhibit 6.12—the weighted criteria method. Only two alter-

Exhibit 6.12. Strategy choice model—weighted criteria method.

Criterion	Reach Goal	Cost/ Profit	Risk	Feasi- bility	Total
Weight	.4	.2	.1	.3	1.00
Alternative:					
Open new sales office	10 / 4.0	6 / 1.2	2 / .2	9 / 2.7	8.1
Not open new sales office	5 / 2.0	5 / 1.0	8 / .8	10 / 3.0	6.8

natives are shown here, but several more could have been included. In our example, one strategy involved opening a new sales office in a market presently served from another location. The other strategy involved continuing to cover the market from a remote office.

Before attempting to choose between the two options, the marketing planner had to decide how he would make the choice—that is, he had to identify his decision criteria and adopt a decision rule. We call this procedure *structuring the decision.* In Exhibit 6.12, the planner selected four criteria:

1. Reach Goal. How well will the alternative achieve the marketing objective?
2. Cost/Profit. What are the cost and profit consequences of the alternative?
3. Risk. What degree of uncertainty does the alternative pose?
4. Feasibility. How workable is the alternative? Can the organization reasonably be expected to make it work?

These, or other criteria the planner might have wanted to include, are probably not of equal importance. To adjust for this, the marketing planner assigned weights to each. The weights in this example are decimal fractions (that is, 0.4, 0.3, and so on). Note that the weights must add up to 1.00.

The next step in the strategy selection procedure is to evaluate each alternative by each criterion. In the example, the planner assigned a number score between 0 (low) and 10 (high). These scores have been recorded on the decision matrix. For example, the new sales office option was assigned a score of 10 on the Reach Goal criterion but only a 2 on Risk. Presumably, if things go well, there is no doubt that opening the new sales office will enable the company to achieve its objective. However, some uncertainty prevails and there is some risk if things do not work out as planned. So the planner assigned a low score (high risk) to the alternative. (Note how the scale reverses polarity in this case.) The planner scored each strategy on each criterion with the values inserted above the diagonal line in each cell.

The next step involves multiplying the scores by the weights previously assigned to each criterion. Thus the score (10) for the new sales office on the Reach Goal criterion was multiplied by 0.4, this criterion's importance weight. The weighted score (4.0) was recorded below the diagonal line in the cell. Similar scores were completed for the remaining criteria.

The final step is to calculate the total weighted score for each alternative. This is simply the sum of the weighted scores for each alternative. In the exhibit, the total score for the new sales office strategy was 8.1, whereas the total score for the other option was only 6.8. Other things being equal, the planner would have opted for the new sales office.

Suppose that when you and the other members of a planning committee have gone through this exercise, some of those people involved cannot accept the decision to open the new office. They begin to raise other questions, to challenge the strategy. Perhaps one person is concerned that since this new office would be in the same city as a major competitor's home office, there was the prospect that this company might retaliate in some way. Perhaps another committee member feels that the money spent to open the new sales office would be better invested in advertising or on developing a new product. How do you deal with this kind of situation? Does the committee just go "round and round"?

This happens quite frequently whenever a planning committee is working together on the development of a marketing strategy. The problem is not necessarily with the committee, or with the committee approach to planning. The difficulty lies with the way in which the strategy choice has been structured. The first objector is really saying, "We have left out a fifth important criterion—competitive reaction." No problem. Go back and add a column to the matrix. Reassign the weights and score each alternative on all five criteria, then recalculate the weighted average score. The second objector is really saying, "We have left out several other viable alternatives to achieve the same objective." No problem here, either. Simply add two rows to the matrix—one for advertising, another for a new product. These two strategies should be evaluated on all five criteria and the total weighted scores determined.

In short, the matrix is only useful when it accurately and completely displays the strategy-choice environment. You will know that it does this when there are no longer any objections rooted in either criteria or alternatives. There may still be people who do not like the answer that the matrix provides, but they can explain their objections

Exhibit 6.13. Payoff matrix.

Alternative Strategies	States of Nature		Expected Value
	Demand is weak	Demand is strong	
	p = .4	p = .6	
Open a new sales office	($1,000,000)	$9,000,000	$5,000,000
Do not open a new sales office	$2,000,000	$5,000,000	$3,800,000

only on the basis of hunch. "I just don't like it," someone may say. Probably true, but that is not a compelling enough reason not to proceed.

Another way of handling the same strategy choice is to deal more directly with the element of uncertainty by structuring the decision somewhat differently. This can be in the form of a payoff matrix, as shown in Exhibit 6.13. The strategy options are the same. However, in this example, the planner deals with only two criteria: payoff and risk. The uncertainty is incorporated into the matrix by stipulating two "states of nature"; in this example, those are the level of demand (either high or low). Since the planner is "uncertain" which state of nature will prevail, he has assigned probabilities to each. In the example, low demand is shown with a probability of 0.4. High demand has a probability of 0.6 (note that these probabilities must add up to 1.0). The numbers in the four cells are the expected payoffs for each strategy, given each state of nature. The decision rule is to adopt the strategy with the highest *expected value*. This value is calculated by multiplying each payoff by the probability of the state of nature associated with it, and then totaling the weighted payoffs for each strategy. The expected value for the new office strategy is $5 million [(0.4 × −1 million) + (0.6 × 9 million)] compared to $3.8 million [(0.4 × 2 million) + (0.6 × 5 million)] for the other option. Again, the choice is obvious.

These decision tools are useful, but they are not necessarily the only way for a marketing planner to choose among alternative strategies. The author remembers the advice of a pioneer operations researcher. He said, "Don't forget that, in the last analysis, the choice of a strategy is more spiritual than statistical." By this statement, he was warning not to go against your best intuitive judgment, even if the numbers say you should. There is an artistry to marketing planning, and there is a place for gut feeling.

You have prepared alternative strategies and have selected one as best suited to your organization's objectives, thus concluding Phase II of the planning process. Now you can begin to work on tactics, the action programs by which the strategy will be carried out. Chapter 7 begins with a discussion of implementation, and concludes with a review of the control process by which you can make sure your marketing program is working well.

7

Tactics, Implementation, and Control

This chapter discusses Phase III of the marketing planning process—the finalization. This phase comprises Steps 10 through 14, as follows:

10. Design the tactics
11. Present the plan
12. Write the plan
13. Implement the plan
14. Measure, evaluate, and control

Step 10: Designing the Tactics

The first major step in the implementation of a marketing plan is the development of action plans, or *tactics*. Strategies are not implemented; tactics are. A strategy cannot achieve the objectives set for it until the tactics to take that strategy into the marketplace are properly prepared.

The Nature of Tactics

Tactics, as just indicated, are action plans associated with a particular marketing strategy. They are distinguished from tasks, which are simply the routine activities people perform as part of their overall job responsibilities. Every salesperson is supposed to call on prospects. The activity becomes tactical only when it is driven by the marketing plan. If a salesman decides where he will go and upon whom he will call on a more or less random basis, this is not tactical; he is just performing his job. If, on the other hand, the salesman makes a call on a particular customer with the purpose of conveying a specific message and of achieving a predetermined result—all of which are triggered by the marketing strategy that the marketing planner has developed—the salesman is engaged in tactical marketing. If the advertising manager tells the agency, "We need to run an ad next month," this is not tactical. In contrast, if next month's ad has already been scheduled as part of an overall campaign which, in turn, was triggered by a marketing plan, the initiation of next month's ad is tactical. It is the implementation of the plan.

Marketing tactics are identified by five specific elements:

1. *What* is to be done. This must be a specific action. It is not a general statement such as, "The sales department will call on customers." Rather, it specifies the accounts to be contacted, the purpose and message content of the calls, the frequency of contact, and so on. The same specificity applies to every tactical element in the plan, whether sales, advertising, or product development.

2. By *whom* it will be performed. The tactical plan must specify, by name, the individual (or at least the department) responsible for performing the action. This is an exceedingly important aspect of tactical planning. Lack of communications is the principal cause of organizational inaction and misaction. The people who will implement a plan must know what they are supposed to do. Getting this information into their hands is part of the planning process, and identifying them in the tactical plan assures that this part of the process has been thought through and that the necessary communications will take place.

3. *When* the action will be started and when it will be finished. Since strategic windows for marketers open and close swiftly, tactics that are not implemented in a timely way cannot be expected to work well. Note the two aspects of scheduling. It is not enough to set completion dates; an activity that is not started on time is not likely to be finished on time. It is far more effective to control starting dates than finishing dates. If an activity is late getting started, there is little prospect of meeting its completion deadline. Once its completion deadline has passed, the opportunity to keep the plan on schedule has probably been lost. If there is any hope at all, subsequent actions must be accelerated—neither wise nor fair to those involved.

4. The *specific results* that are expected. Every tactic must have a purpose—an outcome that is to occur as a result of the action that is taken. Remember that the hierarchy of objectives is still in place. The expected result of any given tactic is derived directly from the objective of the marketing mix component of which it is part. The only purpose of the tactical plan is to carry out its parent strategy. This is important, for it is at this point that the linkage often breaks down. The secret in marketing planning, if there is any, is to preserve the integrity of the hierarchy of objectives. Only in this way can the planner be sure the actions that take place in the field are directed at the same objectives as the overall marketing plan.

The second major reason that tactical goal setting is important is that it becomes the basis of operational control. We have already said that one cannot control a strategy. This is because strategy is too far removed from the point at which action occurs. True, you may know that sales are down or share of market has slipped. But where? Why?

Only when you can trace the deviation back to its point of origin are you in a position to know how to correct the situation.

5. *How much* it will cost. There will be an explicit, or an implicit, cost associated with every action called for in the tactical plan. Explicit costs are direct, out-of-pocket expenses directly traceable to the activity. If the action is not taken, the cost cannot be incurred. Implicit costs are indirect or overhead costs that cannot be traced to the specific activity. Marketing budgets generally are restricted to explicit costs.

This stage in the tactical planning procedure plays a very important part in the overall budgeting and budget control process. If the marketing budget is set by the objective and task method, the chances are that the final budgeting must await the completion of the tactical plan, because the budget is the sum of the expenses needed to carry out the marketing program.

If the budget is set by one of the top-down methods—say, a percent of sales—the costing of the tactics serves two useful purposes. First, as these costs are totaled, you have a good cross-check on the adequacy of the overall budget figure. If there is considerable discrepancy, it will be important to resolve the problem before getting into implementation. The second purpose is satisfied in somewhat the same way. The overall budget, regardless of how determined, must eventually be allocated to the various tactical programs. To avoid purely arbitrary assignments, you should have good documentation to demonstrate where and why the funds should be spent. Costing out the tactical plan provides just this sort of information.

When these five elements have been properly identified for every key marketing activity involved in the execution of the marketing plan, the marketing planner can be reasonably certain that the strategy is actionable and can be confidently sent to the field. On the contrary, if these steps have not been completed, there is the very likely prospect that implementation will be haphazard and ineffective. This is a chance the marketing planner simply cannot take.

Who Should Do Tactical Marketing Planning?

Tactical planning requires street experience. One must know what is involved in performing the tasks of marketing in order to identify the tactics needed to implement any given marketing strategy. An individual who has not spent time in a task-oriented marketing position such as sales, customer service, advertising, or merchandising is seldom well prepared to develop tactical plans. By the same token, the individual with only tactical experience is not always ready to take on the job of developing marketing strategy. Obviously, the talents of both are required. The more or less traditional way of developing marketing planners is to take individuals who have had tactical experience and train them to become marketing planners—that is, product managers, advertising account executives, and so on.

It is quite common for tactical marketing planning to be assigned to functional specialists. The marketing planner should not try to outline for a sales manager or an advertising manager how the people in these departments should go about doing their jobs. Just as the marketing plan is developed out of the requirements of the business plan, so the functional marketing plans are driven by the overall marketing strategy.

The marketing planner may find it most effective to work closely with the managers of functional departments, providing the direction needed for developing functional action plans. Alternatively, of course, the marketing planner with tactical marketing experience can certainly assume responsibility for developing action plans. The balance of this discussion is based on the assumption that this procedure is followed.

How to Prepare the Tactics

Once a strategy has been identified, the marketing planner is ready to begin the development of tactics. For several reasons, it is desirable to break this step into at least four stages, each related to one of the four components of the marketing mix. Tactics will be developed in each mix area in the same order in which the strategy was developed in the first place. While the marketing planner had several options in designing the strategy, the development of tactics should follow that adopted for strategy design. If the planner began the development of strategy with the core component, this is the way tactical planning should proceed. If the order presented in this book (that is, product, distribution, promotion, price) was followed, this is the sequence that should be used in developing the action plans. Regardless of the order in which the mix elements are treated, the tactical planner should complete each of the following steps in the order presented.

To begin, select a marketing mix component from the strategy statement. Then break the component into a detailed list of all the actions necessary to complete the task. These actions must address all the "issues" previously identified during the design of the marketing mix.

There may literally be hundreds of such tasks. If so, it is wise to organize them in some way so that you can first deal with sets and then with the specific actions. Some people need help in structuring and organizing the list; those who have difficulty identifying the tasks either have had insufficient experience to do this or simply have never tried to look at field marketing in this way. In either event, you will have to lead these folks through the exercise.

Arrange the actions sequentially because there is usually a logic to the timing. Some activities must be completed before others can start. You are not trying to schedule at this point, but paying some attention to the chronology as the activities are listed will be helpful subsequently.

Worksheets are included in Exhibit 7.1 to assist you in breaking down the components of your marketing strategy. A worksheet is provided for each of the four marketing mix elements. All are arranged in the same manner. For each mix component, the various strategy issues are indicated, and space is provided to fill in the actions necessary to address each. Since not all the issues described in this book will be germane to your planning assignment, you should first check, in the brackets provided, those that are actually to be addressed in *your* marketing plan. Also, you may need to add other issues that were not mentioned in Chapter 6, but which are important elements of your program. Space has been provided to fill in these unspecified strategy components.

(text continued on p. 205)

Exhibit 7.1.   Strategy (marketing mix) components.

Product Strategy

Check the appropriate box [   ] for those issues listed below which are key results areas in your marketing strategy. In the Actions column on the right, record the specific actions that need to be taken to address the issue. Space is provided for four actions for each issue. If more room is needed, add more rows as required.

Issues	Actions

[   ]   1.   What products should we offer?

1. _____
2. _____
3. _____
4. _____

[   ]   2.   What new products should we add?

1. _____
2. _____
3. _____
4. _____

[   ]   3.   What should be the breadth and depth of our product line?

1. _____
2. _____
3. _____
4. _____

[   ]   4.   What products should be dropped or phased out?

1. _____
2. _____
3. _____
4. _____

[   ]   5.   How should our products be packaged?

1. _____
2. _____
3. _____
4. _____

Exhibit 7.1.   Continued.

| Issues | Actions |

[ ]   6.   How should our products be
           branded?

1. _____

2. _____

3. _____

4. _____

[ ]   7.   What pre- and post-sales
           services should be provided?

1. _____

2. _____

3. _____

4. _____

[ ]   8.   Other: _____

   _____

   _____

1. _____

2. _____

3. _____

4. _____

[ ]   9.   Other: _____

   _____

   _____

1. _____

2. _____

3. _____

4. _____

[ ] 10.   Other: _____

   _____

   _____

1. _____

2. _____

3. _____

4. _____

[ ] 11.   Other: _____

   _____

   _____

1. _____

2. _____

3. _____

4. _____

Exhibit 7.1.   Continued.

Distribution Strategy

Check the appropriate box [   ] for those issues listed below which are key results areas in your marketing strategy. In the Actions column on the right, record the specific actions that need to be taken to address the issue. Space is provided for four actions for each issue. If more room is needed, add more rows as required.

Issues	Actions

[   ]   1.   Should we sell direct?

1. _____
2. _____
3. _____
4. _____

[   ]   2.   What types of channel components should we use?

1. _____
2. _____
3. _____
4. _____

[   ]   3.   How many channel components should be employed?

1. _____
2. _____
3. _____
4. _____

[   ]   4.   Should we use multiple channels?

1. _____
2. _____
3. _____
4. _____

Exhibit 7.1. Continued.

	Issues	Actions

[ ]   5. What special assistance or monitoring will be needed?

1. _____
2. _____
3. _____
4. _____

[ ]   6. What improvements need to be made in our logistical support system?

1. _____
2. _____
3. _____
4. _____

[ ]   7. Other: _____

_____

_____

1. _____
2. _____
3. _____
4. _____

[ ]   8. Other: _____

_____

_____

1. _____
2. _____
3. _____
4. _____

[ ]   9. Other: _____

_____

_____

1. _____
2. _____
3. _____
4. _____

[ ] 10. Other: _____

_____

_____

1. _____
2. _____
3. _____
4. _____

Exhibit 7.1.   Continued.

Promotion Strategy

Check the appropriate box [ ] for those issues listed below which are key results areas in your marketing strategy. In the Actions column on the right, record the specific actions that need to be taken to address the issue. Space is provided for four actions for each issue. If more room is needed, add more rows as required.

| Issues | Actions |

[ ] 1. Is there a promotional
          opportunity?

1. _____
2. _____
3. _____
4. _____

[ ] 2. To whom should we promote?

1. _____
2. _____
3. _____
4. _____

[ ] 3. What should be the promotional
          message?

1. _____
2. _____
3. _____
4. _____

[ ] 4. What promotional media should
          we employ?

1. _____
2. _____
3. _____
4. _____

[ ] 5. What should be the budget? and
          how should the budget be
          allocated?

1. _____
2. _____
3. _____
4. _____

Exhibit 7.1.   Continued.

Issues	Actions
[ ] 6. Other: _____	1. _____
_____	2. _____
_____	3. _____
	4. _____
[ ] 7. Other: _____	1. _____
_____	2. _____
_____	3. _____
	4. _____
[ ] 8. Other: _____	1. _____
_____	2. _____
_____	3. _____
	4. _____

Pricing Strategy

Check the appropriate box [   ] for those issues listed below which are key results areas in your marketing strategy. In the Actions column on the right, record the specific actions that need to be taken to address the issue. Space is provided for four actions for each issue. If more room is needed, add more rows as required.

Issues	Actions
[ ] 1. What should be our basic price?	1. _____
	2. _____
	3. _____
	4. _____
[ ] 2. What discounts and/or extras should be offered?	1. _____
	2. _____
	3. _____
	4. _____

Exhibit 7.1. Continued.

Issues   Actions

[ ]   3. Should we use psychological   1. _____
          pricing?
                                            2. _____

                                            3. _____

                                            4. _____

[ ]   4. How should we price in relation   1. _____
          to promotion?
                                            2. _____

                                            3. _____

                                            4. _____

[ ]   5. What is the proper relationship   1. _____
          of cost to price?
                                            2. _____

                                            3. _____

                                            4. _____

[ ]   6. When and how often should we   1. _____
          consider price changes?
                                            2. _____

                                            3. _____

                                            4. _____

[ ]   7. Should we engage in economic   1. _____
          (not illegal) price
          discrimination?   2. _____

                                            3. _____

                                            4. _____

[ ]   8. Other: _____   1. _____

          _____   2. _____

          _____   3. _____

                                            4. _____

Exhibit 7.1. Continued.

Issues	Actions

[ ] 9. Other: _____

    _____

    _____

1. _____

2. _____

3. _____

4. _____

[ ] 10. Other: _____

    _____

    _____

1. _____

2. _____

3. _____

4. _____

After you have completed the worksheets in Exhibit 7.1, you will transfer the information from the actions column to the tactical worksheet, which is described later. At this stage of the planning it is only necessary to identify the specific issues that must be faced in the development of your marketing mix.

The Tactical Planning Worksheet

Exhibit 7.2 is an example of a tactical planning worksheet. In actuality it is more than a planning worksheet; it is also a control document, about which more will be said later in this chapter. The worksheet is largely self-explanatory, with the various columns containing the critical tactical inputs.

In column 1, insert a brief description of each action; these come from Exhibit 7.1. Remember to keep these in chronological order. One page of the worksheet permits the identification of as many as 20 action items for each marketing mix component. This may exceed the practical number a marketing planner may want to consider, but on the other hand, the tactical planning can be carried just as far as necessary. Theoretically, a backup worksheet could be prepared for each action specified on the worksheet. As a practical matter, this would seldom be done.

Column 2 lets you identify the individual or department responsible for the activity.

Column 3 will contain the scheduling information. It is in three parts: the planned starting date, the planned completion date, and the actual completion date.

Column 4 is also in three parts: The first will show the planned result; the second will be used to record the result as actually achieved; the variance column will show the difference between the plan and the result.

Exhibit 7.2.   A tactical planning worksheet.

Strategy Alternative: _____   ID. No. _____

Marketing Mix Component: _____

Action	Person/Department Responsible	Schedule			Result			Budget		
		Start	Finish	Compl.	Plan.	Act.	Var.	Plan.	Act.	Var.
1.										
2.										
3.										
4.										
5.										
6.										
7.										
8.										
9.										
10.										
11.										
12.										
13.										
14.										
15.										
16.										
17.										
18.										
19.										
20.										

Column 5 is the budget column and is also in three parts: the budget as planned, the actual cost, and the budget variance.

In all, you will complete as many tactical worksheets as there are critical elements in the marketing mix. They become very useful documents from which to prepare agendas for meetings with or memoranda to the persons responsible for the action programs. Ultimately, of course, if action programs are to be included in your written marketing plan, the worksheets become the basis on which this part of the plan is prepared.

Now that the elements of the tactical planning worksheet have been identified, let us examine each of those aspects more closely.

1. Identifying the specific individual responsible for each action. We have already seen why this is important. This step in the planning process gives you the chance to consider how best to use the staff that is available. Generally, don't ask for volunteers. Everybody will want to go to the trade show in Honolulu; no one will want to call on a customer to collect $5,000 in overdue receivables. Assign the task to the best person for the job.

2. Estimating the time necessary to complete each action. Again, here is where street experience tells. Try to be realistic, but remember that any task usually takes longer than it should. Build some margin of safety into your estimates.

3. Scheduling the actions. Working backward from the final completion date, prepare a schedule of starting and completion dates, but recognize the need to coordinate interdependent activities.

4. Preparing cost estimates for each activity. We have touched on this before. Since you will be dealing with explicit costs, you should be able to get acceptable estimates or bids. This will certainly be true for any work commissioned outside the company—a market research project, for example.

5. Identifying the specific, measurable result expected from each action. Remember how you arrived at the decision to undertake this task in the first place. You believed it would accomplish something. This is its expected result. All that remains is to state that objective in an acceptable way. It must be quantitative, realistic, consistent, and hierarchical. You have had plenty of practice doing this; keep up the good work. These expected results will be extremely important in monitoring the program and in isolating areas that have either worked well or need improvement.

6. Grouping all activities for individual managers or departments into consolidated lists for each. Think back over what you have produced up to this point. You have a list of actions, each of which has been assigned to an individual. You also know when each action must start, and the date on which it must be completed. You know what is expected to occur as the result of each action. Now you must get ready to transmit the tactical plans to those who will carry them out. The separation of the tactical plan into separate lists for each person or department is an important step toward implementation.

7. Issuing instructions to each individual or department. Issue instructions together with schedules, budgets, and expected results. You are well prepared to do this. You have just prepared a list of all of the tactical activities that have been identified for each person whose assistance and support is required.

Extensive interaction with nonmarketing departments is often required at this stage. Two complications result from these contacts. First, in some cases, you will actually need approval from the managers of other departments. These departments have responsibilities and priorities other than participating in your marketing program. You may need to rather strongly persuade these individuals to cooperate in order to achieve your purpose. Besides management authorization from the nonmarketing department, you will also need reassurances from the operating personnel that they will support your program. For example, it may be relatively easy to get the vice president of production to agree that, "Yes, this new product looks like a winner. We ought to go ahead with it." It may be quite another thing to get the plant manager to agree to have sufficient quantity on hand by the time the promotion breaks in the late spring. You may have been quite successful in persuading the vice president of human resources that you need to hire three new salespeople to staff the new sales office in Portland. You will also need to make sure that the personnel department has actually scheduled ads, interviews, and so on.

Using PERT/CPM

A useful way of planning and later controlling the tactical marketing plan is by using a network diagram. The two most common methods are PERT (Program Evaluation and Review Technique) and CPM (Critical Path Method). Originally, these terms were used to describe somewhat different techniques, but they have come to be used almost interchangeably, and the general term *network analysis* is applied to both.

The procedure for developing tactics leads directly to the preparation of a network model. An example of a new-product introduction plan is shown in Exhibit 7.3. The circles in the diagram are called *events*. They represent the completion of the various tactical activities. The numbers are the times (in days, weeks, and so on) required to complete the activity. Basically, the events are sequential, although concurrent activities can also take place, as shown in the exhibit.

The network diagram can be used in several ways. First, it is possible to determine the least time-consuming path through the network. This represents the ideal schedule for implementation of the plan. Second, it is possible to identify the most time-consuming path through the network. This is called the *critical path* because, if the project gets behind schedule on this path through the network, the planner can assume that the final implementation deadline will not be met. The third application is the use of either path as a control device for measuring the progress of implementation. The planner knows at any given time just what progress should have been made and can compare that to actual performance. If it is on or ahead of the ideal schedule, this may call for a speed-up of the program—something that might be very important in a new product introduction. On the other hand, if actual performance is behind schedule—particularly if it is behind on the critical path—strong corrective measures may have to be taken. There are a number of computer software programs that enable you to schedule a project, using the concepts involved in PERT and CPM.

Exhibit 7.3. Network model for a new-product introduction.

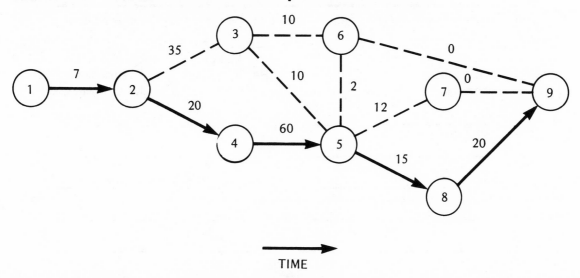

TIME

Event Number	Event
1	Research and development completed
2	Budget for manufacturing and marketing activities approved
3	Initial production completed
4	Overall marketing plan approved
5	Test marketing completed
6	Warehouse stocked with product
7	Salespeople informed
8	Advertising budgeted
9	Product available for sale

Source: From an exhibit in Bell, Martin L. *Marketing: Concepts and Strategy* (Boston: Houghton Mifflin Company, 1979), p. 191.

Exhibit 7.4 is a worksheet for preparing a critical path network diagram. If you have access to a computer and have the necessary software, it will be possible for you to include many more events than the ten that the worksheet provides for. However, the exhibit is useful even for large projects if you program each major event separately. For example, in Exhibit 7.3, one of the events in the new-product introduction process is the development of the marketing plan. A critical path diagram could be produced for the marketing planning activity, as it could for every other event in the new-product planning sequence. In this manner, approximately 100 events could be included.

The worksheet is self-explanatory. There are no particular rules regarding the drawing of the diagram, except to plot the events accurately along the time line. Be careful in identifying the critical path. It must be a continuous sequence which allows the completion of all events on a schedule that provides for the on-time completion of the entire project.

Exhibit 7.4.   Critical path worksheet.

Fill in the information required and then plot the events on the chart below:

Events (listed in chronological order)	Time Required	Events That Must Be Completed First	Events That Must Follow
1. _____	_____	__ __ __ __	__ __ __ __
2. _____	_____	__ __ __ __	__ __ __ __
3. _____	_____	__ __ __ __	__ __ __ __
4. _____	_____	__ __ __ __	__ __ __ __
5. _____	_____	__ __ __ __	__ __ __ __
6. _____	_____	__ __ __ __	__ __ __ __
7. _____	_____	__ __ __ __	__ __ __ __
8. _____	_____	__ __ __ __	__ __ __ __
9. _____	_____	__ __ __ __	__ __ __ __
10. _____	_____	__ __ __ __	__ __ __ __

Time →

Exhibit 7.5. Example of a Gantt chart.

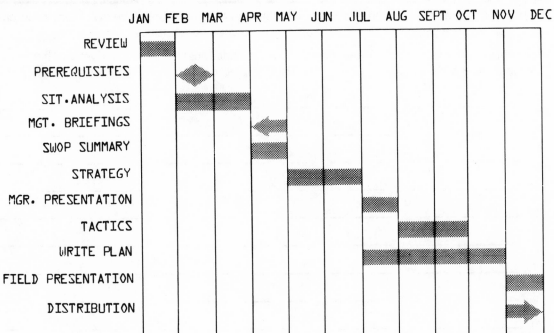

Other Useful Documents

Another useful planning and control document in connection with tactical planning is the Gantt chart. This shows the various activities (action programs) as horizontal bars. Time is indicated on the horizontal scale. Bars are drawn for each activity, showing when it is supposed to start and stop. From such a chart it is possible to identify those activities that threaten to retard the timely completion of the project. An example of a Gantt chart is shown in Exhibit 7.5. You have all the information needed on your planning worksheet to prepare such a chart. A sheet of graph paper, a straight edge, and a pencil are the only tools required.

Exhibit 7.6 is a worksheet for preparing a Gantt chart. It does not differ significantly from the critical path worksheet (Exhibit 7.4), but the chart, of course, is constructed differently. Each event is shown separately and dependencies are implied only by the sequence in scheduling.

Step 11:
Presenting the Plan

You will make numerous presentations of part or all of your plan during the course of your planning activities. Some of these will be within the marketing department; others

Exhibit 7.6.   Gantt chart worksheet.

Fill in the information required and then plot the events on the chart below. More than one event can go on a given line, provided each is performed sequentially.

Events (listed in chronological order)	Time Required	Events That Must Be Completed First	Events That Must Follow
1. _____	_____	___ ___ ___ ___	___ ___ ___ ___
2. _____	_____	___ ___ ___ ___	___ ___ ___ ___
3. _____	_____	___ ___ ___ ___	___ ___ ___ ___
4. _____	_____	___ ___ ___ ___	___ ___ ___ ___
5. _____	_____	___ ___ ___ ___	___ ___ ___ ___
6. _____	_____	___ ___ ___ ___	___ ___ ___ ___
7. _____	_____	___ ___ ___ ___	___ ___ ___ ___
8. _____	_____	___ ___ ___ ___	___ ___ ___ ___
9. _____	_____	___ ___ ___ ___	___ ___ ___ ___
10. _____	_____	___ ___ ___ ___	___ ___ ___ ___

Time →

will be to people outside your department. Some will be quite casual, perhaps workshop in nature, while others will be formal. All these presentations are important steps in the planning process. They have the purpose of reviewing your progress, soliciting assistance and input, communicating your ideas to others, and obtaining approval for the programs you recommend.

A Few Presentation Basics

It is impossible to cover this subject thoroughly in this volume, and simply reading about it isn't going to make you a great presenter, anyway. That comes with experience. Meanwhile, in making your presentations, keep the following basics in mind:

1. Always make sure you understand, and everybody in attendance understands, the purpose of the presentation. Review this ahead of time with your supervisor and communicate it clearly to those who will be present. Begin your presentation with a statement of its purpose and what you expect to occur as a result of it. Developing an agenda for your presentation will help keep the meeting "on track" and help your audience follow your direction.

2. Don't try to accomplish too much at any one meeting or presentation. Have no more than one or two major objectives. Then, make sure that everything you do or say is focused directly on that purpose.

3. Prepare carefully. Prepare both the material you will use and your presentation techniques. Each presentation you make is vital to the completion of the marketing plan. Because it is so important, it is worth preparing carefully. In one sense, this preparation is itself a kind of plan. The things you consider in planning your plan should be considered when planning each presentation.

4. Outline, in detail, everything you want to cover. If it is one of your first presentations, or if it is a particularly important one, you may want to write a script for it. Doing this is especially useful if you are going to be limited to a specified period of time. If you do prepare a script, become so familiar with it that you will not have to read it. Nothing is duller to an audience than having a presenter read from a manuscript. If you talk from an outline, have keynote sentences in the outline—not just a word or two. This will make it easier to use and will achieve much the same effect as a script. Be sure you indicate on your outline just how long you want to spend on each section. Stick to your schedule.

You may want to distribute a short version of your outline to those attending. It will focus attention and help avoid unnecessary interruptions. However, don't hand out exhibits or other materials at the beginning, because they will distract the audience from your presentation. (Some presenters, as well as their audiences, like to have an executive summary distributed before the presentation. Even this practice has some danger in it, since the executive summary may reveal strategic or budget information you would rather present after laying the proper groundwork.)

5. Use visual aids—flip charts, overhead transparencies, and so on. Don't try to put too much on one exhibit; present only the highlights. The purpose of a visual aid is to focus attention on a key point. Seldom will you use a visual to present complex

material, unless by so doing the subject can be made easier to understand. Graphs are always better than numbers, and numbers are better than words.

6. When you use visuals, don't read them aloud. Your audience will get ahead of you. Keep your eyes on the listeners. Talk *about* the visual. Tie your comments directly to it. Repeat its key points, but never turn away from your audience and read what is displayed.

7. Visuals need be only as fancy or formal as the circumstances justify. Strive instead for neatness, legibility, and relevance to your presentation. In general, presentations to top management can be less dramatic than presentations made to implementers of the program.

8. Rehearse your presentation. Do this several times until you feel comfortable with your delivery and the timing is right. Ask someone to critique your presentation—or, better still, videotape it and review it yourself. You can't practice too much, but don't let yourself become matter-of-fact or appear bored. Keep the presentation dynamic and fresh. And, too, as you become more and more familiar with your material, don't speed up your presentation. You will think you're going much too slowly. Your audience generally will not. For the most part, what you say will be new and interesting to them.

9. Take charge and stay in control. This may sometimes be difficult if you are addressing high-level executives. Generally, though, as long as you stick to the agenda, keep going, and appear to be in control, no one will challenge your right to run the show. Discourage interruptions. If they occur, it is your responsibility to get the presentation back on track. Don't abandon your game plan. Handle the question or other interruption, and then pick up where the disruption occurred.

10. Be flexible. No presentation goes completely according to plan. There will be occasions when you will need to modify your presentation on the spot. The important thing is not to lose control or forget your basic purpose. Repeat portions, skip others, and even inject new material *if you absolutely must;* but never abandon the basic objective.

11. Reach closure by the end of your presentation. This means you should obtain some action or response from your audience that will make it possible to proceed with the next stage of the planning process. This may be a formal approval of your proposal. It may be information feedback. Be sure you know what you want to accomplish, and be sure you accomplish it! Don't forget to "ask for the order."

12. Set the stage for the next presentation. As the presentation draws to a close, summarize briefly what has been agreed upon and indicate the next steps to be taken. If appropriate, indicate the assignments for any follow-up actions and suggest a timetable for their completion. Always close the presentation by thanking your audience for its participation. And do this, even if it kills you!

Step 12: Writing the Plan

Someone has said, "It isn't a plan until it has been written down." The statement is true. Recall the definition of the marketing plan that was presented earlier in this book:

"The marketing plan is an organized, documented, written communication that sets forth business goals and action programs required to achieve those goals. . . ." Your plan must be a permanent document. There are several reasons for this:

1. Writing your plan ensures that you have thought it through completely. "Writing is thinking," Anne Morrow Lindbergh once said. Until you have written your plan, you may not have given it the full mental treatment it deserves. Remember, your plan is really your theory of how marketing works. It had better be a good theory. Writing it down will enable you to make sure that it is.

2. A written plan is an unambiguous statement—at least it is clearer than any other form of communication. There should be far less confusion than when the ideas in the plan are communicated verbally.

3. A written plan becomes the historical record. It will always be available for future reference. A number of years ago, when the economy was beginning to tail off seriously, the president of a large industrial company sent instructions to his divisional vice presidents. They should come to a meeting at corporate headquarters prepared to discuss the strategies employed in their divisions some eight years previously, when a similar set of economic conditions prevailed. Actually, none of these vice presidents had been with the company eight years previously. Fortunately, over the years the president had insisted that each division prepare annually a comprehensive, written business plan. All these new vice presidents had to do was refer to the older plans, review their success in dealing with a depressed economy, and come to the meeting prepared to develop strategy for the current situation.

4. A written plan facilitates implementation. This is a parallel situation to good communications, but this time the results are critical to the success of the planning process. One of the commonly expressed criticisms of marketing planning is that after the plan is completed, nothing happens. We are only interested in marketing plans that produce results. The written plan, together with its documention—especially the tactical worksheets—will help assure that implementation occurs.

5. The written plan is the principal instrument of marketing control. The marketing plan states the expected standards of performance required to achieve the objectives. As the control phases of the marketing planning process are carried out, actual performance is compared to expected results; deviations, if any, are noted, and corrective action is initiated. Without the written marketing plan, the control aspects of marketing planning would be severely hampered, if not altogether impossible.

Some Guidelines for Plan Writing

Writing a marketing plan is not like an exercise in creative writing. It is more akin to preparing an engineering specification. Before you start, you know exactly what is going to be in it and how its contents will be arranged.

Your company may have adopted a standardized format for its written marketing plans. If it has, you have little latitude in this regard. If it has not developed a required format, you have considerable leeway in the manner in which you put the elements together. One format was shown in Chapter 2 (Exhibit 2.1). Here is another arrangement for a fairly typical marketing plan:

    I. The Executive Summary
    II. Marketing Objectives
    III. Situation Analysis Summary
    IV. Analytic Summaries
    V. Marketing Strategy
    VI. Marketing Tactics
    VII. Implementation
    VIII. Procedures for Monitoring, Evaluation, and Control
    IX. Expected Results
    X. Contingency Plans (as required)

A number of companies have developed rather comprehensive formats for the preparation of written marketing plans. An example of one that follows the arrangement just described is found in Exhibit 7.7.

The length and style of your plan are up to you. Keep your plan reasonably short—perhaps 15 to 20 pages—but do not be so succinct that your meaning and intent are unclear. The executive summary should not exceed one or two pages. Documentation, if any, should be in appendixes at the back. Preferably, voluminous tables and exhibits should be in another document altogether.

Use a professional style and avoid marketing jargon and stereotyped phraseology. Use section and paragraph headers. Write complete sentences; watch grammar and spelling. Make the text interesting, but never lose sight of the basic purpose of your plan: to communicate clearly what needs to be done (and why) to attain your organization's marketing objectives.

Step 13:
Implementing the Marketing Plan

After your plan has been written and approved, you must concern yourself with its implementation. Why so? Isn't this something that happens *after* the planning—after your job is finished? No, it is simply an extension of the planning assignment. The planning is not finished until the results are in.

It is well to remember that just about everything you have done up to this point will affect your success in getting the plan implemented properly. In one sense, implementation begins the day you start to plan; it is not something done after the planning has been completed. As we have said repeatedly, the purpose of planning is to produce results. Everything in the planning procedure is aimed at this goal. Consider some of the previous planning steps and how they relate to implementation. The objectives have had to meet certain requirements. They had to be quantitative, realistic, consistent, and hierarchical. To a considerable degree, these are tests of successful implementation, too.

(text continued on p. 232)

Exhibit 7.7. Topic outline for a product/market marketing plan.

I. THE EXECUTIVE SUMMARY

    A. Marketing Objectives
    B. The Business Situation
        1. The macroenvironment
        2. Industry and trade
        3. Competition
        4. Customers
        5. The Company
    C. Analytic Summaries
    D. The Marketing Strategy
    E. Marketing Tactics
    F. Expected Results
        1. Financial pro formas
        2. Budgets
    G. Contingency Plans

II. MARKETING OBJECTIVES

State the marketing objectives for each of the next five years:

Net sales	_____	_____	_____	_____	_____
Gross margin	_____	_____	_____	_____	_____
Percentage	_____	_____	_____	_____	_____
Profit contribution	_____	_____	_____	_____	_____
Percentage	_____	_____	_____	_____	_____
Market share	_____	_____	_____	_____	_____

III. SITUATION ANALYSIS SUMMARY

Briefly describe the key elements under each of the situation analysis topic areas (analytic modes):

    A. Macroenvironmental Impacts (Describe each briefly):

        1. Economic: _____

                            _____

                            _____

        2. Technological: _____

                            _____

                            _____

Exhibit 7.7. Continued.

    3. Demographic: _____

                        _____

                        _____

    4. Social/cultural: _____

                        _____

                        _____

    5. Legal/political: _____

                        _____

                        _____

B. Industry and Trade Factors (Describe each briefly):

    1. Demand (market size): _____

        _____

        Market growth rate: _____

        Demand states:
        a. trend: _____

        b. cycle: _____

        c. season: _____

        d. random: _____

    2. Supply (industry capacity): _____

        Rate of utilization: _____

        Cost structure: _____

        Ease of entry: _____

    3. Trade factors
        Channel arrangements:
        a. traditional: _____

        _____

Exhibit 7.7. Continued.

       b. discount structure: _____

                            _____

       c. new developments: _____

                            _____

C. Competitive Factors:
    1. Competitive climate: _____

             _____

             _____

    2. List Major Competitors:

Competitor	Volume	Share	Strategic Thrust
_____	_____	_____	_____
_____	_____	_____	_____
_____	_____	_____	_____
_____	_____	_____	_____

D. Customer Analysis:
    1. List the Major Segments:

Segment	Potential	Growth Rate
_____	_____	_____
_____	_____	_____
_____	_____	_____
_____	_____	_____

    2. Describe the Target Segment:

Demographic Description	Geographic Description	Psychographic Description
_____	_____	_____
_____	_____	_____
_____	_____	_____
_____	_____	_____
_____	_____	_____

Exhibit 7.7.   Continued.

   E. Internal Analysis (Describe each briefly):

    1. Organization and Staffing: _____

                         _____

        Management experience: _____

                         _____

        Mission/charter: _____

                         _____

        Important policies: _____

                         _____

    2. Financial resources: _____

                         _____

    3. Management information: _____

                         _____

    4. Planning/budgeting: _____

                         _____

    5. Cost structure: _____

                         _____

    6. Marketing commitment: _____

                         _____

    7. Marketing evaluation: _____

                         _____

        Products/services: _____

                         _____

        Distribution channels: _____

                         _____

Exhibit 7.7. Continued.

Physical distribution: _____

_____

Promotion: _____

_____

Advertising: _____

_____

Sales promotion: _____

_____

Sales Force: _____

_____

Pricing: _____

_____

F. External Financial Analysis:
   1. Industry sales
       for the past five
       years ($): _____ _____ _____ _____ _____
          Growth
          percentage: _____ _____ _____ _____ _____
   2. Industry sales
       for the past five
       years (units): _____ _____ _____ _____ _____
          Growth
          percentage: _____ _____ _____ _____ _____
   3. Industry
       forecast for next
       five years (units):_____ _____ _____ _____ _____
          Growth
          percentage: _____ _____ _____ _____ _____
   4. Seasonal Index: J F M A M J J A S O N D
                        __ __ __ __ __ __ __ __ __ __ __ __

G. Internal Financial Analysis:
   1. Company sales
       for the past five
       years ($): _____ _____ _____ _____ _____
          Growth
          percentage: _____ _____ _____ _____ _____
          Company
          market share: _____ _____ _____ _____ _____

Exhibit 7.7. Continued.

2. Company sales
   for the past five
   years (units):   _____ _____ _____ _____ _____
   Growth
   percentage: _____ _____ _____ _____ _____

3. Company
   forecast for next
   five years (units):_____ _____ _____ _____ _____
   Growth
   percentage   _____ _____ _____ _____ _____

4. Seasonal Index: J   F   M   A   M   J   J   A   S   O   N   D
                     —   —   —   —   —   —   —   —   —   —   —   —

   Company
   market share   _____ _____ _____ _____ _____

5. Product sales ($) by market for last five years:

   _____ _____ _____ _____ _____ _____

   _____ _____ _____ _____ _____ _____

   _____ _____ _____ _____ _____ _____

   _____ _____ _____ _____ _____ _____

   _____ _____ _____ _____ _____ _____

6. Product sales (units) by market for last five years:

   _____ _____ _____ _____ _____ _____

   _____ _____ _____ _____ _____ _____

   _____ _____ _____ _____ _____ _____

   _____ _____ _____ _____ _____ _____

   _____ _____ _____ _____ _____ _____

7. Product sales forecast (units) by market for next five years:

   _____ _____ _____ _____ _____ _____

   _____ _____ _____ _____ _____ _____

   _____ _____ _____ _____ _____ _____

   _____ _____ _____ _____ _____ _____

   _____ _____ _____ _____ _____ _____

H. Cost-Price-Volume (Breakeven) Analysis:

Volume

I. Last Year—Profit Contribution Analysis by Product Line:

	Product	Product	Product	Product
Net sales	——	——	——	——
Cost of goods sold	——	——	——	——
Gross margin	——	——	——	——
Gross margin percentage	——	——	——	——
Marketing expenses	——	——	——	——
Sales salaries/commissions	——	——	——	——
Sales expense	——	——	——	——
Advertising	——	——	——	——
Consumer promotions	——	——	——	——
Trade promotions	——	——	——	——
Trade allowances	——	——	——	——
Marketing research	——	——	——	——
Total marketing expenses	——	——	——	——
Total contribution	——	——	——	——
Contribution percentage	——	——	——	——

Exhibit 7.7. Continued.

J. Next Year—Profit Contribution Analysis by Product Line:

	Product	Product	Product	Product
Net sales	_____	_____	_____	_____
Cost of goods sold	_____	_____	_____	_____
Gross margin	_____	_____	_____	_____
Gross margin percentage	_____	_____	_____	_____
Marketing expenses	_____	_____	_____	_____
Sales salaries/commissions	_____	_____	_____	_____
Sales expense	_____	_____	_____	_____
Advertising	_____	_____	_____	_____
Consumer promotions	_____	_____	_____	_____
Trade promotions	_____	_____	_____	_____
Trade allowances	_____	_____	_____	_____
Marketing research	_____	_____	_____	_____
Total marketing expenses	_____	_____	_____	_____
Total contribution	_____	_____	_____	_____
Contribution percentage	_____	_____	_____	_____

IV. Analytic Summaries:

A. SWOP Summary:

	Strengths	Weaknesses	Opportunities	Problems
1.	_____	_____	_____	_____
	_____	_____	_____	_____
2.	_____	_____	_____	_____
	_____	_____	_____	_____
3.	_____	_____	_____	_____
	_____	_____	_____	_____

	Strengths	Weaknesses	Opportunities	Problems
4.	_____	_____	_____	_____
	_____	_____	_____	_____
5.	_____	_____	_____	_____
	_____	_____	_____	_____
6.	_____	_____	_____	_____
	_____	_____	_____	_____
7.	_____	_____	_____	_____
	_____	_____	_____	_____
8.	_____	_____	_____	_____
	_____	_____	_____	_____
9.	_____	_____	_____	_____
	_____	_____	_____	_____
10.	_____	_____	_____	_____
	_____	_____	_____	_____

B. Worksheet for Preparing Growth/Share Matrix:

Market Growth Rate:

Current period ( ) _____

Future period ( ) _____

Market Share:

		Current Period			Future Period		
	Product	Sales	MS	RMS	Sales	MS	RMS
1.	_____	___	___	___	___	___	___
2.	_____	___	___	___	___	___	___
3.	_____	___	___	___	___	___	___
4.	_____	___	___	___	___	___	___
5.	_____	___	___	___	___	___	___
6.	_____	___	___	___	___	___	___
7.	_____	___	___	___	___	___	___
8.	All Other	___	___		___	___	

Exhibit 7.7. Continued.

C. Growth/Share Matrix:
    Position major products on the matrix.

Star		Problem Child
Cash Cow		Dog

High

Low

Market Growth Rate

10x   1x   .1x

Relative Market Share

D. Worksheet for Preparing G.E. Screen

Market Attractiveness				Company Capability			
Factors	Weight	Score	Weighted Score	Factors	Weight	Score	Weighted Score
___	___	___	___	___	___	___	___
___	___	___	___	___	___	___	___
___	___	___	___	___	___	___	___
___	___	___	___	___	___	___	___
Total	1.00		___	Total	1.00		___

Exhibit 7.7. Continued.

    E. The G. E. Screen

        Position major products on the matrix:

HIGH (6)   **Market Attractiveness**   LOW (0)

HIGH (6)

Business Strengths

LOW (0)

    F. Forecast and Gap Analysis:

        1. Plot sales for the past five years.

        2. Plot forecast for next five years.

        3. Plot marketing objectives for next five years.

        4. Identify the planning gap.

Exhibit 7.7.   Continued.

G. Financial Pro Forma Statements:
   Attach the following:
   1. Pro forma income statement.
   2. Pro forma balance sheet.
   3. Pro forma statement of change in financial condition.
   4. Marketing budget.

V. Marketing Strategy:
   Attach strategy statements for each product/market (see example next page):
   A. Strategy Statement:
      Product/Market: _____

      1. The target market segment is:

         _____

         _____

         _____

      2. The objective(s) for this product/market are:

         _____

         _____

         _____

      3. The marketing strategy is:
         a. Product: _____

            _____

            _____

         b. Distribution: _____

            _____

            _____

         c. Promotion: _____

            (1) Advertising: _____

                _____

                _____

Exhibit 7.7. Continued.

(2) Sales: _____

_____

_____

(3) Sales promotion: _____

_____

_____

d. Pricing: _____

_____

_____

VI. Marketing Tactics:
Attach tactical worksheets per example on following page.
VII. Implementation:
Attach delegation worksheets per example provided.
VIII. Procedures for Monitoring, Evaluation, and Control:
Describe the procedures that will be used to track the program.
IX. Expected Results:
Attach financial pro forma statements and budgets.
X. Contingency Plans:
A. List the contingent events that exist: ID

_____ ___

_____ ___

_____ ___

_____ ___

_____ ___

_____ ___

_____ ___

_____ ___

_____ ___

_____ ___

Exhibit 7.7. Continued.

B. Plot the IDs on the matrix below.

	1.0	Probability of Occurrence	0.0

```
        1.0          Probability of Occurrence         0.0
      ┌─────────────────────────┬─────────────────────────┐
   10 │ A                       │ B                       │
      │                         │                         │
      │                         │                         │
      │      Include in Plan    │     Contingency Plan    │
      │                         │                         │
      │                         │                         │
Impact├─────────────────────────┼─────────────────────────┤
Level │ C                       │ D                       │
      │                         │                         │
      │                         │                         │
      │     Make Assumptions    │         Ignore          │
      │                         │                         │
      │                         │                         │
    0 └─────────────────────────┴─────────────────────────┘
```

C. Attach a strategy statement for each event in cell B.

Tactical Worksheet

Strategy Component: _____

Action	Responsibility	Schedule			Result			Budget		
		Start	Finish	Compl.	Plan.	Act.	Var.	Plan.	Act.	Var.
___	___	___	___	___	___	___	___	___	___	___
___	___	___	___	___	___	___	___	___	___	___
___	___	___	___	___	___	___	___	___	___	___
___	___	___	___	___	___	___	___	___	___	___
___	___	___	___	___	___	___	___	___	___	___
___	___	___	___	___	___	___	___	___	___	___
___	___	___	___	___	___	___	___	___	___	___
___	___	___	___	___	___	___	___	___	___	___
___	___	___	___	___	___	___	___	___	___	___

Exhibit 7.7. Continued.

Action	Responsibility	Schedule			Result			Budget		
		Start	Finish	Compl.	Plan.	Act.	Var.	Plan.	Act.	Var.
___	___	___	___	___	___	___	___	___	___	___
___	___	___	___	___	___	___	___	___	___	___
___	___	___	___	___	___	___	___	___	___	___
___	___	___	___	___	___	___	___	___	___	___
___	___	___	___	___	___	___	___	___	___	___
___	___	___	___	___	___	___	___	___	___	___
___	___	___	___	___	___	___	___	___	___	___
___	___	___	___	___	___	___	___	___	___	___
___	___	___	___	___	___	___	___	___	___	___
___	___	___	___	___	___	___	___	___	___	___
___	___	___	___	___	___	___	___	___	___	___
___	___	___	___	___	___	___	___	___	___	___
___	___	___	___	___	___	___	___	___	___	___
___	___	___	___	___	___	___	___	___	___	___

Delegation Worksheet

One of these sheets should be produced for each person or department assigned responsibility for one or more of the tactical actions.

For (Name or Department): _____

Action	Schedule			Result			Budget		
	Start	Finish	Compl.	Plan.	Act.	Var.	Plan.	Act.	Var.
___	___	___	___	___	___	___	___	___	___
___	___	___	___	___	___	___	___	___	___
___	___	___	___	___	___	___	___	___	___
___	___	___	___	___	___	___	___	___	___
___	___	___	___	___	___	___	___	___	___

Exhibit 7.7.   Continued.

Action	Schedule			Result			Budget		
	Start	Finish	Compl.	Plan.	Act.	Var.	Plan.	Act.	Var.
——————	——	——	——	——	——	——	——	——	——
——————	——	——	——	——	——	——	——	——	——
——————	——	——	——	——	——	——	——	——	——
——————	——	——	——	——	——	——	——	——	——
——————	——	——	——	——	——	——	——	——	——
——————	——	——	——	——	——	——	——	——	——
——————	——	——	——	——	——	——	——	——	——
——————	——	——	——	——	——	——	——	——	——
——————	——	——	——	——	——	——	——	——	——
——————	——	——	——	——	——	——	——	——	——
——————	——	——	——	——	——	——	——	——	——
——————	——	——	——	——	——	——	——	——	——
——————	——	——	——	——	——	——	——	——	——
——————	——	——	——	——	——	——	——	——	——
——————	——	——	——	——	——	——	——	——	——

In the situation analysis, you looked for internal and external factors that would affect the implementation of your program. You looked at organizational capability and at marketing opportunity. A plan that does not achieve a match between the two will not be implemented successfully. In selecting a strategy, you were concerned with feasibility—can we do it? This is implementation. Finally, in designing tactics, almost the entire thrust was on identifying ways in which to implement the strategy. So, implementation has pervaded the planning process. What you do at this stage is to take the steps to carry through the implementation!

Marketing planners typically do not execute their own plans. Action programs are assigned to functional specialists. In this process of delegation, it is imperative that the marketing planner communicate very clearly with those who will carry out the programs. Implementers not only must understand what is expected of them, but also deserve to know something about the rationale behind the program. A marketing planner has virtually no authority to enforce the proper execution of the plan. But the planner who has done the work well can speak with authority. This power of knowledge is what you have to rely upon to convince functional specialists to execute your plan properly. Of course, after the plan has been approved by top management, it takes on greater meaning for those who are to implement it. In effect, the plan becomes more powerful than the planner. Of course, a marketing planner who has budgetary control over the action components (as some marketing managers do) is in a relatively good position to enforce the proper implementation of the plan.

Here are some suggestions on how to delegate effectively:

Pick Competent People. Be sure the person selected to carry out a task has the ability and resources needed to do the job. Few people will tell you when they do not feel confident about taking on an assignment. Others are overconfident and don't ask the kinds of questions that would assure you they understand the assignment. So, if you get vibrations of either sort, check them out carefully. Recognize when you will have to provide training, assistance, or closer than normal supervision.

Provide Specific Objectives. Use the tactical worksheet. Give each individual a specific, identifiable goal. Make sure that the individual understands that his or her performance will be evaluated, not on effort but on results. Make sure that the importance of the schedule is understood. Achieving the desired result, but not on time, is still a serious performance failure.

Don't Interfere. Once you have given instructions and have confidence that the individual understands the assignment, don't interfere with the process. Nobody will ever go about an assignment in exactly the same way as you might. Don't expect them to. What counts is the result. Besides, in many instances, these people will be specialists—individuals whom you should not try to second guess on matters of detail. You've picked the right people; let them do their jobs.

Do Follow-Up. There is a difference between interfering and following up. Make sure when you give an assignment that the individual knows you will be checking from time to time to see how the work is going, to determine if there are any problems, and to make sure that it will be completed on schedule. Do this and, if necessary, take steps to keep the work going.

Reward Good Performance. There is not a great deal you can do to reward those who perform exceptionally well, but a simple "thank you" is an absolute necessity. A letter written to a superior, with a copy to personnel, is always appreciated. An account executive at an advertising agency followed this practice. As the frequent recipient of "freebees" from media representatives and others, he used these gifts to "thank" the people who had been helpful to him. Whether a ticket to a hockey game or a novelty item, these items became tokens of his appreciation to those who had performed their marketing planning assignments well.

Lest there be a temptation to believe that all there is to implementation is the delegation of task assignments to others, remember that ultimately you, as the marketing planner, are responsible for results. You cannot abdicate that responsibility. You can delegate, but ultimately you will be accountable for the way the plan works. For this reason, you must go to the final step in the marketing planning process: the measurement, evaluation, and control of the plan in action.

Step 14:
Measuring, Evaluating, and Controlling the Implementation

Your role, at this stage, shifts somewhat. Now the marketing planner becomes the marketing controller, whose responsibility it is to monitor and review the results of the plan in action.

There are two basic requirements for control. The first, which you have already attended to, is to state objectives in quantitative (measurable) terms. The second is to measure the results of the program with exactly the same yardsticks. Unless this is done, you will be stuck with two sets of noncomparable data.

Measurement and Monitoring

There are three basic factors that you should follow closely.

Effort

You must have access to some kind of information by which you can tell whether the actions called for in the plan actually occurred. This is obviously most important for tactical assignments that have been given to others. A useful technique to employ at this stage is *debriefing*. You are probably familiar with term as used in the military. When a unit has returned from a patrol or action of some kind, intelligence officers interview members of the team carefully.

In debriefing, usually participants are asked to recount, often several times, the exact sequence of events that took place. Probing questions are asked concerning enemy strengths, tactics, and response to the initiative. The purpose, of course, is to assess the success of the mission, to obtain up-to-date information, and to lay the groundwork for planning future missions. The same technique can be employed in marketing, although probably not after every sales call. Periodically, and not too long after the action, field marketing people should be asked to participate in a debriefing session. This can be handled by a marketing research specialist who is familiar with investigative interviewing, by the field supervisor, or by the planning staff. The results, of course, need to come to you as the marketing planner.

Performance Results

What did you expect in the way of results—that is, what objectives did you seek to achieve? This is what you should look for in evaluation and control. When you review what the program accomplished, it isn't what you *didn't* expect but rather what you *did* expect that matters. For example, suppose your advertising was designed to increase awareness of Product *A* in the Northeast. You can't claim any improvement of awareness in the Midwest (even though it may have occurred), because that was not the *purpose* of the campaign.

The analysis of sales is of vital importance in checking performance results. Sales performance is the principal influence on "top-line" results, although pricing plays a critical role as well and other demand-influencing elements in the marketing plan also contribute to achieving sales objectives. So, when we speak of sales control, we are really concerned with the net impact of the entire marketing mix. Nonetheless, the focal point is the performance of the sales force, so the sales control process usually begins with an analysis of sales data compared to objectives.

The marketing planner is first aware of a potential problem when there is a deviation between forecasted and actual sales. But this information reveals very little as to the location or cause of the difficulty. Sales performance varies along several dimensions, all of which may have to be explored to arrive at the source of the deviation. The most common methods of analyzing sales are by time period, product, territory, and customers. For example, the analyst needs to ask the following questions:

When during the operating period did the sales deficiency first occur?
What product(s) were involved?
Which territories?
Which salespersons?
Which customers?

An example of how a marketing controller might use such questions to analyze sales performance is shown in Exhibit 7.8. The data are hypothetical, although the situation is based on the sales control procedures used by a major company. The example is particularly realistic because it dramatizes how aggregate sales data may cover up serious problems in smaller segments of an operation.

In this example, Holly Hardware Company's marketing manager, B. J. Williams, has only a slight initial indication that anything is wrong. A routine quarterly review of sales against the forecast reveals that the program appears to be running smoothly. However, Williams knows that a thorough sales control review requires that sales performance be checked at several key results areas. Accordingly, he checks sales in relation to quota, beginning with the first of the company's eight marketing regions. It is immediately apparent that the overall sales picture is somewhat misleading. The Mideast region is actually slightly off its objective. One half of one percent may not seem like much, but the dollar amounts are significant. More important, this is a danger signal that a far more serious problem may lurk lower down in the management hierarchy.

Exhibit 7.8.   Sales analysis—Holly Hardware Company.

Sales Analysis Activity	Focus	Sales Data				Comment
		Sales ($000)	Goal ($000)	Over or Under ($000)	Percent Over or Under	
1. Williams conducts a quarterly sales review, comparing actual with goal for the overall marketing program	Total company	7,741	7,650	91	1.2	No apparent problem
2. Microanalysis by reviewing sales in eight regions	Mideast	1,493	1,500	−7	−.5	Mideast region off by $5,000, which is 0.5% of goal
	Midwest	1,575	1,500	75	5.0	
	Northeast	451	450	1	.2	
	Plains	606	600	6	1.0	
	Southeast	1,571	1,575	−4	−.3	
	Southwest	765	750	15	2.0	
	Mountain	144	150	−6	−4.0	
	West	1,136	1,125	11	1.0	
3. Microanalysis by reviewing sales in the Mideast region at four districts	Baltimore	405	375	30	8.0	All of the Mideast region's problem is in the Pittsburgh district
	Philadelphia	473	450	23	5.0	
	Pittsburgh	210	300	−90	−30.0	
	Richmond	405	375	30	8.0	
4. Microanalysis by reviewing sales in Pittsburgh at three focal points:						
a. Customer	U-Do-It, Inc.	23	23	—	—	The problem in Pittsburgh is centered in two large customers— one of which bought nothing during the quarter
	ABC Hardware	0	60	−60	−100.0	
	Great Eastern	15	60	−45	−75.0	
	Home Center	38	23	15	66.7	
	All other	134	134	—	—	
b. Salesperson	Johnson	15	90	−75	−83.0	Johnson and Spivey are the focal points of the problem, with Johnson alone accounting for $50,000 loss in sales
	Spivey	38	75	−37	−50.0	
	Kurtz	68	68	—	—	
	Carlson	89	67	22	32.8	
c. Product line	Hand tools	45	60	15	−25.0	Sales loss is concentrated in the builder's hardware line—a highly competitive area; Housewares showed unexpected strength, primarily due to a new line of microwave cookware.
	Builder's hardware	30	105	−75	−71.4	
	Garden tools	60	90	−30	−33.3	
	Housewares	75	45	30	66.7	

Source: From an exhibit in Bell, Martin L. *Marketing: Concepts and Strategy* (Boston: Houghton Mifflin Company, 1979), p. 477.

The next step, accordingly, is to inspect sales performance in the sales districts making up the Mideast territory. This inspection shows that sales are off drastically in the Pittsburgh district. This is apparently where the problem lies, but what is the reason for it? There are three dimensions to sales in any district: (1) sales to specific customers, (2) sales of specific products, and (3) sales by specific salespersons. Any one or some combination of these elements might be at the root of the problem. Williams first looks at sales to customers. What he discovers is that almost all the sales deficiency is centered on two customers: ABC Hardware, a major hardware chain; and Great Eastern, a large independent. Records by salesperson reveal that two senior representatives, Dick Johnson and Bill Spivey, who carry the load of the district, are 83 and 50 percent below quota, respectively. A quick check confirms that their major accounts are the same ones whose purchases are far below expectations. The product analysis further reveals that the builder's hardware line accounts for most of the district's sales problems.

Thus, the Pittsburgh district's sales deficiency centers on two salespeople and their inability to keep two major customers going and to produce orders for the most important product line. At this point, the marketing planner would involve the territorial and district managers, asking them to investigate and determine the reason for the sales problem. This could be important information. If the problem is localized—that is, if it is unique to the Pittsburgh district—the remedy lies largely in tactical implementation. If the problem relates to the builder's hardware product line or its price, the same kind of difficulties should be cropping up elsewhere in the field. So, Williams continues the exploration of the sales data base.

As it turns out, none of the other territories shows any of the same symptoms as the Mideast. The Great Lakes region is $50,000 over its forecast. What is happening there? Is there a clue to an emerging marketing opportunity? The analysis of this region's sales leads to the Chicago district, where an unexpected order from Ace Hardware sent the district far beyond its forecast. (This development does, in fact, lead to a focused effort to build even greater volume with Ace. The effort, however, requires more service-selling effort than the district can afford. The account is turned over to the national sales manager to develop.)

And so, Williams proceeds with the inspection of other territories and districts. No important deviations are identified, and the sales controllership task is suspended until receipt of the next quarterly sales report.

Ideally, you should measure the results of every aspect of the marketing plan for which you established a quantitative objective. Your company's marketing information system may not yet be set up to do this, and you may have to arrange special data-gathering activities. If your firm has a marketing research department, this is probably the best place to go for this type of assistance. But, as a last resort, you can probably set up some informal measurements yourself. Normal sales information should be available from the accounting or sales departments.

Environmental Monitoring

As you recall, the environmental scan was an important part of the situation analysis. You may well have identified major external factors that eventually shaped the strategy you selected. Unfortunately, the environment does not stand still. In fact, some aspects of it (say, economic or political factors) can change significantly without much warning. The same is true to an even more considerable degree of industry and competitive conditions.

Because of such changes, and their serious implications for the effectiveness of your marketing program, you must monitor these factors continuously. When any significant change occurs that might alter the outcome of your plan (for good or bad), immediately consider if it calls for a modification in the program.

Evaluation

The process of evaluation has been implied in the discussion of monitoring and measuring. Specifically, this step involves comparing measured results with expectations and noting any variances (differences) between them.

Variances can arise because of failures in the effort (performance) area, because of ineffective tactics, or because the wrong strategy was selected. It may have been a weak choice to begin with, or there may have been important changes in the external environment. If some aspect of tactical planning or performance lies behind the variance, the marketing planner can reasonably hope to bring results into line by making some fairly quick and obvious changes. If the fault lies with the strategy, the problem is more serious and may require quite drastic action. Because of this, the planner will usually first concentrate control efforts on performance and tactical issues, in two steps.

Identify the Variance

Identify the magnitude, direction, and trend of the variance. Exhibit 7.9 presents a useful way of tracking such information. It plots cost performance on a key marketing input: field sales expense (not commissions or salaries, but such things as travel, entertainment, and so on) as a percentage of sales. The budget is shown as a broken line at 5 percent. Because it is common for actual sales expense to fluctuate from this budgeted figure by as much as 2.5 percentage points, and these are judged to be the limits to which such deviations can be tolerated, two additional horizontal lines are drawn—one at 2.5 percent and the other at 7.5 percent. Actual sales expense figures are plotted monthly on the chart. In general, as long as the actual figure is within the two boundary lines, the variance is assumed to be acceptable. But there are exceptions. In the exhibit, several hypothetical patterns are shown. In Pattern A, sales expense has been increasing monthly until it has reached a figure of 7 percent. It is still within an acceptable range, but what might this predict? That in the next period, it will be greater than 7.5 percent. Why wait to find out the cause before taking corrective action?

Pattern B shows that sales expense over a period of five months has been consistently below the budget of 5 percent. Is this good? Not necessarily. There is a reason for budgeting a sales expense level of 5 percent. It is to assure that the funds are available to do those things which are necessary to develop and serve customers. If the money

Exhibit 7.9. Example of a budget variance analysis.

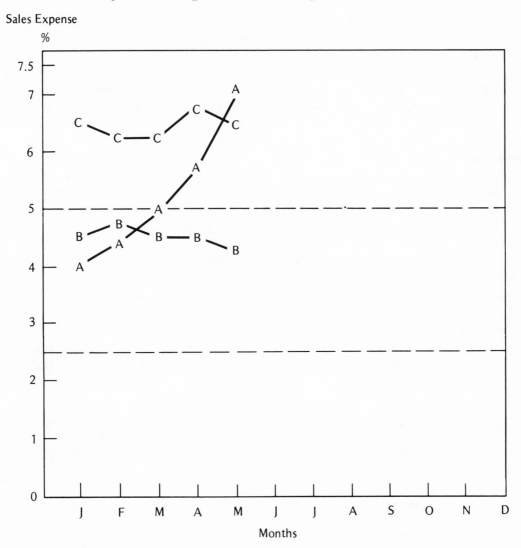

Source: Adapted from an exhibit in Kotler, Philip. *Marketing Management*, 5th Edition (Englewood Cliffs, N.J.: Prentice-Hall, 1984), p. 749.

is not being spent, it is unlikely that the work is being done. A successful sales manager prides himself on his ability to use the sales expense account as a barometer of how effectively his sales force is working the field.

Pattern C shows a consistently high sales expense percentage, hovering around 6.5 percent. There seems to be no danger that it will go over the upper limit. But it is equally clear that, by the end of the year, total sales expense as a percent of sales will be over budget. Halfway into the year it will be time to do something about this variance.

Explain the Variance

You will have to determine what part of the variance is owing to internal performance factors and what part to external factors. (This is where debriefing and environmental monitoring become important.)

This process, even when dealing with a fairly specific tactical element in the plan, is not simple. For instance, in the above example, there may be several factors at work explaining the variances in the patterns. For example, if sales expense was budgeted in actual dollars, as it needs to be for control purposes, this tends to be viewed by the sales force as a fixed cost. Suppose, however, that sales volume is down. Then this fixed outlay per month is going to show up as an increase in the percentage of sales spent on sales expense. Of course, the opposite could explain the low rate of sales expense in Pattern B. But it is possible that other factors have been at work. Perhaps a district manager has either been too tough or too lenient in approving expense accounts. This alone could have caused the deviations. Only an investigation will reveal the facts.

To show how the analysis of variance is applied, let us examine a sales variance. An aspect of sales control is the diagnosis of a difference between actual sales and projected sales, when these values are expressed in monetary terms. When the sales data involve physical units, the variance is most likely to be because of the kinds of problems identified in the Pittsburgh district of Holly Hardware Company. However, if sales are reported in dollars, a decline in sales can come from either a decline in physical volume, a decline in average price paid, or both. To illustrate how this analysis is made, consider this example.

	Plan	Actual	Variance
Physical volume	1,000	800	200
$ Price per unit	50	45	5
Dollar volume	50,000	36,000	14,000
Variance Analysis:			
Variance because of volume (200 units at $50)			$10,000
Variance because of price (800 units at $5)			4,000
Total variance			$14,000

In this example, profit is going to be less than anticipated, by a $14,000 sales revenue variance. The most serious factor, of course, is the volume loss; this is the kind of situation in which sales control analysis is critical. But the planner would also be concerned about two aspects of the pricing situation. First, the sales force has not been able to preserve the $50 price that was built into the marketing plan. Can they sell quality? But at the same time, even though price was off by 10 percent, volume was off by 20 percent. What would the volume have been if the price had been held? This marketing planner clearly has some tough decisions to make about pricing strategy and tactics for the future.

When you have completed these two steps, you are ready to begin the task of modifying your program—a requirement that you should have anticipated from the very beginning of the planning process. It was precisely because of this probable need to adapt the program that we earlier stressed the importance of flexibility in your plan.

Control

"Control" means being able to exercise a continuing influence over the outcome of your plan. The need for it arises because few plans ever work out as they were intended. We have indicated why this is so, and how variance analysis is employed to determine when and why some modifications in a plan are required. Three kinds of modifications might be needed. They are discussed below in the order of their seriousness, with the least troublesome first:

Effort Corrections. If actions called for in the plan were not taken by those responsible for them, your response is clear. Reasons for the collapse in effort must be identified, instructions clarified or reissued, or new assignments made. You must be careful to determine if the delay caused by the failure threatens any subsequent actions or events—for example, is it a delay on the critical path? If it is, appropriate alterations may have to be made in subsequent activities.

Tactical Fine-Tuning. The easiest, and most practical, place to begin actually modifying your program is with its tactical elements rather than with the strategy itself. If performance is below expectation and there is no indication of an environmental change, tactics are certainly the place to start. But where to begin? Which tactics to change?

Fortunately, if you insisted that each action component of your program be assigned a specific expected result, you need only begin to inspect the various tactical components to discover where the breakdown occurred. Remember, you stated a measurable result to be achieved by a specific date for every action on the tactical worksheet. Go back to those worksheets to determine just where each action program failed to meet its goals. Your task as marketing controller is to find out why this happened and to determine what can be done about it. You may want to get out into the field.

Once you have some idea about the circumstances surrounding the performance variance, you can decide (on the basis of your original planning) whether your overall strategy is still viable. And even if you begin to suspect that the strategy is weak, you should first fine-tune the tactics, attempting to improve the situation as much as possible until such time as a replacement strategy can be brought to bear.

Strategy Change. This should be your last resort in dealing with performance variance. Only after you have exhausted the fine-tuning options should you abandon your strategy. Months of effort, considerable money, and tremendous thought went into its preparation. It is not to be cast off lightly.

However, if your variance analysis or your monitoring of external factors reveals that a change of significant proportions has occurred in the external environment, you have little choice. Your strategy, based on a different set of assumptions, will have been compromised. A different strategy is required. And where does this new strategy come from? Either you call up an existing contingency plan, or you go back to Step 4 in the planning process: a review of the marketing situation. Obviously, any changes made in the strategy should be described and explained in an addendum to your written marketing plan.

Putting a Contingency Plan Into Action

The contingency plan was a strategy that you previously considered as one of your strategy alternatives. Specifically, it was a plan intended to cope with a potentially threatening external event. At that stage of the planning process, it was judged to have a low probability of occurring. But, as succeeding developments have proved, that judgment was incorrect. What was an inferior strategy has become the appropriate one. All that remains to be done is to develop the tactical details of the contingency plan and put it into action.

How do you know when to invoke a contingency plan? The following steps may be helpful in answering this question.

Identify a Contingent Event. This has already been done in the planning sequence. You analyzed impending events and classified those for which contingency plans would be necessary.

Prepare a Strategy Statement. Using your best judgment as to the likely impact of the event, you prepared a strategy to deal with it. A strategy statement, similar to those which you prepared for the plan itself, should now be prepared. It will include, as you recall, the following elements: (1) the target market, (2) the objective, and (3) the marketing mix.

Select a Tracking Indicator. You must have some way of forecasting arrival of the contingent event. If the event is an economic one, such as a downturn in the economy, it is relatively easy to select a tracking indicator. You can pick one of the government's leading economic indexes and use it to determine when the trend toward recession is sufficiently serious to warrant a change in strategy. For instance, if your business is involved in capital goods, you might well track a series on new equipment orders.

If the event is less likely to be traceable through public information, you may have to construct your own tracking device. For example, if the event involves the introduction of an improved product by a major competitor, you will want to know how far down the new-product development path this competitor has progressed. Some steps in this process are hard to detect, since they are all performed internally. But once the competitor begins concept or product testing, your marketing research people should be able to pick up this information.

Identify an Early Warning Signal. In selecting a tracking indicator, you have determined *how* you will decide to invoke your contingency plan. *When* you take this step depends upon locating two key trigger points. The first is an early warning signal—a clue that is detected early enough for you to put together the tactical plan necessary to implement the contingency plan. The second is the actual point at which the program is initiated. It is similar to the steps taken by the captain of a fishing vessel who is watching the approach of a coming storm. He or she knows that when the wind rises to gale force, the boat should be in port, safely moored. Knowing how long it takes to retrieve the nets and reach the safety of the anchorage and how fast the storm is approaching, the captain sets an early warning signal based on wind velocity to allow adequate time to prepare for the storm.

Develop Tactics. Knowing full well that the contingency plan will be invoked, your next step is to prepare the tactical plan. There is no point in doing this sooner, since up to this point there was no firm indication that the strategy would be needed. But the time has come to be prepared to implement it.

This task is exactly the same as preparing tactics for any strategy. You will complete the tactical planning worksheets and be ready to issue instructions for implementation as soon as the final decision to change strategies has been made.

Institute Advance Actions. Some aspects of the tactical plan may require lead times that may not be available later. In this situation, it is probably a good idea to institute advance actions that will permit the swift invocation of the plan later on. For example, in an example used earlier, the president of an industrial products company called a meeting of the divisional vice presidents to discuss how to deal with an expected decline in the economy. To give these executives time to prepare for the meeting, the president had to mail the instructions before it was even certain that the meeting would be held or a contingency plan required. This kind of advance action saves time and avoids the danger of acting precipitously under pressure from a rapidly deteriorating situation.

Invoke the Contingency Plan. In developing tactics, the trigger point was identified. Once it has been reached, the system really takes over. The contingency plan is called up. Of course, management always reviews each major step of this kind to make sure it is appropriate. But if the analysis has been well done, the decision is probably a foregone conclusion. The contingency plan becomes the new company strategy.

Once under way, events do not slow down. At this point it is wise to take another look at the external environment to determine the need for yet another contingency plan. A corporate planner at a major company, referring to a period in the early 1970s in which the energy crisis and a deepening recession combined to create an increasingly uncertain business climate, once said, "We started the year with A, B, and C plans. By the end of the first quarter, the C plan was the A plan. By the end of the year, we ran out of the alphabet." Obviously, this corporate planning staff was engaged in a rapid cycle of plan, evaluate, and plan again.

However, relatively few marketing planners develop contingency plans, and it is not likely that you will have done so. Accordingly, your only move is "back to square one" to begin the planning process anew. The task is not, however, as frustrating as it might appear. The next section on the management cycle explains.

Amending Your Planning Document

Should you invoke either a tactical or strategic change in your plan, you must amend your written plan accordingly. This may be done by editing the original text or by inserting new material. Do not be reluctant to "mess up" your written plan. It is a tool you are expected to use. As a tool, it may need sharpening or to be replaced. And,

Exhibit 7.10.   The cycle of planning, implementation, and control.

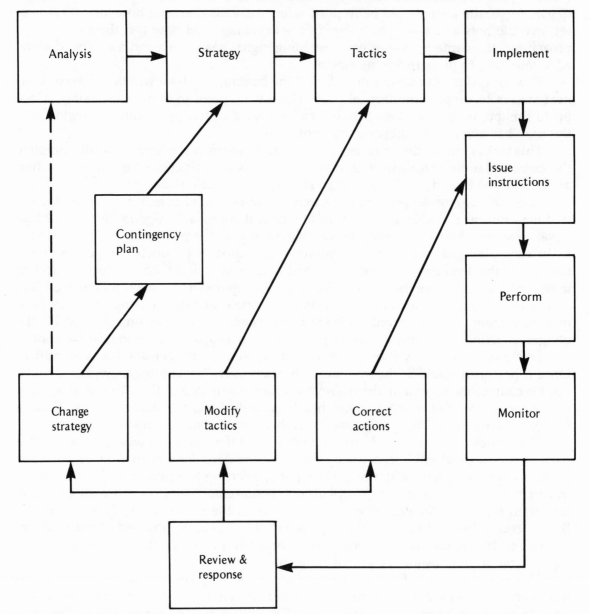

Source: Adapted from an exhibit in Bell, Martin L. *Marketing: Concepts and Strategy* (Boston: Houghton Mifflin Company, 1979), p. 54.

in use, it is bound to show signs of wear and tear. It is part of your job to keep your plan in working order. As a matter of fact, if you don't find yourself making modifications in your plan, you probably aren't using the planning process correctly.

The Cycle of Planning and Control

Marketing planning is an annual event. It begins, as you recall, with a review of the previous year's plan. This usually takes place only six months or so after your previous year's plan went into the field. It could well be midyear before your control process indicates that a strategy change is needed. The first step in the new planning season will produce exactly the same conclusion. In other words, the control phases of one planning process merge naturally into the planning phases of the next. The process really never ends. This cycle is depicted in Exhibit 7.10. In brief, the exhibit portrays the entire marketing planning process—a process in which planning, implementing, and controlling go on almost continuously.

PART III

Beyond the Planning Process

Part III contains three chapters that go beyond the nuts and bolts of planning. They are intended to broaden your perspective and to help you become an even better marketing planner. Chapter 8 presents an overview of the financial aspects of marketing planning. Its coverage of the use of accounting and financial information represents the level of familiarity a marketing planner should possess. In Chapter 9, the human side of planning is discussed. Plans are developed by people and implemented by people. The planning exercise involves a great deal of personal involvement, and the interaction between the marketing planner and the rest of the organization is an important factor in determining the success of the planning effort. The last chapter in the book briefly reviews a number of planning pitfalls—things that can destroy the effectiveness of your planning efforts.

8

Financial Aspects
of Marketing Planning

The need to understand the financial implications of marketing arises often during the development of a marketing plan. Some of these circumstances were discussed as the marketing planning steps were described. Others, however, were temporarily side-stepped, awaiting fuller discussion in this chapter. We will not attempt here to tie these financial concepts and tools to specific steps in the planning process. Instead, the chapter will cover basic aspects of accounting and finance that are important to marketing and therefore are important to marketing planning. It should be quite obvious how and in what ways these concepts are employed in the marketing planning process. Examples are, of course, provided to illustrate the application of these concepts.

Two Kinds of Accounting

There are two kinds of accounting and financial analysis employed in management. Each has its place, and each is pertinent to marketing planning. The first type is generally referred to as *financial accounting;* the second is called *managerial accounting.*

Financial accounting is undertaken largely on behalf of the controller or other chief financial officer of the business. The concern is to protect shareholders' equity and, if possible, to improve it. Since this is often the primary financial goal of a business, it is not surprising that the accounting system is designed primarily to address issues that relate to the financial condition of the business. The reports issued periodically are intended to display the financial health of the business and to show how it has changed since the last reports were issued.

The financial issues of concern to top management find their way, sooner or later, into the marketing plan. This is because the hierarchy of objectives typically begins with a statement of corporate financial objectives. As we have seen, these objectives are soon transformed into operating objectives, and plans are developed to achieve them. But these operating plans are successful, at least in the eyes of top management, only to the degree that the financial objectives of the business are met. Thus it is that the marketing plan typically includes the traditional financial statements: profit-and-loss statement, balance sheet, and statement of sources and disposition of funds.

Accounting systems are designed for the uses to which the information is to be put. As long as the uses are almost exclusively in terms of traditional financial reporting, there is no need to enter and store data in ways other than those necessary to prepare periodic financial reports. Because of the traditional, dominant importance of financial reporting, most accounting systems, and the data bases upon which they are built, have been designed to meet the needs of financial planners—not necessarily those of marketing planners or other executives concerned with managing the business.

Managerial accounting deals with information needed by operating managers in their decision making. Frustrated by the inapplicability of data collected primarily for financial reporting, managers found ways to reshape traditional reports to make them more useful for plotting strategy and evaluating performance. A number of the large, national accounting firms took the lead in developing these approaches. A type of managerial accounting of particular interest to marketing planners is called *profitability accounting*.

As you might suspect, financial accounting systems are not very good at reporting the profit (or loss) of specific products. They also do not consider customers or customer segments, geographic territories, programs, sales representatives, dealers, and so on. But these are the objects of marketing efforts. Managerial accounting, which permits the analysis of financial variables as they relate to these objects or to segments of the business, is far more useful for our purposes than purely financial accounting.

In the balance of this chapter, we will look first at the ways in which traditional financial analysis is employed in marketing planning. Then we will probe more deeply into those aspects of managerial accounting that bear directly on marketing planning.

Traditional Financial Analysis

Financial analysis is used in marketing planning in three ways. First, it is used to assess the financial performance and capability of the business; this involves the inspection of prior years' financial reports. The second use is in estimating the financial outcome of a proposed strategy; it is in this context that the planner prepares pro forma financial statements. The third use is in control. The principal control instrument is the budget, of which there are two types: the capital expenditure budget and the expense budget.

The Balance Sheet

The balance sheet is a statement of the financial condition of a business. An example is shown in Exhibit 8.1. The balance sheet has two parts which, by design, must balance. On the top half are the assets of the business; on the bottom half are the liabilities and

Exhibit 8.1.   The balance sheet.

Emanem Manufacturing Company
Balance Sheet
December 31, 1987

	1987
Assets	
Cash	$92,000
Accounts receivable	127,000
Inventory	78,000
Total current assets	297,000
Land	60,000
Buildings	1,000,000
Equipment	891,000
Total fixed assets	1,951,000
Less depreciation reserve	706,000
Net value of assets	1,245,000
Total assets	$1,542,000
Liabilities	
Accounts payable	92,000
Salaries payable	21,000
Total current liabilities	113,000
Notes payable	45,000
Mortgage on buildings	450,000
Total long-term liabilities	495,000
Total liabilities	$608,000
Capital	
Common stock	779,000
Retained earnings	155,000
Total capital	934,000
Total liabilities and capital	$1,542,000

owner's equity (capital). The balance sheet is affected by every revenue- and cost-impacting event that occurs. Some of these events simply represent shifts in the mix of assets and liabilities as, for example, when a company sells one of its trucks. A current asset—cash—replaces a fixed asset—the truck. Or reverse the process. The company buys a new welding machine, for which it pays cash. The asset account—equipment—is increased, and the cash account is reduced. In other cases, transactions affect both sides of the balance sheet, as when a company pays one of its suppliers. Cash is diminished, but so is the current liability—accounts payable.

These are not inconsequential changes, as any financial manager will affirm, but they are not primarily related to marketing. Marketing actions—for instance, the sale of a product—affect the balance sheet in much more fundamental ways. Cash (or accounts receivable) is increased and finished-goods inventory is diminished. But these are not equal values. It is hoped that the sales price will exceed the inventory value of the product. This is profit. Where does it go? It increases the owner's equity. Specifically, it increases retained earnings, from which dividends are eventually distributed.

Almost all marketing decisions are aimed at making a profit, and thus at improving the shareholders' equity. But the ability to do this may depend upon how well equipped the business is to undertake the necessary marketing program. It is for this reason that the marketing planner looks closely at the balance sheet to determine financial strengths and weaknesses that may affect the kinds of marketing programs which can be undertaken. One way of doing this is to inspect a set of balance sheet ratios.

Liquidity Ratios. These are used primarily to assess the solvency of a business, but can be applied to marketing planning to evaluate the capability to engage in short-term marketing activities. The best known of the liquidity ratios is the *current ratio:*

$$\frac{\text{Current assets}}{\text{Current liabilities}}$$

This ratio indicates the degree to which the immediate claims of creditors can be covered by cash or assets that could be quickly converted to cash. A ratio of 1:0 is a bare minimum for solvency, whereas a ratio of 2:1 is quite satisfactory.

Quick Ratio. Sometimes called the *acid-test ratio,* this is determined by the relationship:

$$\frac{\text{Current assets } - \text{ inventory}}{\text{Current liabilities}}$$

This is an even tougher test of liquidity. It assumes that inventory cannot be swiftly converted to cash without considerable sacrifice, if at all. Thus the test is whether cash and receivables exceed current liabilities. A company that cannot pass the acid test is probably in very serious short-term financial difficulty.

Inventory to Net Working Capital. This ratio addresses the same problem as the quick ratio. It relates the value of inventory to the level of working capital:

$$\frac{\text{Inventory}}{\text{Current assets } - \text{ current liabilities}}$$

The higher this ratio, of course, the less the liquidity of the firm's current assets. In marketing terms, there is reason not to let inventories of finished goods climb too high. First, there is the ever-present threat of obsolescence. Second, there is at least an implicit cost in holding inventory. On the other hand, the ability to promptly fill customers' orders argues for maintaining an adequate assortment of the most rapidly moving items.

Leverage Ratios. These deal with the relationship of long-term debt to other items on the balance sheet. The *debt-to-asset ratio* compares total debt to total assets.

$$\frac{\text{Total debt}}{\text{Total assets}}$$

This ratio indicates the extent to which the firm has borrowed to finance its operations. In contrast, the *debt-to-equity ratio* compares debt to stockholders' equity:

$$\frac{\text{Total debt}}{\text{Total stockholders' equity}}$$

This ratio indicates the extent to which the business already relies on funds from outside the business. A highly leveraged business is at some risk of being taken over by its creditors, but the use of debt to finance growth may be the most feasible (or only) way to expand. A low debt-to-equity ratio, in the absence of a policy to the contrary, should suggest to the marketing planner that obtaining outside funds may be feasible. It is a much less likely prospect for a company that is already highly leveraged.

The Income Statement

The income statement, often called the *profit-and-loss statement,* shows the financial results of business operations over a period of time. It is issued at least annually, but most companies issue income statements each quarter or more frequently. An example of an income statement appears in Exhibit 8.2. The income statement is a primary input to marketing planning, since the purpose of the planning is usually to achieve goals that relate to sales, margin, or profit. The ultimate purpose, of course, is to improve the balance sheet—to increase the worth of the business.

As a marketing planner, you will study previous income statements to identify company strengths or weaknesses. These comparisons can be expedited when industry data are available. While the absolute values may differ significantly from one company to the next depending upon size, the relationships tend to be quite stable. Therefore, you can be very legitimately concerned if cost of goods, gross margin, or any of the expense categories for your company are out of line with the industry average. Also useful is to compare the income statements over a period of time. In making such comparisons, of course, you should concentrate on percentages rather than absolute figures, because changes in price level can affect dollar values. If necessary, use a price index to eliminate the effect of price changes on various income statements.

Operating Ratios

Now that you have a picture of the operating results for a given period of time, it is possible to employ another set of analytic ratios. There are two types of operating ratios.

Exhibit 8.2.   The income statement.

Emanem Manufacturing Company
Income Statement
Year Ended December 31, 1987

Sales	$2,340,000
Cost of goods sold	
Materials	654,000
Direct labor	600,000
Other manufacturing expenses	150,000
Total	1,404,000
Gross margin	$936,000
Expenses	
Administrative	317,000
Sales salaries and commissions	306,000
Depreciation	64,000
Interest expense	38,000
Total	725,000
Profit before taxes	211,000
Less income tax liability	74,000
Net profit after tax	$137,000

The first deals with profitability, the second with the efficiency with which assets are managed.

Profitability Ratios

These compare various aspects of the income statement or compare income data with balance sheet information. The *gross profit margin* is variously referred to as *gross profit, gross margin,* or simply *margin.* It is the percentage of sales represented by the difference between sales and cost of goods sold:

$$\frac{\text{Sales} - \text{cost of goods sold}}{\text{Sales}}$$

From the marketing planner's point of view, this may be the single most important number on the income statement. Protecting gross margin, or planning to achieve a targeted level of gross margin, can be at the forefront of a marketing strategy. Since it is a residual (sales − cost of goods sold), both of these elements must be studied. The culprit from the sales end is usually the discounts that are awarded to move inventory. It is easy to give away the store in order to move merchandise. Remember, unless otherwise stated, the "sales" item on the income statement is *net sales*—sales after discounts and allowances.

The other causal factor is cost of goods. Can a marketing planner have any impact on cost? It is hoped, yes. A variance from standard on material or labor cost, or in productivity, can increase cost to the point at which gross margin is endangered. This needs to be watched carefully. A product manager at Ralston-Purina spent almost six months in the accounting department learning about cost accounting and trying to find ways to eliminate the negative variances caused by rapidly escalating costs of a major ingredient.

The *net profit margin* is the percentage of net income to sales:

$$\frac{\text{Net income}}{\text{Sales}}$$

This is the "bottom line." It displays what the company has been able to accomplish in the operating period. Is the company better off? The net profit percentage (and the dollars it represents) is often the primary goal of the marketing planner.

The difference between gross margin and profit is that group of expenses not related to the production of goods and services. But these costs are not unmanageable; they can be budgeted and controlled. They also include all the costs of marketing and, therefore, have considerable impact on sales. You will be very much concerned with these expenses in your marketing plan. As you develop a strategy to achieve a targeted profit, you will need to address them.

A related ratio, *operating profit margin*, uses income before taxes. This has the advantage of displaying the actual profit-generating capacity of the business. Tax liabilities can vary owing to a number of nonoperational considerations. It is sometimes useful to exclude the tax line from the ratio.

Return on Assets (ROA). There has been much interest in this particular ratio in recent years. It shows the relationship between net income and the assets employed:

$$\frac{\text{Net income}}{\text{Assets}}$$

The ratio is far more useful than the net income figure alone. The real test of management's skill is how well assets are employed to produce profit. What appears to be a very high profit in absolute dollars may prove to be quite low when related to a costly asset base. Return on assets is a principal measure used by corporate strategists to compare the performance of divisions of differing size and technology. The critical strategic issue is, how can a company deploy its assets most profitably?

Return on Investment (ROI). This ratio compares net income to the owner's equity:

$$\frac{\text{Net income}}{\text{Owner's equity}}$$

This ratio is of principal interest to the owner of a business. It tells how well the investment in the business is paying off. This can then be compared to other investment opportunities. In a conglomerate organization, the parent company might well use ROI to evaluate its investment in each subsidiary. Operating managers typically prefer to use *Return on Assets Managed* (ROAM) because of its more direct relevance to the kinds of decisions they must make.

Earnings per Share (EPS). This ratio is also of principal interest to the investor community. It relates net income to the number of common shares outstanding:

$$\frac{\text{Net income}}{\text{Number of common stock shares outstanding}}$$

The ratio has a bearing on marketing planning to the degree that the financing of a strategy may depend on the ability to sell common stock. EPS is a principal determinant of how a stock is valued by investors. This may well be the form in which the hierarchy of objectives gets started. The finance committee of the board of directors may charge the president with the objective of increasing earnings per share. This in turn starts the hierarchy in motion. Ultimately, marketing objectives must be developed that relate back to the finance committee's expectations.

Activity Ratios

Managers use many different ratios to evaluate the performance of various functions. Four such ratios, which are closely related to the operating statements, deal with the turnover of inventory, assets, and receivables.

Inventory Turnover. This is the ratio of sales to average inventory:

$$\frac{\text{Sales}}{\text{Average inventory}}$$

When compared to industry averages, the ratio provides a very quick indication of whether the company is maintaining too much inventory or too little. Suppose the industry average is, say, 6—indicating that the inventory is moved roughly every two months—and the company's turnover ratio is 4. This suggests that more inventory is on hand than necessary to support a given level of sales, or else the assortment is not sufficiently attractive to produce adequate sales volume. (Of course, there may be other reasons for low sales volume, but the meaning of the ratio in terms of inventory level is not changed.) Marketing planners pay careful attention to inventory. It is an important aspect of the logistics of marketing strategy.

Asset Turnover. This is the ratio of sales to assets, either total assets or fixed assets:

$$\frac{\text{Sales}}{\text{Assets}}$$

Typically, successful firms in an industry operate with sufficient assets to produce a given volume of business. It is a rough way of estimating whether a given company is operating in relation to capacity. If the ratio of sales to assets is low, chances are the asset base is too high and excess capacity exists. From other ratios, such as ROAM, one would probably discover that the return on that asset base is also small.

Receivables Turnover. This is a measure of the average length of time required for a firm to collect sums due from credit sales. Specifically, it is the ratio of credit sales to the average amount of accounts receivable. Thus, if the ratio is 4, it means that on the average it takes three months to receive payment. A low ratio such as 3—which extends the repayment period to four months—indicates either poor credit and collection procedures or a softening of the economy, forcing customers to delay paying their bills as a way of conserving cash. This is not typically a marketing planner's concern, except to the extent that actions taken to increase the turnover may create problems with customers, which marketing would prefer to avoid.

Cash Flow

Because of the manner in which financial accounting records are kept and the form in which operating results are reported, it is possible for a company to show a net profit and still be short of cash—cash needed to meet obligations and to fund new programs. What happens, of course, is that the profit is imbedded in unsold inventory, in accounts receivable, or in expanded capacity.

Interest in managing cash flow arose in the 1970s, when the need to generate cash internally became critical. Concern has not abated, even though the cost of borrowing has become more reasonable as interest rates have fallen. It is not unusual for a marketing planner to be asked to demonstrate the impact of a proposed program on the cash flow of the company. It is useful, therefore, to be familiar with the concept and the way in which to analyze changes in working capital.

In its simplest version, *cash flow* refers to cash flow from operations and simply involves adding any noncash expenses (for example, depreciation) to net income.

A more comprehensive view of cash flow is expressed by the relationship:

$$CF = (NI + depreciation) + dP\&E + dWC, \text{ where}$$

$$
\begin{aligned}
CF &= \text{cash flow} \\
NI &= \text{net income} \\
dP\&E &= \text{change in plant and equipment} \\
dWC &= \text{change in working capital}
\end{aligned}
$$

The changes in plant and equipment and the changes in working capital involve an inspection of the balance sheets at the beginning and end of the operating period. Exhibit 8.3 presents the 1986 and 1987 balance sheets for Emanem Manufacturing Company. The changes in cash and the working capital accounts are summarized in Exhibit 8.4. The one item in this exhibit not obtained either from the income statement or the balance sheet is the amount of the shareholders' dividend. This distribution of earnings was made after the books were closed but before the balance sheet was prepared. We can see that the operating profit of $137,000 resulted in the payment of $100,000 in dividends. The balance of $37,000 is found in the increase in retained earnings.

Exhibit 8.3. Comparative balance sheet.

Emanem Manufacturing Company
Comparative Balance Sheets
1986 and 1987

	1987	1986
Assets		
Cash	$92,000	$67,000
Accounts receivable	127,000	90,000
Inventory	78,000	95,000
Total current assets	297,000	252,000
Land	60,000	60,000
Buildings	1,000,000	1,000,000
Equipment	891,000	841,000
Total fixed assets	1,951,000	1,901,000
Less depreciation reserve	706,000	642,000
Net value of assets	1,245,000	1,259,000
Total assets	$1,542,000	$1,511,000
Liabilities		
Accounts payable	92,000	74,000
Salaries payable	21,000	30,000
Total current liabilities	113,000	104,000
Notes payable	45,000	60,000
Mortgage on buildings	450,000	450,000
Total long-term liabilities	495,000	510,000
Total liabilities	$608,000	$614,000
Capital		
Common stock	779,000	779,000
Retained earnings	155,000	118,000
Total capital	934,000	897,000
Total liabilities and capital	$1,542,000	$1,511,000

Based on the examples in Exhibits 8.3 and 8.4, the simple cash flow estimate is $137,000 + $64,000 = $201,000. This is somewhat misleading, since a number of balance sheet transactions took place. Using the expanded equation, the cash flow is:

$$\$137,000 + \$64,000 - \$50,000 - \$36,000 = \$115,000$$

The Budgets

The last of the traditional financial documents used by marketing planners are the budgets. There are two kinds: the expense budget and the capital expenditure budget.

The Expense Budget

The *expense budget* is a forecast of the operating costs that will be incurred for a given period of time, usually one year. It differs from a forecast only in the extent of the commitment implied. The marketing planner, in submitting a budget, in effect says, "This is what we agree to spend." Management approves the budget, and operating managers are held accountable for keeping expenses within the budget. In common with all other forecasts, of course, the future frequently holds surprises, and deviations of actual expenditures from the budget will occur.

For convenience in administration, budgets are usually developed for operating departments, not for total plans, although there are project accounting systems that approximate this. This is one reason the planner must spend a great deal of time with nonmarketing departments to make sure that budgets are prepared sufficient to fund the activities called for in the marketing plan. Accordingly, one of the major uses of the marketing plan is to provide nonmarketing departments with the information they need to prepare and document their budget requests.

Exhibit 8.4.   Changes in working capital.

Emanem Manufacturing Company
Changes in Financial Condition
1986 and 1987
(OOO)

Sources of Working Capital

Funds provided by operations		
Net income	$137,000	
Add back noncash items	64,000	
Working capital from operations	201,000	

Uses of Working Capital

Repayment of note	15,000
Payment of dividends	100,000
Purchase of equipment	50,000
Increase in working capital	36,000
Total uses of working capital	201,000

Schedule of Changes in Working Capital

	Increase	Decrease
Increase in cash	25,000	
Increase in accounts receivable	37,000	
Decrease in inventory		17,000
Increase in accounts payable		18,000
Decrease in salaries payable	9,000	
Total changes	71,000	35,000
Net increase in working capital		36,000
	$71,000	$71,000

Exhibit 8.5.   The marketing expense budget.

	2 Years Ago	Last Year	Current Year	Approved Next Year	Actual	Variance
Summary						
Net Sales	_____	_____	_____	_____	_____	_____
Cost/Goods	_____	_____	_____	_____	_____	_____
Margin	_____	_____	_____	_____	_____	_____
Mkt. Expense	_____	_____	_____	_____	_____	_____
Allocations	_____	_____	_____	_____	_____	_____
Contribution	_____	_____	_____	_____	_____	_____
Marketing Expense						
Advertising						
Magazines	_____	_____	_____	_____	_____	_____
Newspaper	_____	_____	_____	_____	_____	_____
Radio	_____	_____	_____	_____	_____	_____
TV	_____	_____	_____	_____	_____	_____
Outdoor	_____	_____	_____	_____	_____	_____
Trade Pubs.	_____	_____	_____	_____	_____	_____
Other Media	_____	_____	_____	_____	_____	_____
Production	_____	_____	_____	_____	_____	_____
Fees	_____	_____	_____	_____	_____	_____
Sales Promotion						
Consumer						
Price	_____	_____	_____	_____	_____	_____
Non-price	_____	_____	_____	_____	_____	_____
Other	_____	_____	_____	_____	_____	_____
Trade						
Co-op Adv.	_____	_____	_____	_____	_____	_____

Exhibit 8.5. Continued.

	2 Years Ago	Last Year	Current Year	Approved Next Year	Actual	Variance
Deals	————	————	————	————	————	————
Free Goods	————	————	————	————	————	————
Other	————	————	————	————	————	————
Sales Force Compens'n	————	————	————	————	————	————
Sales Exp.	————	————	————	————	————	————
Incentives	————	————	————	————	————	————
Meetings	————	————	————	————	————	————
Marketing Research Salaries	————	————	————	————	————	————
Services	————	————	————	————	————	————
Projects to Other Departments R & D	————	————	————	————	————	————
Engineering	————	————	————	————	————	————
Total Marketing Expense	————	————	————	————	————	————

Much of the marketing plan is implemented by the marketing department, and the marketing department budget is driven directly by the marketing plan. The starting point is the "expenses" section of the pro forma income statement. These expenses, as they appear in the income statement, are actually aggregates of line-item expenditures as developed from the tactical plan. Since you have already broken down the costs of implementing the plan, both by department and individual, it is largely a matter of proper summation to develop the totals necessary for inclusion in the budget.

In addition to the direct costs involved in implementing the marketing plan (such as advertising expense, sales commissions, sales expense, and sales promotion expense), the various marketing departments have fixed costs that are incurred simply to provide the human resources and equipment necessary to perform the marketing functions. These costs include the salaries of managers and support staff, as well as expenses such as rent, depreciation of office equipment and vehicles, and the like.

An example of a marketing budget is found in Exhibit 8.5. This budget form is really more of a worksheet, since it displays the actual expenditures for the past two years, the budget for the current period, and tentative projections for the next three years. The line items on the budget should meet two requirements. First, they should be derived from the tactics the company will employ in implementing its program. (Budgeting and controlling the costs of these activities is important.) Second, the line items on the budget must correspond to the accounting department's chart of accounts, since this is the way in which actual expenditures will be tracked. Every outlay voucher is coded with its appropriate account number, and the expenditures in the various accounts are summed to determine the total expenditure in a given category. These totals eventually appear on the income statement as expense items.

The preparation of the budget is an integral part of the planning process. True, it is driven by the marketing plan, and the plan was developed to achieve the objectives of the business. But there always exists the possibility that a given plan will simply be too costly. This may show up in the early drafts of the pro forma income statement. Within limits, the planner may find a way to accomplish the same objective at less cost—and this effort should always be made. (In fact, a criterion for the evaluation of alternatives should be its projected profitability.)

But what if there is no less costly approach? A case can be made that the stream of future profits will be sufficient to justify the lesser profits (or even a loss) in the short run. (This is similar to the payback analysis of a capital expenditure. The application of payback analysis in capital budgeting is described in the next section.) More likely is the decision to scale back the objective, at least for the upcoming period. This will have repercussions up the hierarchy, but there is no more vital issue to deal with. The viability of the company's overall objectives depends on its ability to implement programs, and funding is a necessary condition for implementation. The conflict must be resolved.

Unfortunately, some companies never come to grips with this situation. The budgeting process is kept separate from the marketing planning process. Departmental budgets are approved with only general relevance to the demands the marketing plan will make. The result is that funds are misallocated and budget variances are considerable. Actual expenditures tend to follow the marketing plan. All too often the budget is gone before the fiscal period is over. Then long and unfriendly hassles arise as marketing managers seek supplemental budget approval to complete the plans that have been under way for many months. Avoid this kind of situation.

The Capital Budget

A capital budget is an estimate of the funds needed to acquire a fixed asset. Almost all expenditures for land, structures, and equipment are capital expenditures. The costs of these items are not included in the operating budget. Instead, a separate appropriation request is submitted to cover their costs. A number of reasons explain the difference in the way the budgeting for capital expenditures is handled. First, the amounts of money are usually very substantial. Second, the responsibility for managing assets is typically not delegated to functional managers. Third, the sources of funding are quite different. Operating budgets are covered by the income generated during the fiscal period. The funds to acquire assets tend to come from debt or equity accounts, thus they affect the balance sheet directly. Over time, of course, the original cost of these assets is charged to current operations through depreciation.

When your marketing plan requires the acquisition of assets, this will have to be a decision reached in concert with top management, including the chief financial officer. Remember, though, that the decision to make a particular capital outlay depends on factors beyond the merits of your marketing plan. Decisions to acquire any assets, and particularly to acquire the assets you need, are really determined by the intersection of two forces: the cost of the money required and the relative profitability of the investment. As a marketing planner, you will seldom be involved in capital budgeting decisions, but you should know enough about the process so you can present your spending request in an appropriate way.

Your company will have its own forms for submitting capital-spending requests. The information requested usually goes beyond the amount and purpose of the expenditure. You will be asked to forecast the income and/or cost savings that the new asset will produce. You will be asked to estimate its expected life, as well as any scrap or resale value it may have at the end of its usefulness to the company. Although it is seldom requested, your marketing plan should provide the documentation necessary to support the capital budget request. With this rationale, the chances for approval should be good.

Those responsible for making capital-spending decisions employ a number of criteria or decision rules in determining which requests will be approved. You are not responsible for making these evaluations, but you may want to know a little about the way they are made. These evaluations can be very complex, and only those with extensive training and experience in financial analysis are asked to make them. In fairly basic terms, these are the criteria usually employed:

Payback. Payback is an estimate of the time (in years) that will be required to return to the company the funds invested in the asset. Usually it is calculated on a cash flow basis:

$$\text{Payback} = \frac{\text{Net investment}}{\text{Average annual operating cash flow}}$$

Financial managers use this estimate either: (1) to compare the payback to a stipulated maximum number of years, or (2) to compare it with other investment opportunities. Because of the dynamics of marketing opportunities, some companies are very conservative in making capital investments required to seize them. Expected paybacks of one or two years are common.

Return on Investment. This is the reciprocal of the payback formula:

$$\text{ROI} = \frac{\text{Average annual operating cash flow}}{\text{Net investment}}$$

Note here that the net investment figure is really the cost of the asset, so the criterion should really be called "return on assets employed." This calculation will yield a percentage figure, say, 25 percent. The decision on the appropriation request is then made by comparing this figure to some cutoff or by comparing it to the ROIs associated with other projects.

Present Value Analysis. The decision rule in this analysis is that if the present value of the cash flow from the investment is greater than its cost, it should be acquired. To calculate the present value of the investment, you must forecast the cash flow for the life of the asset. Then, using the appropriate discount table, you compute the present value of that cash flow. The basic concept is that a dollar of cash in the future is worth less than a dollar in hand today. Exactly how much less depends upon the discount rate employed. For example, at a discount rate of 5 percent, a dollar of cash flow five years from now would be worth only 78 cents. The effect of this analysis is to extend the payout period and reduce the ROI figure. The decision maker can use these estimates in exactly the same way the payback and ROI estimates are employed.

What if your asset requirements fail to pass these tests? You will have to respond in much the same way as if an operating budget is judged excessive. Back to the drawing board. Another plan, perhaps even a different set of objectives, may be required. And this is the correct procedure, painful as it may be. Marketing is not a panacea. It cannot make up for the financial deficiencies of the company. You should not undertake projects the firm cannot afford. If the marketing program is sufficiently attractive, it will generate the rationale for the expenditure. If it cannot do this, then the program has to be redesigned.

Marketing Cost and Profitability Analysis

Marketing cost and profitability analysis is an application of managerial accounting. It involves the use of accounting information to make strategic marketing decisions. Helpful as the analysis of traditional financial information may be, it is often inadequate for the manager who needs to know the cost and profit impacts of specific decisions, such as a choice among products, the selection of a market segment, or the approval of an advertising campaign.

The Behavior of Marketing Cost

Marketing costs behave quite differently, depending on the time period under consideration. The economist thinks generally in terms of the short run and the long run, and these concepts have their parallels in marketing planning. The short run, in economic reasoning, is a period of time too short to change capacity. The long run is any period longer than the short run—that is, of sufficient length to increase or decrease capacity. We have looked at marketing planning from both its strategic and tactical dimensions. In tactical planning, for the most part you must use the resources at your disposal. In strategic planning, which covers a period of three to five years, you can think in terms of increasing, or decreasing, resources. Thus, there is a parallel with the economist's perspective.

In the short run, there are two kinds of costs: fixed and variable. *Fixed costs* are those that remain constant in total, regardless of the level of output. *Variable costs* are those that, in total, vary directly with output. There are also costs that fall between these two extremes. *Semivariable costs* do increase with output, but not directly; usually they increase in steps, as when an additional supervisor is needed for every additional ten workers employed.

Exhibit 8.6.   Short-run total cost.

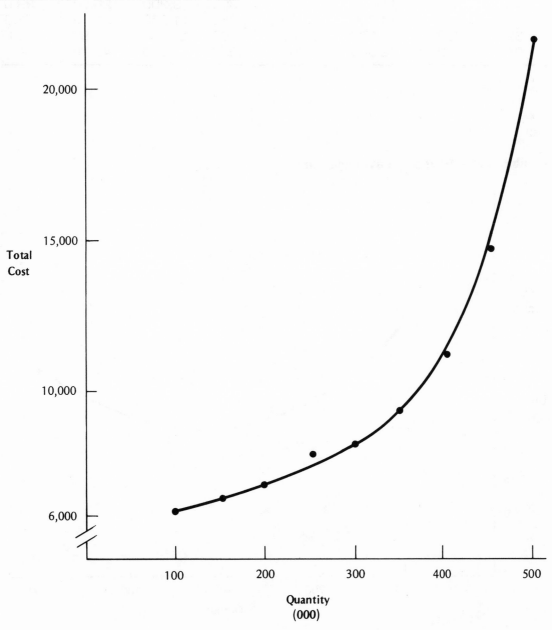

Exhibit 8.7. Short-run cost data.

Price	Quantity (000)	Revenue	Fixed Cost	Variable Cost	Total Cost	Average Cost	Marginal
$65	100	$6,500	$5,000	$1,000	$6,000	$60.00	$8.00
60	150	9,000	5,000	1,400	6,400	42.67	9.00
55	200	11,000	5,000	1,850	6,850	34.25	11.00
50	250	12,500	5,000	2,400	7,400	29.60	15.00
45	300	13,500	5,000	3,150	8,150	27.17	23.00
40	350	14,000	5,000	4,300	9,300	26.57	39.00
35	400	14,000	5,000	6,250	11,250	28.13	71.00
30	450	13,500	5,000	9,800	14,800	32.89	135.00
25	500	12,500	5,000	16,550	21,550	43.10	———

Exhibit 8.8. Short-run average cost.

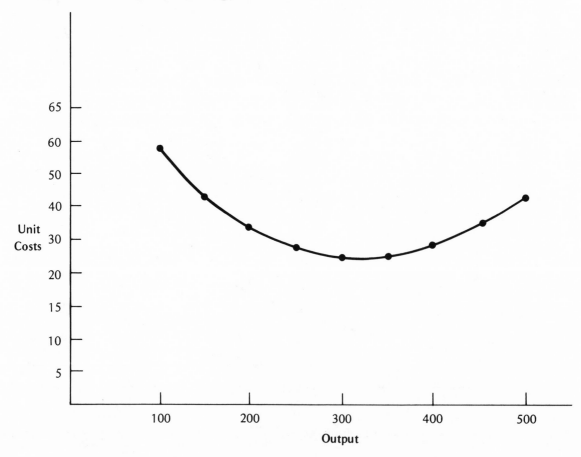

Exhibit 8.6 is a graph of short-run costs. The data supporting the chart is found in Exhibit 8.7. As is obvious, fixed costs remain constant regardless of output. Variable costs are constant per unit, and so vary directly with output. Another version of the same cost relationships is shown in Exhibit 8.8. This is a unit (or average) cost curve, and its shape is helpful in understanding the cost impact of marketing decisions. As output (sales) increases, presumably as the result of your marketing plan, unit costs fall, reach a low point, and then begin to rise again.

There are a number of explanations for the shape of this cost curve. First, since fixed costs do not vary with volume, the average fixed cost falls sharply as output increases. The second major factor affecting the shape of the curve is the law of diminishing returns. You have been introduced to the concept with regard to the marketing response function. Because decreasing marginal productivity pervades almost all marketing activities, there is going to be constant upward pressure on average cost.

Exhibit 8.9. Breakeven analysis.

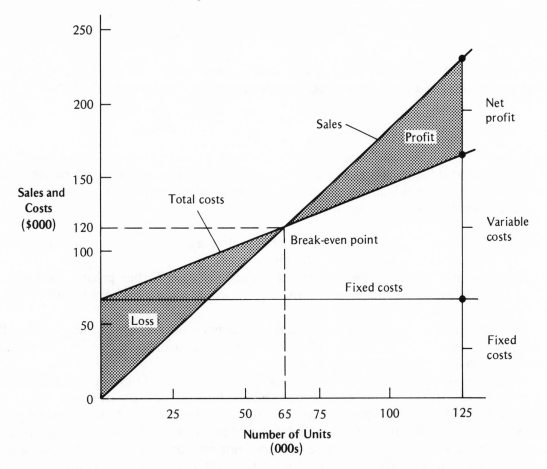

Source: Cravens, David, and Charles W. Lamb. *Strategic Marketing: Cases and Applications* (Homewood, Ill.: Richard D. Irwin, Inc., 1986), p. 30.

How does the marketing planner use these relationships? In several ways. First, the curve can be used to estimate what costs will be at any forecasted level of output. Second, assuming there are no other factors to consider, a planner might select the output that has the lowest average cost. Still another application is to find the most profitable output level. This is done by locating the output at which there exists the greatest spread between total revenue and total cost.

Breakeven Analysis

Breakeven analysis is a technique for examining the relationship between sales and costs.[1] An illustration is provided in Exhibit 8.9. Using sales and cost information, you can easily see from a breakeven analysis how many units of a product must be sold to cover total costs. In this example, 65,000 units at sales of $120,000 are equal to total costs of $120,000. Any additional units sold will produce a profit. The breakeven point can be calculated from this formula:

$$\text{BE (units)} = \frac{\text{Fixed cost}}{\text{Price} - \text{variable cost}}$$

Price in the illustration shown in Exhibit 8.9 is $1.846 per unit, and variable cost is $0.769 per unit. With fixed costs of $70,000, this results in the breakeven calculation:

$$\text{BE (units)} = \frac{\$70,000}{\$1.846 - \$0.769} = 65,000 \text{ units}$$

Note that this analysis is not a forecast. Rather, it indicates how many units of a product at a given price and cost must be sold to break even. Here are some important assumptions that underlie the analysis.

1. Fixed costs are constant and variable costs vary at a constant rate.
2. All costs are either fixed or directly variable.
3. The analysis considered only one selling price. A higher price would yield a lower breakeven point, and a lower price would yield a higher breakeven point.

When these assumptions do not apply, the marketing planner must modify the basic breakeven model. The model can be expanded to include nonlinear sales and costs, as well as alternative price levels.

Used in connection with breakeven analysis, estimates of market demand can approximate profit-maximizing decisions. Exhibit 8.10 is an example in which fixed costs are $200,000, the unit variable costs are $2.50, and demand forecasts are given for prices of $5, $10, $15, and $20. Of the four prices considered, the $15 price yields the highest profit ($360,000). Although this example does not attempt to get into the complexities of cost behavior, you should remember that the total cost function is also nonlinear. This is owing to the declining marginal productivity of the variable inputs.

Exhibit 8.10. Breakeven analysis with market demand schedule.

Unit price	Market demand (units)	Total revenue	Total costs	Break-even points (units)	Expected profits
$ 5	65,000	$325,000 (*d'*)	$362,500	80,000 (*d*)	$ (37,500)
10	55,000	550,000 (*c'*)	337,500	26,667 (*c*)	212,500
15	45,000	675,000 (*b'*)	314,500	16,000 (*b*)	360,500
20	30,000	600,000 (*a'*)	275,000	11,429 (*a*)	325,000

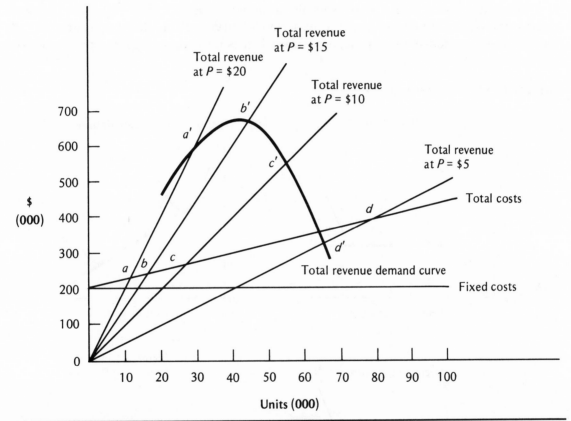

Source: Cravens, David, and Charles W. Lamb. *Strategic Marketing: Cases and Applications* (Homewood, Ill.: Richard D. Irwin, Inc., 1986), p. 31.

In the long run, all costs are variable, even costs that one might think of as fixed. For example, in the long run, capacity can be added or reduced. As this is done, the cost impact of adding or decreasing the asset base will change. The long run is, therefore, really a succession of short runs, each at a different level of capacity. Examples are shown in Exhibit 8.11. This cost curve is often called a *planning curve*, because of its usefulness in planning capacity changes. The curves are created by drawing a line tangent to each of a set of short-run cost curves. The curve marked D in Exhibit 8.11

shows stages of both increasing and decreasing cost. On the decreasing side, the assumption is that larger plant sizes are more efficient than smaller ones. Accordingly, if the market is large enough, the company should select that size plant with the lowest long-run average cost. If there is still opportunity to provide output, it does not build an even larger plant, because this would have higher costs. Instead, the company builds a second plant of optimum size. The relation of this kind of analysis to long-range marketing planning should be obvious. So also is its relevance to the capital-budgeting issues mentioned previously.

Somewhat akin to the long-run cost curve is the so-called *experience curve*. Instead of relating cost to output at any given size of plant, the experience curve plots *cost per unit versus cumulative output*. An example is shown in Exhibit 8.12. Besides the scale effects, which are inherent in it, the experience curve reflects another source of cost reduction—experience. Over time, a business learns how to manage its operation more

Exhibit 8.11. Long-run cost.

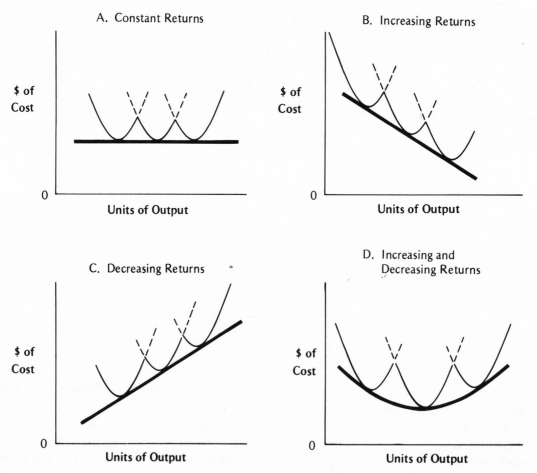

Source: From an exhibit in Bell, Martin L. *Marketing: Concepts and Strategy* (Boston: Houghton Mifflin Company, 1979), p. 505.

Exhibit 8.12.   The experience cost curve.

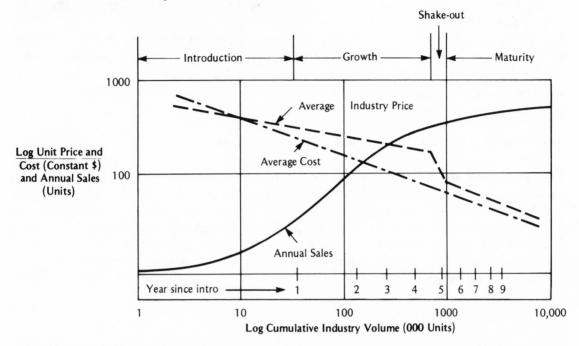

Source: Day, George S., and David B. Montgomery. "Diagnosing the Experience Curve," *Journal of Marketing* (Spring 1983), p. 44.

and more efficiently. This learning results in cost savings, savings that are reflected in total costs and, therefore, in average costs.

It does not appear that very many companies use the experience curve in connection with marketing planning, although some have done so with telling effect. Texas Instruments pursued a strategy of penetration pricing based on the expectation that cost of manufacturing would drop significantly with experience. But the strategy that worked well for calculators did not achieve the same dramatic results with digital watches and home computers. The secret seems to lie in being the first to achieve the low cost advantage.

Analyzing Marketing Cost and Profit

Analyzing marketing costs with traditional accounting data presents some serious problems. The difficulty is that almost all marketing costs are incurred in support of several products, customers, territories, or salespeople. They are, therefore, what we refer to as *common*, or *shared*, *costs*. For example, the marketing manager is responsible for planning, directing, and controlling the entire marketing function. How much of this person's salary is incurred on behalf of sales management, how much to supervise the advertising effort, how much to oversee new-product development? It is even more complex when we begin to think about specific products, territories, or customers. The accounting system is simply not set up to tell us the cost of these separate functions or segments of the business, let alone their profitability.

To estimate the cost or profitability of a particular part of the business, it is necessary either to allocate the common costs or to adapt the accounting system so that the costs can be charged directly. The second approach is preferable, but less feasible; so we start the discussion with methods of cost allocation.

Traditional Methods of Marketing Cost Analysis

Marketing costs can be analyzed at three different levels, each consistent with traditional methods of financial accounting and each representing a different level of analytic sophistication. The most basic type of analysis is taken care of by the financial analyses we have already discussed. The second type of analysis centers on the cost of performing specific marketing functions. The third, and most complex, approach focuses on the analysis of marketing costs by segments of the business—that is, products, territories, customers, and so on.

Functional Cost Analysis

The purpose of functional analysis is to plan and control the internal operations of the marketing department with greater precision. A cost is always incurred for a purpose, and we can think of the marketing functions as the purposes for which expenditures take place. This gets away from the great problem of just looking at the expenditures in relation to the budget. The budget may tell you that you went over the limit on electricity, but it cannot tell you why the electricity was needed or by whom.

Although there are a number of ways in which functional costs can be assembled, the method frequently employed is as follows:

1. Natural (P&L) expenses are reclassified according to the functions of the organization for which they are incurred. Various classifications of marketing functions have been devised. A useful set might be: selling, advertising, credit, warehousing, and delivery. The important point to remember is that any given function should represent a group of relatively homogeneous activities. Of course, the extent to which this is possible depends entirely on how difficult it is to trace the expenditure back to a particular function. For some expenses, this is not difficult. All sales salaries and expenses go to the selling function. Warehouse rent goes to warehousing. Even an expense like electricity can be apportioned reasonably on the basis of the number of square feet occupied.

2. A service unit (a unit by which functional output is measured) is identified for each function. For example, the service unit for selling might be the completed order. For warehousing, it could be a volume unit of some kind, such as a case or pallet load. The total number of service units produced in the period must be measured or estimated.

3. The final step is to determine the unit cost for each function by dividing the total cost of that function (Step 1) by the number of service units produced (Step 2). This produces a unit functional cost.

The unit functional cost can be used for planning or control, as the need arises. In anticipating an increase in the employment of a function, the expected workload (in service units) can be multiplied by the unit cost to estimate the budget impact. Or, when reviewing operations, the manager might compare actual unit functional cost to the standard or to the budget to identify where variances have occurred.

Segment Analysis

When we speak of marketing cost by segment, we refer to that part of the business for which the cost or profitability estimate is being made. For example, as a marketing planner you might want to know the past profitability of various products. Or your concern might be with alternative channels of distribution. Again, you might be looking at sales territories or specific customers. These segments are the object of your marketing cost analysis.

The procedure of segment cost analysis is:

1. Any costs incurred directly on behalf of the segment under analysis should be assigned to it immediately. For example, if salespersons are paid on a straight commission basis, this cost of selling can be charged directly to products on the basis of product sales.
2. With respect to the segment being studied, subdivide the marketing task into homogeneous functions capable of being related to specific items of cost. This is similar to the first step in functional cost analysis described previously.
3. Reclassify the remaining P&L expenses according to the functions selected in Step 1. Determine the total cost for each function.
4. Identify a service unit for each function.
5. Calculate a unit functional cost for each function.
6. Ascertain the number of functional service units required by the segment under study. For example, in the allocation of warehousing expense to products, the number of square feet of storage space devoted to the product should be determined.
7. The functional cost to be assigned to the segment is calculated by multiplying the number of service units utilized (Step 6) by the unit functional cost (Step 5).
8. The total marketing cost for the product is determined by adding the sum of the functional costs to the direct costs already assigned.
9. Product profitability is measured by subtracting the total product marketing cost (Step 8) from its gross margin.

This method of marketing costing enables the marketing planner to determine the actual cost of marketing particular products or brands, of selling to specific customers, of serving given markets, and so on. The cost information can then be studied in other ways. For example, the costs (or profits) of one product can be compared to those of another. Or changes in cost or profit can be analyzed from one year to the next or over a period of time. And, certainly, actual costs can be compared to predicted costs included in the pro formas in your marketing plan.

An Example of Marketing Cost Analysis

The Kane Wholesale Hardware Company sells two separate lines of merchandise to the retail hardware trade. Both lines are sold by the same sales force. Some of the hardware customers carry both lines, while others buy only one. Salespeople are paid a straight commission of 3 percent of net sales. The company delivers both lines of products directly to customers. No advertising is done, but merchandising aids such as display cards, posters, and so forth are furnished to hardware dealers. Gross profit taken by the company has always been the same (15 percent) on both product groups, on the theory that any differences in the cost of distribution must be negligible and that competitive forces have never dictated lowering or raising markups.

During 1986, however, the marketing manager of the Kane Wholesale Hardware Company noted a decline in sales of Product A. Also, the president of the firm was concerned because the net profit of the business the previous year had not been satisfactory. The income statement for the Kane Wholesale Hardware Company is shown in Exhibit 8.13. In this statement, sales of the two product categories are presented separately, but marketing costs are reported only for the overall operation.

In the hope of obtaining information on which to base possible changes in marketing strategy, the marketing manager decided to attempt a reasonably accurate cal-

Exhibit 8.13.   Income statement for the KANE Company.

Kane Wholesale Hardware Company
Income Statement

	Company	Product A	Product B
Net sales	$2,875,000	$1,725,000	$1,150,000
Cost of goods sold	2,443,750	1,466,250	977,500
Gross margin	431,250	258,750	172,500
Expenses			
Sales commissions	86,250		
Sales expenses	8,050		
Salaries	28,750		
Promotion expense	11,500		
Warehouse	247,250		
Credit	28,750		
Total expenses	410,550		
Profit	20,700		

culation of the costs of marketing each of the product groups. The method of cost analysis by segment was followed.

- Step 1: The manager selected the marketing functions shown in Exhibit 8.14, part A.
- Step 2: Marketing expenses as shown on the income statement were reclassified according to function. This is illustrated in Column 2 of Exhibit 8.14, part A.
- Step 3: Costs incurred directly for products were assigned. These included salespeople's commissions and promotional materials.
- Step 4: Since all functional costs were to be allocated to commodities, none was excluded from the analysis.
- Step 5: Appropriate service units were selected for each function. They are shown in Exhibit 8.14, part B.
- Step 6: Unit functional costs, excluding those costs assigned directly to product, were calculated; see Exhibit 8.14, part A.
- Step 7: The number of functional service units required for each product was ascertained. These are shown in Exhibit 8.14, part C.
- Step 8: The total cost of performing each function for Product A and Product B was calculated by multiplying the number of service units by the unit costs. This is shown in Exhibit 8.14, part A.
- Step 9: The total marketing cost of Product A and Product B was determined by adding the direct and functional costs. The total marketing costs of the two products are shown at the bottom of the last two columns of Exhibit 8.14, part A.

The profitability of each product is found in the recapitulation, Exhibit 8.15. It indicates, contrary to management's prior opinion, that in spite of its declining sales, Product A accounted for all the company's profit. Product B, on the other hand, had been marketed at a loss. Clearly, some type of management action was called for. Whether the action should relate to methods of selling Product B or to its pricing became a matter of executive concern. Eventually, the company increased prices and adopted a tighter cost-control system.

Profitability Accounting for Marketing

Up to this point, we have been considering the traditional methods of marketing cost analysis. A more sophisticated method has received attention in recent years.[2] Profitability accounting is a total accounting system that reports only those revenues and costs directly related to a particular product, territory, or other object of profit control.

The starting point of profitability accounting is a reclassification of expenses in such a way as to permit their identification as direct or fixed with respect to particular profit centers in the business. A *direct cost* is a variable cost—one that varies with the volume or activity. A *fixed cost* is one that does not vary with volume or activity. Implicit in these definitions is the idea that a variable cost is incurred because activity has taken place, and that this cost would not have been incurred if the activity had been elimi-

Exhibit 8.14.   Other facets of the marketing profitability analysis for the KANE Company.

A. Product line income statement

Functional Cost Groups	Cost	Service Units			Allocation to Products		
		Total	A	B	Unit Cost	A	B
Maintenance							
A. Investment	$11,500	400,000	160,000	240,000	$0.029	$4,600	$6,900
B. Storage	57,500	300,000	100,000	200,000	0.192	19,167	38,333
Movement							
A. Physical handling	80,500	120,000	55,000	65,000	0.671	36,896	43,604
B. Order entry	74,750	200,000	80,000	120,000	0.374	29,900	44,850
C. Delivery	23,000	120,000	55,000	65,000	0.192	10,542	12,458
Promotion							
A. Sales commissions	86,250	Direct				51,750	34,500
B. Sales expenses	8,050	2,500,000	1,500,000	1,000,000	0.003	4,830	3,220
C. Salaries	28,750	2,500,000	1,500,000	1,000,000	0.012	17,250	11,500
D. Dealer promotions	11,500	Direct				5,750	5,750
Reimbursement							
A. Clerical	14,950	2,500,000	1,500,000	1,000,000	0.006	8,970	5,980
B. Credit	13,800	250,000	140,000	110,000	0.055	7,728	6,072
Total Cost	$410,550					$197,383	$213,167

B. Bases of allocation

Functional Cost Groups	Bases of Allocation
Maintenance	
A. Investment	Average inventory value
B. Storage	Floor space occupied
Movement	
A. Physical handling	No. of standard handling units
B. Order routine	No. of invoice lines
C. Delivery	No. of standard handling units
Promotion	
A. Salespeople's commissions	Direct—3% of sales
B. Sales expenses	Dollar value of sales
C. Management salaries	Dollar value of sales
D. Dealer helps, etc.	Direct to product group
Reimbursement	
A. Clerical	Dollar value of sales
B. Financial & collection	Average amount outstanding

C. Functional cost allocation

Service Units	Company	Product A	Product B
Dollar value of sales	$2,500,000	$1,500,000	$1,000,000
Average value of inventory	400,000	160,000	240,000
Number of handling units	120,000	55,000	65,000
Average amount outstanding	$250,000	$140,000	$110,000
Floor space occupied	300,000	100,000	200,000
Number of invoice lines	200,000	80,000	120,000
Promotions	$10,000	$5,000	$5,000

Exhibit 8.15. KANE Wholesale Hardware Company summary.

	Company	Product A	Product B
Net sales	$2,875,000	$1,725,000	$1,150,000
Cost of goods sold	2,443,750	1,466,250	977,500
Gross margin	431,250	258,750	172,500
Expenses	410,550	197,383	213,167
Profit	$20,700	$61,367	($40,667)

nated. If a decision maker is really interested in controlling costs, fixed costs should not be assigned to profit centers. Variable costs of selling and standard manufacturing costs are assigned, however, as are certain other costs incurred specifically for the profit center involved.

These latter costs are called *programmed,* or *specific, costs.* They may be of a nonvariable or a semivariable character. They are not necessarily directly variable, but they are escapable in the sense that, if an activity is not undertaken, no expense is incurred. Examples of such programmed marketing costs might include sales promotion and advertising costs planned for particular products or territories. In addition, a particular department or profit center may have other types of programmed costs that properly are charged against it in profitability accounting. The expense of maintaining a department marketing research staff would be an example.

Exhibit 8.16 compares a profitability-accounting earnings statement with a profit-and-loss report prepared in the traditional manner. Two notable differences can be seen. First, the profitability statement is a partial statement. It emphasizes a product's contribution to profit, not its net profit *per se.* Second, the classification of expenses and the order in which they appear in the statement are different. The reason for this should be clear. The traditional statement mixes costs between marketing and manufacturing so that the resulting profit figure cannot be used solely for marketing planning or control purposes. The profitability-accounting statement isolates those costs that are the specific responsibility of the marketing decision maker. Manufacturing overhead and general administrative expenses are not charged against the marketing department.

An Example of Profitability Accounting

The discussion of marketing profitability accounting can be clarified with an example of a hardware manufacturing company. Hefty Hardware makes three lines of products. Its small household appliance line is composed of fans, small space heaters, kitchen toasters, and waffle irons. This line is sold through hardware wholesalers, department stores, and discount houses. Hefty also manufactures a line of power lawn mowers, which it sells direct to mass merchandisers and to hardware wholesalers. The third line is industrial shelving, which is sold to industrial distributors, large direct buyers, and the government. All lines are sold by salaried company salespeople.

Exhibit 8.16.   Comparison of traditional and profitability-accounting earnings statements.

Traditional Accounting		Profitability Accounting	
Net sales	$29,733	Gross sales	$29,964
Cost of goods sold		Variable costs	19,072
Direct materials	13,100		
Direct labor	2,057		
Manufacturing overhead	4,217		
	19,374		
Gross profit	10,359	Profit contribution	10,892
Selling expenses			
Salaries	3,091		
Advertising and promotion	1,104	Specific product expenses	
Shipping	970	Discounts and allowances	231
Other	1,202	Advertising and promotion	2,068
	6,367		2,299
General and administrative expenses	2,000	Product earnings	$ 8,593
Earnings before taxes	1,992		
Provision for taxes	956		
Net profit after provision for taxes	$ 1,036		

Source: From an exhibit in Bell, Martin L. *Marketing: Concepts and Strategy* (Boston: Houghton Mifflin Company, 1979), p. 515.

At the end of 1986, the director of marketing received a year-end profit-and-loss statement for the company as a whole. With some dismay, it was noted that not only had Hefty failed to achieve its target sales volume of $37 million, but net earnings for the year actually were below the 1985 level. Return on investment was below the goal set by top management. The director of marketing believed that a thorough analysis of marketing costs should be made. The company's accountant was asked to prepare a profit-and-loss statement by major product lines. Because of the detailed analysis involved, it took about two months to complete this report; and it was not until March 15 that the new statement of earnings was available. This statement is shown in Exhibit 8.17. The controller sent a memorandum with the analysis, indicating that a meeting should be called to discuss the immediate dropping of industrial shelving. "We're losing money on this industrial shelving line even before it leaves the factory" was the memo's opening sentence.

The director of marketing was not so sure about this, believing that the report did not accurately reflect the actual profit picture. This marketing executive was familiar with profitability accounting and asked the accountant to revise the product-group profit-and-loss statement to show variable and specific costs and the profit contribution of each product group. Although this involved another time-consuming examination of accounting documents, the report was prepared. The new statement, shown in Exhibit 8.18, revealed some interesting things. First, the shelving line actually made a

Exhibit 8.17. **Hefty Hardware Company income statement by product lines, year ended 12/31/86.**

	Company	Housewares	Lawn Mowers	Industrial Shelving
Net sales	$35,680	$24,061	$6,006	$5,612
Cost of goods sold				
Direct materials	15,720	9,318	2,383	4,019
Direct labor	2,468	1,622	366	480
Manufacturing overhead	5,060	3,343	544	1,174
Total	23,248	14,283	3,293	5,673
Gross margin	12,433	9,778	2,713	(61)
Percentage	0.35	0.41	0.45	−0.01
Selling expenses				
Salaries	3,709	2,653	452	604
Advertising and promotion	1,325	942	317	66
Shipping	1,164	786	198	180
Other	1,442	1,086	278	78
Total	7,640	5,467	1,245	928
G & A expense	2,400	1,620	408	372
Profit	2,390	2,690	1,060	(1,360)
Percentage	0.07	0.11	0.18	−0.24

Exhibit 8.18. **Hefty Hardware Company profitability accounting statement earnings by product group, year ended 12/31/86.**

	Company	Housewares	Lawn Mowers	Industrial Shelving
Net sales	$35,957	$24,286	$6,019	$5,652
Variable costs	22,886	14,320	3,472	5,095
Profit contribution	13,071	9,966	2,547	557
Percentage	0.36	0.41	0.42	0.10
Specific product expenses				
Discounts and allowances	277	224	13	40
Advertising and promotion	2,482	832	1,344	306
Total	2,759	1,056	1,357	346
Product earnings	10,312	8,910	1,190	211
Percentage	0.29	0.37	0.20	0.04
General expenses	7,921			
Profit	2,390			
Percentage	0.07			

contribution to factory and general overhead in 1986. Unless another product could be found to take its place, the immediate removal of industrial shelving would lower Hefty's profits even more. Nevertheless, the shelving line was not contributing nearly as much as the other two lines. Its overall profit contribution was only 9.8 percent, compared to over 40 percent for the houseware and lawn-mower lines. The production department maintained that its costs were not out of line, however. Raw materials were purchased competitively, and the cutting, stamping, and painting operations were routine and well controlled.

The director of marketing believed that the problem was in the pricing of the line. Before making a decision to raise shelving prices generally, another report was prepared that showed the sales of shelving by type of customer. Three major types of accounts were served: large, direct-buying industrial users; industrial distributors; and government departments and agencies. Exhibit 8.19 shows the breakdown of sales and the profit contribution for each shelving customer group. At last the culprit emerged! Direct sales of shelving to the government actually cost Hefty Hardware Company $208,000 in 1986. On further investigation, the reason became all too clear. Prices quoted in bids on government contracts were low—too low, in fact, even to cover the direct cost of manufacturing. Most government orders, it was discovered, were for eight-foot-high shelving, which required 20 percent more steel than the standard six-foot-high units on which the firm's standard costs were based.

As a result of this study, Hefty's director of marketing immediately initiated a policy of pricing on government orders to yield a profit contribution of 25 percent. The sales force objected at first, maintaining that it could not get any business at the higher prices. As it turned out, however, Hefty was able to compete favorably on some of the patented items in its line, and was even able to obtain orders for its standard line of shelving because of its history of quality and prompt delivery. The executive committee of Hefty Hardware was so impressed with the improved information provided by the profita-

Exhibit 8.19. Hefty Hardware Company earnings for industrial shelving by customer group.

	Industrial Shelving	Industrial Direct	Industrial Distributors	Government
Net sales	$5,652	$565	$1,696	$3,391
Variable costs	5,095	424	1,187	3,485
Profit contribution	557	141	509	(94)
Percentage	0.10	0.25	0.30	−0.03
Specific product expenses				
Discounts and allowances	40	10	24	6
Advertising and promotion	306	36	120	150
Total	346	46	144	156
Product earnings	211	96	365	(250)
Percentage	0.04	0.17	0.22	−0.07

bility accounting reports that it instructed the accountant to convert the entire system to this basis.

The Control of Marketing Cost and Profit

No area of financial analysis is more critical to the marketing planner than that of marketing cost and profit control. While the specific responsibility for monitoring and reporting cost and profit information lies with the finance department, the marketing planner needs to be closely informed and involved in decisions that are made as the result of cost and profit reports. Two areas in which performance evaluation and program modification are likely to present important issues to the marketing planner are in expense control and profit control.

Expense Budget Control

The principal tool for controlling marketing costs is the expense budget. Actual expenses are compared to the budget each time an income statement is produced. See the example in Exhibit 8.20. Differences from the budget are noted and explanations are sought. If necessary, actions are taken to correct the situation. We have already noted how important it is to track expenditures continuously, and not to wait until a budget limit has been exceeded.

The major difficulty that arises in connection with expense budget control is that the variances which occur are seldom the result of flagrant deviations from the marketing plan. To the contrary, marketing managers in the field take actions to address problems or seize opportunities not anticipated originally. We have continuously stressed the importance of flexibility in order to adapt swiftly to change. The problem is that in most companies the budget doesn't change, even if the plan is altered. Instead of living with the obsolete budget, there are two ways to get it into line with reality.

The first method is to reissue the budget. This implies, of course, that a completely new set of operating pro formas has been created. If the events leading to the change are of sufficient importance to warrant a change in the budget, they probably also require a change in strategic direction and tactics. Not only the financial aspects, but the entire thrust and scope of the plan may need to be amended.

Another approach involves flexible budgeting. In this method, it is anticipated that a change on volume may occur and, if so, a different budget would be necessary. The company may actually publish an A Budget and a B Budget, or even A, B, and C budgets, each suited to different levels of business. If a change in volume does occur, the organization immediately shifts to the next higher or lower budget level.

Profitability Control

We have seen how profitability accounting can be used to report those costs and revenues for which the marketing planner is responsible. It should be relatively easy to

Exhibit 8.20.   Budget control analysis.

Item	Current year Dollars	Current year Percent	Budget Dollars	Budget Percent	Variance (dollars)	Previous year Dollars	Previous year Percent
Gross sales	5,000,000	100.5	4,800,000	100.4	−200,000	4,500,000	100.4
Less: Returns and allowances	25,000	.5	20,000	.4	−5,000	20,000	.4
Net sales	4,975,000	100.0	4,780,000	100.0	−195,000	4,480,000	100.0
Cost of goods sold							
Beginning inventory	200,000	4.0	200,000	4.2	—	180,000	4.0
Cost of goods purchased	2,500,000	50.3	2,400,000	50.2	−100,000	2,250,000	50.2
Total merchandise handled	2,700,000	54.3	2,600,000	54.4	−100,000	2,430,000	54.2
Ending inventory	250,000	5.1	200,000	4.2	−50,000	200,000	4.0
Cost of goods sold	2,450,000	49.2	2,400,000	50.2	−50,000	2,230,000	49.8
Gross profit	2,525,000	50.8	2,380,000	49.8	−145,000	2,250,000	50.2
Direct marketing expenses							
Sales salaries	750,000	15.1	700,000	14.7	−50,000	680,000	15.2
Sales expenses	500,000	10.1	450,000	9.4	−50,000	430,000	9.6
Advertising	250,000	5.0	200,000	4.2	−50,000	190,000	4.2
Warehousing and shipping	360,000	7.2	350,000	7.3	−10,000	330,000	7.4
Payroll taxes and insurance	35,000	.7	30,000	.6	−5,000	30,000	.7
Regional and district office expense	150,000	3.0	150,000	3.1	—	140,000	3.1
Total direct marketing expenses	2,045,000	41.1	1,880,000	39.3	−165,000	1,800,000	40.2
General administrative expense							
Executive salaries	150,000	3.0	150,000	3.1	—	140,000	3.1
Clerical expense	100,000	2.0	100,000	2.1	—	95,000	2.1
Payroll taxes and insurance	2,500	.1	2,500	.1	—	2,500	.1
Office expenses	60,000	1.2	55,000	1.2	−5,000	54,000	1.2
Depreciation	12,000	.2	12,500	.3	+500	12,500	.3
Credit and collection	35,000	.7	25,000	.5	−10,000	20,000	.4
Other expenses	50,000	1.0	55,000	1.1	+5,000	51,000	1.1
Total general administrative expenses	409,500	8.2	400,000	8.4	−9,500	375,000	8.3
Total expenses	2,454,500	49.3	2,280,000	47.7	−174,500	2,175,000	48.5
Net profit	70,500	1.5	100,000	2.1	−29,500	75,000	1.7

Source: Bell, Martin L. *Marketing: Concepts and Strategy* (Boston: Houghton Mifflin Company, 1979), p. 508.

understand how profitability accounting might be used to plan and control profits in the future.

In the Hefty Hardware case, we saw how profitability accounting isolated the problem of the industrial shelving sold to the government. Looking ahead, the director of marketing decided to use the same cost concepts as a basis for controlling profitability in 1987. He prepared a complete marketing plan, utilizing the process presented in this book.

A detailed forecast of sales for the first six months was made. Next, the accounting department established standard costs of direct material and labor at the expected rate of operations (based on the forecast). Given the unit forecast and the pricing structure contained in the marketing plan, it was possible to estimate the profit contribution of each product line. Product managers were required to submit detailed tactical plans for 1987, including budgets for advertising and sales promotion. The director of marketing discussed these promotional plans with each product manager. Agreement was reached with the general sales manager on the limits to which special deals and allowances would be made. With these commitments, it was possible for a pro forma contribution income statement to be prepared, broken down by quarters.

By comparing the quarterly reports of actual performance against this plan, the director of marketing was able to identify when the profit goals were threatened. As needed, he was able to work out changes in promotion and pricing tactics that resulted in the achievement of Hefty's profit goal, even though a number of the assumptions made about the economy and competitive behavior had to be altered during the year.

Marketing Cost Standards

As in manufacturing and in some service operations, there are aspects of marketing that can be made routine and for which cost standards can be set. These include telephone selling, order entry, warehousing, and the like. Of course, there are other tasks that cannot be made so routine—such as personal selling and advertising. However, where repetitive operations are common, it is feasible to set up marketing cost standards. The following steps might be involved:

1. Establish the most efficient, but realistic, work procedure.
2. Compute the standard input required. It might involve such factors as labor, materials, power, and so on.
3. "Cost out" the standard input to determine the cost of performing the most efficient procedure.
4. Compute the standard output—that is, the number of output units created in a given time period when the required procedure is followed.
5. Compute the standard cost per unit of output. By dividing the total cost of a given procedure by its standard output, it is possible to estimate the standard cost per unit. No attempt is made here to allocate a portion of general marketing overhead or administrative cost to a particular task, although this is sometimes done by companies using absorption accounting procedures.
6. Compare actual cost to standard cost. At the end of an accounting period, actual unit costs of the function are compared to standard. To do this, of course, it is necessary to keep records of the actual amount of functional output.
7. Analyze the variances. The difference between actual and standard must be analyzed. A favorable variance means that a function was performed more efficiently than was anticipated in the preparation of the standard. This may have been owing to a reduction in the cost of some purchased factor or service, or it may be because of improved productivity. An unfavorable variance suggests the reverse. Variance resulting from changes in the quantity of materials or services purchased or the prices paid for them can be identified.

An example may be useful. Suppose an in-store sampling program has been conducted. The company has had extensive experience in this kind of activity and has

Exhibit 8.21. Comparison of actual to standard cost.

	Actual	Standard	Variance
Materials used			
Amount used	750	700	50
Price	$10	$8	$2
Material cost	$7,500	$5,600	$1,900
Labor used			
Amount used	180	160	20
Price	$8	$9	$1
Labor cost	$1,440	$1,440	0
Total cost	$8,940	$7,040	$1,900
Output	900	1,000	100
Unit cost	$9.93	$7.04	$2.89

Cost Variance Analysis		
Material		
50 units at $8	− $400	(50 more units of material used than planned)
Price		
750 @ $2	− $1,500	(750 units cost $2 more than standard)
20 @ $9	− $180	(20 more units of labor used than planned)
180 @ $1	$180	(180 units of labor cost $1 less than standard)
Total	− $1,900	
Cost of 900 units		(900 × $7.04 standard unit cost)
should be	$6,336	
Actual was	$8,940	(900 × $9.93 actual unit cost)
Difference was	$2,604	
Difference due to volume variance	$704	(100 units @ $7.04)
Difference due to cost variance	$1,900	(See Cost Analysis above)
Unit variance due to volume	$ .78	
Unit variance due to cost increase	$2.11	
Total unit variance	$2.89	

established a standard cost for performing a two-week sampling program in a major supermarket. The standard calls for the distribution of 750 cases of the product, costing $10 per case. Two persons working 40 hours each week can handle the schedule. Cost per hour is budgeted at $9.

The sampling program was conducted. The results and variance analysis appear in Exhibit 8.21. Because of difficulties encountered in the field, the actual program deviated somewhat from the plan. Store hours were longer than normal, and the cost of sample materials was higher than expected because the product had to be express-shipped to the store location. Fortunately, the labor cost was somewhat lower, which offset the increase in hours. However, in view of the lesser output and the higher cost per output unit, the marketing director asked for a complete report from the sales promotion manager on the reasons for the productivity decline and recommendations on how the problems in this situation might be avoided in the future.

We have looked at a lot of numbers throughout this book, especially in the last three chapters. Important as they are, they cannot of themselves make a plan work. Marketing plans are made by people and are carried out by people. There is a human side to planning. We will look at that in the next chapter.

9
The Personal
Side of Planning

We have looked at the marketing planning process in some detail. It is not necessarily an easy process, but it is a manageable one. The system does work. The only thing that interferes with its working well is the failure of people involved to cooperate in producing a results-driven marketing plan everyone can enthusiastically support.

It is well for the marketing planner to recognize from the very beginning that this cooperation takes a great deal of work and patience. It doesn't occur naturally. Indeed, it may seem at times that there is a giant conspiracy to thwart your efforts. The planning assignment may challenge your best management skills, your patience, and your sense of humor. But stick with it; the job is important and it is worth doing well.

The purpose of this chapter is to explore the types of relationships the marketing planner has with others whose input is critical to the development of the plan. We will review some of the typical problems and why they occur. Finally, we will look at some human skills you need to produce your marketing plan.

Interconnections of the Marketing Planner

With whom does the marketing planner interact? The answer is simple: just about everybody in the organization. This is because marketing pervades the entire business. More specifically, the marketing planner must establish communications in three directions: upward with top management; downstream in the organization with those who can provide information and who will be involved in implementation; and crosswise with peers in other functions.

Contacts with Top Management

There are several steps in the planning process in which top management plays a key role. First, and really most important, top management must be supportive of and directly involved in the planning process. This means you should be looking to the CEO for the initiative in getting the planning process started. But since the marketing plan is simply one of many items on the CEO's agenda, it is a good idea to implant a reminder, with sufficient lead time, to get the process under way.

Your first functional contact with top management should probably be in connection with a "briefing" session held prior to or early on in the planning process. At this session you can present an update on the external environment, especially those developments you believe will be of sufficient interest to trigger strategic thinking. The session has the great advantage of enabling you to begin to orient top management to the issues that will have to be addressed in the plan, and you can do this in a setting free of the pressure involved when top managers are asked to approve programs and budgets.

Once the planning process gets under way, your principal contacts with top management will involve the planning prerequisites. These were, as you recall: mission, objectives, policies, organization, and business unit strategies. The only serious problem you encounter here is that top managers do not often think in these terms, and they may not be sure why you need to be privy to such information. It is hard to say one of these prerequisites is more important than the others, but it is certain that there is virtually nothing you can do without a proper statement of objectives.

Ultimately, the most important occasion for contact with top management occurs when you present your plan for approval. A great deal hinges on the outcome of this session. You will undoubtedly be anxious about the outcome. But as a television commercial reminds us, "Don't ever let them see you sweat." The "upstairs" presentation needs to be tailored to the concerns and management style of your management group. If they prefer short, to-the-point presentations, do it this way. If they like to see the tactics, as some do, then run out the old "dog and pony show." Each company has its own culture, and each top manager has an individual management style. You must determine what is best for your situation.

The major difficulty you face in dealing with top management is getting sufficient time with them to really explore and explain your needs. Sometimes it is next to impossible to see them at all. This is one reason that top management's commitment to planning is so essential. Unless the president thinks that marketing planning is important, virtually nobody else will either.

Relations Within the Marketing Department

Your relationship to the functional groups within the marketing department will depend largely on the position you hold. If you are the marketing director and the managers of sales, advertising, sales promotion, marketing research, and so on report to you,

you can exercise considerable direct authority over them. This means that while you may consult with them and solicit their input to the planning process, you are in charge. You can assign tasks and evaluate performance. The same applies to implementation, although you will probably be more willing to delegate responsibility for performing specialized functional tasks once they have been properly defined in the marketing plan.

The dilemma arises when your relationship to the rest of the marketing department is advisory. If you are in a staff position, you have almost no authority to direct anybody to do anything. If the planning process depends upon the direct involvement of these these people, it will be up to you to find ways to elicit their participation.

Sales Management

Your primary contact will be with and through the sales manager. Preserve this relationship. Do not go around the sales manager, tempting and timesaving as this may appear. You will rely heavily on information from the sales department. Salespeople are in the field and can be a fruitful source of information about customers and competitors. However, watch for bias and selective screening in the information passed on to you.

The sales department is a key factor in your arsenal of competitive weapons. Unquestionably, the successful implementation of your plan will depend greatly on how well the sales force performs. How you go about communicating with these people, how you motivate them, and how you track performance will have much to do with the final outcome of the marketing plan.

Again, you will work through the sales management structure. But you cannot afford to assume that, without effort on your part, the sales plan will "take care of itself." How hard should you push? This is a touchy area, and must be handled wisely. The sales department can be your strongest ally or one of the most serious impediments to the success of your plan. Remember, as marketing planner *you* are responsible for results. Whether the sales department does its job or not depends in large part on how well you do yours.

Advertising

The structure of the marketing department determines where the responsibility for advertising lies. If a product-manager system is in place, each PM develops an advertising plan. There may or may not be an overall advertising director. As in the case of sales, the nature of your relationship to the advertising decision makers will determine how you work with them in developing and implementing the marketing plan. If you have line authority, as would a marketing director, you will rely primarily upon the product managers to develop the plans for their respective product lines. This will include the advertising. You must make sure these product managers are working at objectives that relate to the overall marketing objectives. They will bring their proposed plans to you for approval, and they will be held responsible for the outcomes.

If there is an advertising manager who reports directly to you as a marketing director, your relationship is just about the same as with product managers, except that the scope of the advertising manager's responsibility is much narrower, dealing only with the communications function.

On the other hand, if as marketing planner you fill a staff role, your relations with product and advertising managers will be quite different. They actually will be responsible to your superior, the director of marketing. However, because of your special role as planner, you may be given "dotted line" authority over product and advertising managers. This means that they are expected to report to you in matters concerning planning. Other than in this capacity, you have no direct authority over their work. This can be a problem, since implementation may not be seen as part of the planning assignment, and you may have difficulty enforcing performance, even though you were instrumental in the development of the plan.

Marketing Research

If your company has a marketing research department, you will need to establish very close working relations with its manager. The information requirements of your marketing plan can seldom be met with data you already have. It is doubtful that a year could go by in which you do not get involved with marketing research in order to generate data for completing the situation analysis. In general, these people are better able to undertake research than you will be. Use their services. They know where to find information. They should have a better grasp of the marketing information in the company's data base than even the MIS people have. They usually have good computer skills. They know statistics. But do not assume you can expect instant service. Plan ahead, and get on their schedule. Make sure you have budgeted funds, otherwise even an internal department tends to do what it wants to with its own money.

If you need to go outside for marketing research assistance, you will find an over-populated field of suppliers. Be careful in making your choice. Find a company interested in solving your problem, rather than one interested in doing the things in which it specializes. Ask to see samples of their work. Get competitive proposals. And be willing to pay what is necessary. Above all, monitor the project from beginning to end to make sure the work is done properly and on time. You will be on a tight planning schedule, and it will be impossible to go back and repeat research done improperly or finish work not started on time.

Relations With Other Departments

MIS

You will need to understand the exact capabilities of your company's information services group. They will also need to understand your needs. You must establish a dialogue with the person in charge. Find someone who is especially interested in your situation, and bring this individual onto your planning team. As soon as you have specified your planning information needs, together work out a plan of fact gathering, analysis, and reporting.

You are likely to encounter only two serious problems in working with MIS personnel. First, they tend to talk their own language, which may seem like jibberish to you. Try to master it, because they don't have nearly the same incentive to acquire marketing vocabulary. Second, these people tend to want to write their own programs; that is their thing. Unfortunately, writing and debugging a program is usually time consuming, and MIS people are kept pretty busy. You may have to do some persuading to get them to bring in packaged software, but this is really the better way to go. And, interestingly, this enhances the value of the MIS person, for the person who has a working understanding of the capabilities of several software programs is far more useful than someone who has to start from scratch each time a new problem comes along.

If you decide to use personal computers, you may encounter some resistance from traditional data processing people. Do not antagonize them, for you will still need to access the data base. Start by emphasizing the word processing capabilities, then the report writing, and finally the computational features. Eventually, true computer buffs will respect your interest in personal computing, and you will find them of great help in interpreting instructions on software packages, in fixing crashed programs, and in keeping the hardware going.

Corporate Planning

If your organization has such a group you need to form a particularly good working relationship with it. You may encounter some resistance, however, if the corporate group feels that you are usurping its role. The situation should not arise if top management has properly determined the role of planning in the company and how it wants corporate strategic planning to relate to the planning done in the operating areas, such as marketing. But problems do arise.

The corporate planners may have functional responsibility for all planning in the organization. If so, then make sure the head of the department understands what you are doing and approves it. Beyond that, the relationship really depends on whether you are also staff or are a line manager. A principle to keep clearly in mind is that *staff does not plan;* managers plan. The staff facilitates and assists. This is as true of corporate planners as of staff marketing planners. Do not let your first obligation get lost in the confusion. Even if corporate planners think they are planning and behave as if they were, and even if top management lets them do so, you must constantly remind yourself that your first obligation is to the director of marketing and, through him or her, to the general manager of your business unit. If you do get caught between "a rock and a hard place," you will have to muster all your patience and persuasion to work your way out of a delicate situation.

On a more positive note, you may often be able to look to corporate planning for help. The top-management planning prerequisites often come through the corporate planning group. These are often very talented and highly qualified people. In some companies, corporate planning also functions as an in-house consulting group, helping divisions develop planning procedures and analyzing their business situations.

Production

The path between marketing and production is a two-way street. The functions are so mutually dependent that one wonders why they often seem to be at odds with each other. Marketing cannot deliver the goods unless production has made them. Marketing will not have the goods on time unless production has scheduled the work. Marketing cannot assure customers that they will be satisfied with the product unless manufacturing enforces a good quality-control program. Marketing cannot produce sales at a profit unless manufacturing can control costs. Could there be more compelling reasons for the marketing planner to court the favors and help of manufacturing?

At the other end of the street, manufacturing is also dependent upon marketing. What manufacturing makes, marketing must be able to sell. Manufacturing cannot schedule anything until marketing has provided a reliable forecast. Manufacturing does not even know what "quality" is supposed to be until marketing tells them what customers need. Manufacturing has no idea what its target costs should be until marketing has determined what the price should be.

But the system does not always work this way. Manufacturing managers often want to produce long runs of very uncomplicated products. Marketing wants short runs of highly differentiated products. Manufacturing defines quality in terms of conformance to engineering specifications. Marketing is more interested in whether the product works once it is in the customer's hands. Manufacturing thinks marketing should take its costs, add some profit, and price the product. Marketing wants to price the product competitively and have manufacturing produce the item at a cost that also generates a profit.

This is the classic dilemma in manufacturing-marketing interaction, and it affects the marketing planning process. It is not peculiar to planning as such, and so it should come as no surprise to encounter it in working out your marketing plan. The great advantage you possess is that at least you have a new opportunity to make the system work better each time you prepare a marketing plan. The marketing plan should be the place where these conflicts are resolved. But you must communicate; you must empathize. And you will probably have to compromise. In one company, an inexperienced marketing manager went to the president and asked that the entire quality-control function be turned over to marketing because of the conflict between how manufacturing was handling the function and how marketing thought it should be done. The president wisely refused and told the young man that the problem was with his marketing plan—that he hadn't anticipated the problem and devised a way to solve it. You can be sure that the next marketing plan contained an entirely new approach to quality assurance, an approach that satisfied both manufacturing and marketing.

Research and Development

Marketing has virtually no voice in basic research. It might alert the scientists to long-range technological and market developments, but it would be unusual for marketing to be involved in deciding what direction basic research should take. But the moment a breakthrough occurs, which offers any hope of commercial application, marketing should be involved. Marketing should manage the new-product development process, including the screening of ideas. Sometimes projects from basic research have a way of sneaking into the system without a thorough screening. As marketing planner, you should ask for periodic briefings on the company's basic research program to determine if and when new-product ideas are likely to emerge.

There is much need for close involvement and coordination of marketing with applied research and development. This type of research is done to serve markets, and should only be undertaken as part of an overall marketing plan. It means that the marketing planning process must involve R&D. The situation analysis should include an audit of its capability. Any strengths or weaknesses should be identified. Objectives involving the development of new products or the improvement of old ones should be addressed in the product-strategy component of the marketing mix.

R&D people are usually very cooperative, but they do not always have the same priorities or concern for schedules as do marketing planners. R&D frequently gets behind schedule, partly because of interruptions, but also because of overly optimistic estimates of the time required. These people are also very poor estimators of cost. The original cost estimate for the development of a new design should probably be tripled if you want it to come anywhere close to what the design will eventually cost. All of these tendencies create problems for the marketing planner. They should be anticipated and factored into the planning effort. Since you really can't control what R&D does or how it is done, about the only thing you can rely on is your ability to convince these folks of the critical importance of both the schedule and the budget.

Accounting and Finance

Chapter 8 positioned the marketing planner as sort of a junior financial executive, capable of using tools of financial analysis and of making finance-related decisions. You may not need—or want—to be so involved in the financial part of the planning process. There is no question that if the accounting and finance people are as interested in marketing aspects of finance as you are in the financial aspects of marketing, you will find people who are willing and able to participate directly in the planning process. You should certainly scout around to locate peers in accounting and finance who are interested in helping you work out the financial portions of your plan.

As when working with all outside departments, it is probably a good idea to clear what you are doing with the financial people. At first, they may not like the idea of a marketing planner doing financial analysis. But if you can involve them, at least to the extent that they review your methodology and meaning, you can probably smooth any ruffled feathers. Since it is becoming more and more common for top management to expect to see financials in the marketing plan, the finance department really shouldn't be surprised to find you on its doorstep. If they volunteer to help, let them; but keep control. Get the analyses and reports you need, and get them on time. Otherwise, you will have to do it yourself.

The finance departments in some companies have people actually assigned to work with marketing planners. In a very few, there are controllers in the marketing department. However, the great majority of planners are on their own. Again, because you are not in a position to insist on anything, give finance and accounting plenty of lead time. Their schedules are usually full, and at certain times of year it would be impossible for them to help you. Annual closing time, for example, is when you don't even go near the accounting and finance departments.

Legal

Without doubt, the worst thing that could happen to a marketing executive would be to go to prison for a violation of the Sherman Antitrust Act. It can happen; it has happened.

The legal environment of marketing is complex and constantly changing. Get regular briefings from the legal department on trends and developments. As you explore alternative strategies, ask legal people to review the general scope of each. There may be some hidden legal implication you have missed. By all means, submit formal documentation for legal review. All contracts, pricing agreements, and even advertising copy should be approved. Factor time for these reviews into your schedule, because they may not be on the top of the lawyer's do list. Finally, have the legal department review the draft of your marketing plan. Occasionally, these documents end up in court as evidence of strategic or tactical intent. The legal advisor to a company suggested that the language of one of its objectives be changed. It originally had read "It is our objective to drive *XYZ* Company out of business by the end of the year." This was not a very prudent way to state a market share objective.

Why the Human Side Gets Messed Up

There is no doubt about it. Not every planning exercise goes smoothly. The schedule is often delayed. The plan itself may be incomplete. Others in the organization refuse to "sign off" on it. Management won't approve the program until they do. Everything grinds to a halt.

Are You the Problem?

It is very tempting to place the entire blame on others. This would be a mistake. In Chapter 10, a number of the pitfalls in planning are briefly described, and we will not anticipate that discussion. Instead, let us consider a few of the things that may happen to you as a person, which will affect your ability to drive the plan on to its proper completion.

You may get disillusioned about the process. This is most likely to happen the first time around, unless you intentionally keep it simple and are willing to accept the fact that completing the plan may actually be more important than having the best plan possible. The search for instant perfection is fruitless. Be patient. Don't expect the impossible. Work to achieve the possible, and go on from there.

There is no doubt you will become frustrated, even angry, with the obstacles, delays, lack of commitment, and misunderstanding you will encounter. These things will happen; expect them to. But don't count the pieces. Pick up and start again. As they occur, you will learn better how to deal with them. You should expect that these problems will grow less and less burdensome as time goes by and as others in the organization get used to what you are doing and feel less threatened by it. If, by chance, the resistance gets worse, interrupt the process long enough to discover the reason. It may be your approach; it may be the lack of commitment from higher levels in the company. Whatever the cause, address it or the planning process will have little hope of working.

You may find yourself resenting the time and effort it takes to get the planning done. It will take much more time than you expect. You undoubtedly have other responsibilities. As these jobs get postponed, you will feel greater and greater pressure to take shortcuts in the planning process. Don't do it. Later, as you become more familiar with the procedure, you will be able to expedite the process; but don't do it until you know what the consequences will be. A good example is the temptation to avoid meeting with peer managers to solicit their cooperation. You will surely regret this later, for it will be the very department you slight at the planning stage that will be the problem spot later on.

As all of these things happen, you too will be inclined to lose your zest for the project. Like a captain determined to sail your yacht across the Pacific, you will doubt whether you really wanted to do it after a few weeks at sea. Anticipate the probability that your enthusiasm will wane. At certain stages, especially the situation analysis, you will feel you will never get on to the next (and more exciting) steps. But you must persevere. Research and analysis may not be your favorite tasks, but develop an interest in them and the work will be less onerous. Approach the task as a detective or a diagnostician. Savor the information as you gather it. Don't make any decisions, but don't be reluctant to speculate about the strategic meaning of what you discover. A professional baseball player who later became a very successful salesman found the key to his success in simply trying to be enthusiastic, even though he was not. "If you act as if you were enthusiastic," he said, "you'll soon be enthusiastic."

On the other hand, you may find the creative aspects of planning particularly frustrating. You may think you are not very good at creating ideas. Don't believe it. Creativity is a skill, like skating or typewriting. It can be taught; it can be learned. If this is a problem for you, look into the literature on creativity or attend one of the popular seminars. It could help.

Some planners find it difficult to make decisions. Eventually you will have to make up your mind on both strategy and tactics. If "decisions get you down," make sure you approach the task in the right way. Decide first on *how* you will decide. Structure the assignment, select the criteria, pick a decision rule, then evaluate the alternatives. Pick the one alternative that the decision structure indicates is "best." Remember, though, that you have to feel right about the choice. And, if the decision is still a problem, recall that the choice of a strategy may turn out to be more spiritual than statistical.

When Others Are the Problem

Realistically, even if you are part of the problem, others will also be to blame if the planning process goes astray. Unfortunately, there are a number of organizational gliches that get in the way of marketing planning. If marketing were to take place solely within its own area, the problems would be much less serious. But, as we know, marketing pervades a business from top to bottom and from side to side. Let us discuss a few of the problems that organizational structure creates.

First, there is the conflict between line and staff. Staff people think they are planners, whereas line managers should be. Staff people try to take over the function, and line managers resist. Managers don't do the job, so staff steps in and gets it done. Then the managers take the credit.

Or consider the problem when levels are involved. Top management thinks one way; divisional management thinks another way. Top managers lay down the ground rules; divisional managers ignore them. The program works, and nothing is said. The program fails, and everyone blames each other. A marketing planner spends a great deal of time studying the situation and presenting a carefully thought-out plan. Top management does something quite different and never bothers to explain its action. What Derek Abell refers to as "we-they" battles emerge. The marketing plan is the real victim, because the disillusioned marketing planner probably leaves and top management wonders why.

The rejection of recommendations from the planning staff is a matter of genuine concern to most marketing planners. Nobody likes rejection. Nobody likes to spend time preparing a good plan, which is then trashed for unexplained reasons. Even more frustrating is when a carefully worked-out plan, designed to achieve the stated objectives, is rejected because it is too "risky," while a more conservative plan is substituted. Not only does the substitute fail to achieve the goal, but the opportunity to enter and close a strategic window may be lost.

Closely related is the disappointment that the marketing planner feels when top management takes strategic actions without regard to what has been approved in the marketing plan. It is not so much that one strategy is replaced by another, but that the same care and thought is not given to the replacement action. When this occurs, the planner rightly wonders about both the commitment to planning and the degree of respect top management has for the work of the planning staff.

The marketing planner often finds that there is difficulty in getting others even to provide the needed information. Sometimes it "isn't available." Sometimes it is delayed. Often it is provided grudgingly. Not infrequently it is "slanted." The information may not be false, but it can easily be incomplete. There is always the fear that bad news will upset somebody. "Kill the messenger" phobia prevents people from reporting poor performance—lost customers, missed opportunities, and the like.

The sidewise organizational problems have already been mentioned in discussing the various interactions of the marketing planner. The difficulties are largely those of misunderstanding and conflict in goals. In general, the marketing planner has a much better chance of resolving these conflicts than conflicts that arise with top management. However, none is easy to resolve and all will require constant efforts to diminish their impact on the planning process.

Why Organizational Conflicts Arise

Before attempting to deal with the organizational conflicts that interfere with the marketing planning process, it is useful to review why these differences occur. Without trying to tie them to particular levels or functions within a business, we can identify some of the basic causes for conflict.

Differences in Goals. One reason the hierarchy of objectives is so important is that it forces a linkage among the goals at different levels of a business. When objectives have been set without meeting the hierarchical test, there may well be conflict. This is especially true when subordinate levels or functions are allowed to set their own goals. They will tend to set objectives that optimize the local situation but have little bearing on the higher-order goals of the organization.

Even if hierarchically related to objectives above and below in the organization, the goals of peer groups and functions at the same level may be in conflict. Thus they fail to meet a second test, that of consistency. For example, if manufacturing, in the interest of lowering cost, sets a goal of maximizing output of one product, this may be in direct conflict with the goal of marketing to increase sales of another.

Short-run versus Long-run Perspective. If, for example, the marketing plan calls for the development of business with a category of customer the company does not presently serve, this may conflict with the short-term interests of both manufacturing and sales. Salespeople will not give up calling on customers who are presently buying to call on prospects who need products the company does not yet have. Manufacturing wants orders for products that can be scheduled next week, not next year.

The Reward System. Most reward systems do not recognize planning activities. Most managers do not attribute product sales to the plan, but to the sales department. They assume the credit for profits for themselves. So the salesperson gets the bonus, and the managers share the profits. A thoughtful person might conclude that it doesn't pay to spend time in planning and that he or she should devote just as little time and attention to it as possible. Obviously, this thinking gets in the way when a marketing planner sallies forth to rally the organization for a comprehensive marketing plan.

Differences in Management Style. There are genuine differences in the way managers operate. If you are dealing with the newer breed of manager who understands the role of planning, you will have little difficulty. However, you will face a different situation with the action-oriented manager who "shoots from the hip." He or she spots a situation that needs attention and goes right at it, often with uncanny perceptiveness. Rather than taking the more careful and cautious approach of assessing the situation, this manager's approach is to organize a posse and hit the trail. There are probably fewer of these types around today than formerly, but there are still enough of them to give the marketing planner fits. Remember that you have little chance of changing these managers' style. You will have to adapt to it. If you have very many of them in your organization, you had better learn to ride!

Lack of Understanding of Planning. Very few managers, even though they understand the role and importance of planning in general, grasp the scope of marketing planning. First, they may not be marketing oriented, and the whole approach of starting with the customer may seem peculiar. Second, since they are so accustomed to thinking of planning in forecasting and financial terms, they do not understand why marketing planners have to make it so much more complicated.

The manager who is task-focused, as is often true of people in operations and research, sees his or her job as operating a department as efficiently as possible. Linking those efforts to that of other departments is quite foreign. "You do your job, and I'll do mine" is the prevalent attitude. Educating these people to the planning process is difficult. Help them see the benefits of planning their own work; then they will be more receptive to participating in the marketing planning process.

Marketing Planning Is Seen as a Threat. Back when the idea of a "marketing orientation" was first touted, managers of other departments were extremely apprehensive that marketing people would take over the business. Of course that never happened, and probably could never have happened. Marketing people were no better equipped to run the entire business than financial managers were qualified to run the marketing department. The latent fear remains because, as this book demonstrates, marketing must be the lead function. People in nonmarketing areas still see the effort to develop an overall marketing plan as a threat to their autonomy. Since the threat is not real, the marketing planner must find ways to reassure other managers that the process is actually intended to make their jobs easier, more productive, and more secure. It is a challenge to face a hostile director of research who is convinced that he will lose all control over what his department does. If you ever think marketing planning is boring, just give this one a try.

Uneven Distribution of Knowledge. Have you ever realized that the people who know least about the full scope of marketing are either at the very top or the very bottom of the organization? The president is too far, and too long, removed from the field really to know what is going on in the market (assuming he or she had ever had any experience in that part of the business). True, the president may talk to a customer now and again, but usually it is a social acquaintance or a disgruntled user who has managed to get through to the top of the organization. At the other end of the business is the rank-and-file salesperson, perhaps new on the job, who sees only as much of the business as his or her territory and training have touched. Interestingly, these are the two levels of a business at which the most important marketing decisions are made. The president approves strategy; the salespeople make tactical choices upon which marketing results eventually depend.

The place where the greatest knowledge of the business and of its markets exists is in the middle of the organization—where marketing planning is usually done. This is where the marketing planners—the marketing managers, the product managers, the market research managers, and the advertising managers—are to be found. But these people are only the recommenders of strategy and the suggestors of tactics. When the marketing planner goes upstream to talk about strategy, he or she runs into a general lack of understanding of the situation. When that planner goes downstream to suggest tactics, he or she finds people who are either very fixed in their routines or who are unable to see the bigger picture. Given these differences, it is easy to see why the marketing planner encounters problems in establishing a communications link with people at both the top and bottom of the company.

Politics. An organization is a political structure. Where one stands in it or how one is perceived very much influences how that person responds to any efforts to include him or her in the planning process. Is it the thing to do to get ahead? Should I really be working with this department, with this person? All organizations have informal networks and alliances that can be used either to advantage or to get in the way of achieving some goal. By knowing something about these networks, the marketing planner can use them advantageously. The problem is that various networks are in competition with each other. At worst, one alliance may attempt to sabotage the work of another. At the very least, the networking makes it difficult to affect cross-fertilization of efforts and ideas. Unfortunately, almost every upwardly mobile individual in an organization is expected to take sides, to join one network or another. The loner really doesn't get along with anybody.

The only saving feature of these alliances is that they often cross departmental and functional lines. This means that the marketing planner, having chosen a network within which to work, should have at least a point of contact at every key place in the business. With this kind of entrée, you may then be able to work within the more formal organizational structure.

Communications Failures. The secret of working with others in the organization is good communications. The problem is that the system can fail to function properly. Much of the contact involved in marketing planning is verbal—quick conversations at lunch or in the elevator. Few of these communications are followed up in writing. Third parties are relied on to transmit information or requests. Distortion occurs. The message may not even be delivered. Or it may arrive along with other bits of information that confuse or diminish its importance. The noise in business communications is always at a high level.

Written memoranda are preferable, but even these can create problems. They may be dictated, but never get typed. They may be typed, but never get sent. Likewise, they may be sent but not received, received but not noted, noted but ignored. And the response faces the same hurdles. Sometimes written memos can cause problems in their own right. An instruction can be misunderstood, a meaning misconstrued. When visiting personally, you can tell if the message is registering the wrong way— an arch of the eyebrow, a frown. You quickly sense that you have said something the wrong way or left something out. The mistake is quickly corrected. But you may never know why a memo goes unanswered.

The only safe course is to initiate all communications in person, and then follow up with written confirmation. This may seem burdensome, but is really the only way to make sure messages are sent, delivered, received, and understood. "Marketing is communications," someone once said. The "inside" marketing you do within your own organization to get others involved is almost all communications. Make sure that the channels are open and being used.

Competition for Resources. Reduced to its common denominator, the marketing plan is the manager's way to make a good case for the allocation of resources. Management support and funding go to the projects it feels are best for the company. Other managers in the business who understand this aspect of planning may well suspect that their support of the marketing plan will give you a better shot at a share of the scarce resources. At the extreme, for example, a plant manager might think, "Why should I help you develop a plan that will result in an expensive marketing program for your products? All that will do is make it harder for me to get the money I need for a new boiler." Of course, this is short-sighted, parochial thinking; but it is easy to understand why someone might think this way.

How to Deal With Conflicts

The array of problems presented and the deep-rooted reasons for them may raise tremendous barriers to effective marketing planning. They are serious, but there are things you can do to deal with them. They will not go away overnight. Some may never disappear completely. But you can lessen their impact. As you succeed, you'll find your marketing planning assignment becoming easier and more personally rewarding.

Get Top Management Involved. Here your objective is twofold. First, you must accept that unless marketing planning has the whole-hearted support of the president, it can never function very well. Marketing planning cannot be mandated from the top. It has been tried, but it doesn't work. But if top management sets the right climate, sees that people are properly trained, and becomes personally involved, the planning process will work.

Educate. Marketing planning works best when the organization understands what marketing is and how the marketing planning process works. This education should start at the top and filter down the organization to the heads of functional departments. One large company, which entered into the marketing planning process without any previous experience or knowledge about marketing, went about the process in this way. First, the new company president spent several months in informal conversations with a pair of marketing professors. They sat in front of the fireplace in the president's family room on Sunday afternoons discussing the philosophical, organizational, and operational meaning of marketing. Next, a training seminar was held for the divisional presidents. The president attended and participated. Again, the nature of marketing as the driving force of the business was discussed. Strategic marketing decision-making and marketing planning procedures were reviewed. Following this, short courses in various aspects of marketing management were held throughout the company. Both the practice of marketing and the tools of marketing planning were covered. Eventually, after this program was completed, the company undertook its first pass at the development of marketing plans.

Process First, Then Plan. Don't start planning without first getting agreement on the process. As this book has demonstrated, there is a logical sequence to the marketing planning activities; to undertake them on a haphazard basis will probably kill the project.

When a management group responsible for marketing planning was established at a large agribusiness firm, a three-year project was developed to establish a planning culture and routine. The first phase involved a comprehensive educational program to train a group of managers in the techniques of marketing planning. The balance of the first year was spent in a dry run, practicing the planning process with no intention of implementing the plans. This approach was used to meet two needs: (1) to provide experiential training, and (2) to build bridges to nonmarketing departments.

The second year, marketing planners went through the process under close tutorial supervision. Training sessions were continued, and formal presentations were made at every stage of the process. Some plans were exceptionally well done and were implemented; others required much modification; a few were held over for further refinement the next year.

The third year was a real-world exercise. Supervision was relaxed, although the process was monitored, and individual performances were evaluated regularly. Eventually, the separate marketing planning department was disbanded and the planning responsibility was assumed by the operating departments. But the planning procedures remained virtually intact, and the people who had been trained assumed important planning assignments in the departments.

Get General Involvement. If planning is going to work, and if the plans are going to succeed, almost every function in the business will be involved in some way. It is important for you to set the stage for this by getting everybody involved as early as possible. In planning your planning, define the steps to be taken and identify the people or departments to be involved. You will have a master list of those whom you want to contact to make sure they are ready, willing, and able to participate. As a cross-check, take an organization chart and contact every function or department that intersects with marketing. Make sure that everybody is properly introduced to what the planning process will involve.

Use Staff Assistance. If you are a line marketing manager, this instruction is meant specifically for you. Use help wherever and whenever you can. Delegate as much of the intelligence gathering and analysis as you can. Don't get tied to your personal computer. Remember, staffers don't plan; managers do. It is your job to set objectives, select strategies, and approve budgets.

If you are a staff planner, the opposite is true for you. Stand ready to be of assistance to the manager responsible for planning. If the manager is reluctant to get into the planning, help get it started. But once started, make sure the manager understands the respective role of staff and line management. Do not make the decisions the manager should make. This may be very frustrating, but it is the only correct way to function. As staff, you cannot hope to affect implementation. Planning is part of the manager's job.

Keep It Simple. You can quickly overwhelm your organization if you attempt to implement a complex planning system too quickly. Take it step by step. Begin with the easiest, not the most difficult planning assignment. You will find it easier to get cooperation, the schedule will go faster, and there will be less frustration and confusion.

Respect the Numbers. Your plan will be only as good as the data upon which it is based. Remember: garbage in, garbage out. Draw a distinction between marketing information and marketing intelligence. Intelligence is data that have been collected for a purpose, then screened, interpreted, and presented in a form the manager can use. As you go about the situation analysis, make sure you are dealing with intelligence, not just words and numbers. Keep an open audit trail from your plan back through your situation analysis summaries to the original sources.

Remember the Purpose of Planning. Planning has no purpose in and of itself. It is a useful exercise, but if it fails to produce a plan, it has not served its ultimate purpose. The fundamental purpose of the plan is to produce results; so this is the purpose of planning, also. You might think that the planning is finished when you produce the plan. But the planning is not over until the results are in.

Use the Reward System. It was pointed out that the reward system sometimes works against getting people to participate in the planning process. You can turn this around to your advantage. If you are a line manager, you can easily build rewards and incentives into the system. If you are a staff planner, this is a bit more difficult, but it is not entirely impossible. You must see that those in a position to employ the reward system are aware of the contributions people in the planning system have made. In discussing implementation in Chapter 7, a number of ways of rewarding performance were mentioned.

Be Flexible in the Way You Work With Others. Different strokes for different folks. Fit your approach to the management or work styles of your colleagues. A corporate planning director once sent a short memorandum to a number of divisional heads, in which he instructed them to appear at corporate headquarters on a certain date with a particular analysis. It happened that nobody in the company was familiar with the form in which he wanted this information, and being divisional vice presidents, they reacted with expected irritation. Before it was over, the company president had to get into the act. If the memorandum had been preceded by a telephone call, had been written in a different tone, or had gone to the financial departments of these divisions, the reactions would have been quite different.

Employ Positive Collaboration Techniques. Ed Roseman, a senior executive with a major company, has suggested ten ways in which a marketing manager can build better relations with others. He calls them tools of positive collaboration.[1]

1. Exchange problems. Discuss each other's situations. Outside and inside points of view generally enrich the solutions.
2. Give credit. Instead of fighting each other for the credit when something works out well, give the other person credit—even more than he or she may deserve.
3. Avoid memos. Use person-to-person verbal communications.
4. Bank goodwill. Build a reserve of trust with others. Save the goodwill for a rainy day when you need a favor.
5. Keep the other person informed. Avoid the trauma that results when you pull surprises on your colleagues. Withholding information simply makes a bad situation worse.
6. Accept responsibility for failure. Don't play Ping-Pong with the "who's to blame" game. Share the risks of failure and enjoy the glory of success.
7. Acknowledge suggestions. Give a fair hearing to all ideas—good and bad. Encourage creativity. Don't screen out any idea until it has had a fair hearing.
8. Be humble. You will get much more cooperation if you approach others with a good dose of humility. Treat the other person as an equal, intellectually and organizationally. Don't be condescending. Find something you can appreciate about the other individual and concentrate on that.
9. Recognize others' needs. You can build a healthy relationship with another human being only if you are sensitive to that individual's needs and try to respond to them.
10. Build a record. Work at building a collaborative relationship with one or two people. Others will see this and respond. Before you know it, you will have built a network of people whom you work well with and who work well with you.

Find Ways to Exercise Power. If you are a staff planner, this will be very important in your interpersonal relations. If you are a line marketing manager, it will help you deal with nonmarketing personnel. Gemmill and Wilemon suggest several ways of exercising practical, if not formal, organizational power.[2]

■ Exercise *reward power.* You may be able to gain support because others perceive you as capable of directly or indirectly dispensing rewards they value. Your ability to do this may be severely limited.

■ Exercise *coercive power.* In some instances, you can probably gain support because others perceive you as capable of dispensing punishments they wish to avoid. This source of power is closely linked to the first, and you will probably be very restricted in the degree to which you can, or will want to, employ it.

■ Employ *expert power.* Your expertise as a manager, as a marketing specialist, and as a planner will be respected. You will be perceived as a person having special skills and abilities. Others will respect this and want to be associated with you. They may see in your expertise skills that can help them. This will probably be your most viable source of power within the organization.

■ Use *referent power.* This is the ability to gain support from others because people feel personally attracted to you. It is probably true that you will not be able to accomplish much if people do not like to be with you. Try to develop a pleasant personality; use it to your advantage in working with others.

Plan Your Planning. A complete chapter on this topic appeared early in this book. We underscore its importance in getting the cooperation of others. You must anticipate where you are going to need assistance and prepare the way for getting it. The plan for planning also organizes your own work. Your enthusiasm for the plan may wane; the plan for planning will keep you going.

Keep Going. Keep your attention riveted on the marketing planning process. Let nothing interfere with your part in the process. As noted before, enthusiasm is catching. When the smoke subsides and the battle is over, you will see what you have accomplished. So what if nobody ever thanks *you* for your part in it all? The important thing is that the plan worked, and you will know why.

If you do these things—if you follow the planning procedure, if you understand what sound marketing is all about—your marketing planning will be successful. It will fulfill its purpose: You will have produced a marketing plan that gets things done. The only remaining problem is that you might tumble into one or more of the marketing planning pitfalls. These are described briefly in the next chapter.

10
Pitfalls in Planning

It may seem something of a downer to close this book with a chapter on the pitfalls in planning. But planning is not an easy task, and the people assigned to prepare marketing plans are all too often untrained or inexperienced. Things can go wrong for many reasons, and part of your assignment as a marketing planner is to make sure your planning does not fall victim to one of the several pitfalls that lie along the path. All of them have been discussed in earlier chapters, but the following brief summary can serve as a handy checklist as you pursue your goals.

No Plan for Planning. You must approach your planning assignment in an organized, disciplined manner. Plan your planning. You will find that to the extent you do this, you will become the master rather than the servant of the planning process. Those planners who do not plan the planning inevitably find that they produce plans that are not or cannot be implemented, that they get little or no top management support, and that their plans are frequently late.

Not Enough Time. Estimates of the time spent on marketing planning activities vary considerably, but 200 to 300 hours is not uncommon. It is not unusual for product managers to spend one-third to one-half of their time annually on planning-related activities. That amounts to 700 to 1,000 hours a year. You must be the final judge as to how much time you can and should devote to planning. But if you do not put in the time, you cannot expect much of a marketing plan to come out of the process.

Failure to Integrate the Planning Stages. Marketing planning is a continuous process with numerous feedback loops. It is not a set of 14 independent steps to take, robotlike, until the task is completed. Every time you take a new step in the process, link it to those you have already completed. And think of the implications of what you are doing for the steps that still remain.

Inadequate Data Base. This can be the most crippling deficiency in a planning exercise. Once a disciplined process has been installed, lack of an adequate data base is inexcusable. Your plan will never be any better than the facts upon which it is based. You may find the situation analysis to be the least exciting part of the process, but it is absolutely essential.

Lack of Assistance and Cooperation. You may often feel alone, even rejected, as you pursue the planning process. You may be frustrated by the indifference or outright hostility of those whose input you need. This is one of the most challenging parts of the entire process. All your interpersonal skills will be required, and they may be severely tested. If you find yourself unable to cope and ineffective in getting the necessary support and assistance, bring this problem to the attention of your supervisor. The situation will have to be corrected, or the entire planning process may be jeopardized.

Strategic Drift. This is a special aspect of the failure to integrate the planning steps. It is especially critical because it affects the content of the plan. Strategic drift most obviously occurs when the execution of a strategy deviates seriously from the marketing plan's basic thrust. A very clever advertisement to promote a special price represents strategic drift if the overall campaign is intended to develop an image of quality and reliability. Strategic drift also occurs when a stated opportunity is unsupported by the facts in the situation analysis, when an objective is unrealistic, or when a strategy statement only vaguely addresses a major marketing objective.

Taking Shortcuts. Leaving steps out of the planning process or cutting back on the effort applied to them is a serious pitfall. It is usually done because of time pressure, lack of input from others, or a failure to appreciate the importance of each step in the process. This is superficial and dangerous. Leave nothing out of your plan. Give each part of the process your full and best effort.

Failure to Develop Tactics. One of the fairly common mistakes in marketing planning is not to carry the process through the tactical planning stage. As has been mentioned, strategies do not accomplish results; tactics do. Make sure that tactical plans are developed, whether you do this yourself or others do so. Without tactics, you do not have a complete marketing plan.

Being Hypnotized by the Numbers. Do not get trapped into believing that the statistical analyses you have performed are a substitute for the creative problem solving that is the essence of marketing planning. There are several places in the planning process where this is apt to occur. First, in the situation analysis there is a temptation to concentrate only on what can be counted, leaving out those qualitative factors that may be even more important in describing the marketing situation. In the data analysis stage, it is possible to get so caught up in the elegance of the quantitative manipulations that the subjective aspects are neglected. For example, simulation models are extremely useful in exploring "what if" questions. But the models are only as good as the assumptions behind them, and they are in no way complete replications of the real world. Remember, the choice of a strategy may be more spiritual than statistical. Finally, there is the common failure of putting undue emphasis on the financial aspects of the planning. Sales forecasts, pro forma financial statements, and operating budgets are necessary. But these are not marketing plans, although they should be included in a complete planning document. They are simply ways of recording useful information about the results that are expected.

Failure to Control. If you stop the planning process before the results have been measured and evaluated, you will have shirked a major planning responsibility. You are both marketing planner and marketing controller. Together, these tasks comprise the most important and most time-consuming elements of any marketing manager's job.

Failure to Modify the Plan. The perfect plan has never been conceived. Don't plan for the ages. Plans often must be changed to accomplish their desired results. General Eisenhower once said, "Plans are nothing. Planning is everything." Begin with a flexible plan, and be willing to change it. Be willing—even anxious—to abandon a plan that is not working for one that will. Dogged determination to stick with an ineffective plan is sheer folly. Better to lose a little face, than to lose the battle in the marketplace.

Not "Selling" Your Plan. It's already been said many times, "The purpose of planning is to produce results." But, if top management or another department does not accept your plan, there will be no results. You've simply wasted your time. Your challenge is still to produce plans that will deliver results, and not just to "sell" your plan to somebody else. But sell you must, and it would be inexcusable for your plan to fail because you were unable or unwilling to persuade others of its merit.

Planning Becomes a Ritual. There is the danger that planning will lose its vibrant character and be reduced to a ritual—something done every year. This happens when planners and line managers begin taking the process for granted. The routines of planning are followed almost by rote, and the sense of urgency and expectancy that characterized the early days of marketing planning are gone. One year's plan looks pretty much like the one before. Watch for the first signs of this. If it happens, you may need to jolt the system. Fortunately, the dynamic nature of marketing and the market itself should supply endless opportunities to trigger concern.

Now, on to your plan . . .

And don't forget,

The purpose of planning is not to produce a plan.
The purpose of planning is to produce results!

Appendix 1
Situation Analysis Questionnaire

The body of the text explained a general approach to the marketing situation analysis. Here is a set of questions that might be used in a comprehensive situation audit. The marketing planner would seek answers to these questions (as edited to fit the particular situation) and record the responses in some accessible format. The data then becomes the information base from which analytic summaries are prepared.

Questionnaire

I. The Company

1. Provide a brief history of the company.
2. Provide an organization chart of the entire company, and briefly describe each top management and functional position.

mission statement 3. Describe the business your company is in.

4. Does the business as it is differ from the kind of business you want to operate? If so, in what ways?
5. What has been the company's progress in sales and earnings over the past five years? Provide a recap of sales and earnings by major product categories for the past five years. (If there is a convenient way to report sales in physical units for this period, do so. If not, provide the average percentage increase in price which occurred for each of the past five years.)
6. Is the growth which you have experienced in the past five years satisfactory to your management? If not, what growth would have been acceptable?
7. If the growth over the past five years has not been satisfactory, what are the factors that have, in your opinion, hindered it?
8. State the company's objectives for each of the next five years for each of its major product categories.
9. Does your company have a basic business philosophy? If so, what is it?

✓10. What are the company's basic operating policies regarding markets to be served, product lines, services to be offered, quality level, prices, costs, channels of distribution, and so on? (Note, this is not a description of what you do, but rather a statement of rules concerning decisions which might be reached in these or similar areas.)

11. What is your management's attitude toward expansion in sales, services, markets served, facilities, personnel, capabilities, and so forth?

12. Do you anticipate any significant near-term changes in the company as it now exists? If so, describe them.

13. Describe the company's present strategy to achieve its long-term (five-year) objectives. (Note: Even if you do not have a definite plan, you probably have some ideas about how you think you should go about addressing your five-year objectives.)

14. Describe the company's plans for achieving its objectives for next year.

II. The External Environment

✓1. What are the major external factors that have affected your industry and business in the past five years? (Be as specific as you can in each of the following areas. If there are areas not listed below but important to your business, include them under "other.")
   a. Economic
   b. Legal/political
   c. Technological
   d. Cultural and life-style
   e. Other

2. What is the outlook for the next five years in each of these same areas? (For each prospective development, indicate (a) how seriously it will impact on your company, and (b) the probability that it will actually occur.)

III. The Industry

✓1. Briefly describe the industry in which your company operates.

✓2. What has been the five-year sales history of the industry? Provide this in dollars and in physical units, if possible.

✓3. What has been the average increase in prices in the industry for each of the past five years?

✓4. What are the major influences upon industry demand? List and describe each briefly.

5. What is your forecast of these demand influences over the next five years?

✓6. What new or additional demand influences do you see having an impact on your industry in the next five years?

7. Are you aware of any sales forecasts for the industry? If so, what are they? Do you agree with them? Why or why not?

✓8. What are the things about your industry that make it attractive to your company?

✓9. What are the things about your industry that make it unattractive to you?

10. Has industry demand been cyclical? If yes, with which economic indicators has it been most closely related? Have any lead/lag relationships been discovered?

11. Is industry demand seasonal? If so, provide some statistics that measure the seasonality. To what do you attribute the seasonal character of demand, if any?

✓12. At what stage in the product life cycle is the industry? Does this have any apparent implications to your company's methods of operation?

13. What is the production capacity of the industry, and at what percentage of capacity has the industry operated over the past five years?
14. How easy is it for a new competitor to enter the industry? Explain.
15. Are there any compelling limitations on supply, such as labor, raw materials, energy, and so on that afflict the industry?
16. What is the general competitive situation in the industry? Specifically,
    a. How many competitors are there?
    b. What is the degree of concentration—that is, what percentage of industry sales do the top three firms enjoy?
    c. Is there any regional or market segment specialization by the different competitors?
    d. Is the competition characterized by two or more different kinds of firms (for example, vertically integrated, high vs. low technology, low cost/price vs. quality/high price, full-time vs. short-line, and so on?
    e. What are the general competitive methods employed—that is, price, new products, trade promotion, advertising, and so forth?
17. In general, what are the key factors for success in the industry? What seems to have made some firms more successful than others?

IV. The Customer

1. Who are the end users of the products you sell? Describe briefly.
2. Who are your customers—for example, end users, wholesalers, mass merchandisers, and the like.
3. For each major type of customer to whom you sell, provide the following information:
    a. Where are these customers located geographically?
    b. What is the present size of this customer group?
    c. Is this customer group increasing or decreasing in size? If so, explain.
    d. How does this type of customer use or resell the products?
4. Besides the customer groupings identified above, is there evidence of segmentation in the market? If so, what are the various segments?
5. Are there any potential customer types your company has not been successful in selling? If so, what are they? To what do you attribute your difficulty in selling to them?
6. In what ways has the type of customers you have served changed over the past five years or so? To what do you attribute this change? What impact has it had on your company?
7. Have you specifically lost ground with any particular customer type over the past five years? If so, which type and why?
8. What image do your various types of customers have of your company? How does it differ from the image they hold of your competitors? Is there some way in which you would like to have your image changed? If so, what aspect of it? Why?
9. In general, what are the buying motives of the customers for your types of products?
10. How do your types of customers make their buying decisions regarding the type of product to purchase, where to buy it, and which brand to select?

V. The Competition

1. List your important (and potential) competitors.
2. Rank these competitors according to their overall strength, and indicate whether each is getting stronger or weaker. Explain your ranking for each.
3. Identify specifically the companies you expect might enter your industry in the next

few years. What would be the principal strength each would bring and what entry strategy would each be likely to employ?

4. Which company (companies) is your most vulnerable competitor? Why?
5. What important competitive changes beyond your control do you anticipate within the next few years?
6. Rank the changes listed in question 5 in order of their likely impact on the market and on your company in particular.
7. Give one or two examples of how your company has responded to major competitive changes in the past.
8. For the most important competitors listed in question 1, provide the following information:
   a. What is its principal competitive strength? Others?
   b. What overall marketing strategy does it employ?
   c. What products and services does it offer and what are the competitive advantages and disadvantages of each?
   d. What is the company's method of selling—direct, reps, and so on?
   e. To what market segments does it sell?
   f. What form and amount of advertising and sales promotion does it utilize?
   g. What is its pricing approach?
   h. Explain why customers prefer this competitor's products in preference to yours.
   i. What is its present market share and share trend?
   j. What specific opportunity or threat does this competitor pose?
   k. What kind and amount of reaction would this competitor present if its market share were threatened?

VI. The Products and Services

1. List the products and services your company sells.
2. What is each product's and service's reason for existence?
   a. Is it a need or a want for the customer?
   b. Is it a long-existing or a new need or want?
   c. At what stage in the product life cycle is it?
3. What are each product's or service's advantages and disadvantages vs. the competition in each of the following areas?
   a. Market potential
   b. Profitability
   c. Suitability to the market
   d. Suitability to the company
   e. Quality
   f. Materials
   g. Features
   h. Design/style
   i. Color
   j. Variety
   k. Packaging
   l. Price
   m. Positioning
   n. Safety
   o. Durability
   p. Performance

 4. Are there any other product/service characteristics that distinguish your products/services from the competition? If so, list them and indicate how your products differ from those of competitors.
 5. What makes each of your products unique?
 6. Why do people buy your products instead of competitors'?
 7. Describe how customers use and maintain your products.
 8. Provide sales and profit contribution data for each product. If these data are not available, rank each product by (a) sales volume and (b) profit contribution.
 9. What product improvements have been made recently?
 10. What improvements are presently contemplated?
 11. What new products or services are being considered?
 12. Describe briefly the procedure your company uses to develop new products.
 13. What kinds of products are generally substitutable for your products? Are these products making headway in the market? Why or why not?
 14. Are there any technological or other developments taking place in the market that are beyond your control? If so, describe and indicate what threat or opportunity each development poses for your company.
 15. What procedures do you follow to review the marketing status of each item in your product line?
 16. What products, if any, have you dropped in the last year or so? Why?
 17. Are there any other products you are considering deleting? Which ones? Why?

VII. The Distribution Channels

 1. Describe the distribution channel(s) used by your company.
 2. Do any of your competitors use different methods? If so, describe and explain the reasons for the different approach. Do you see any new trends developing? If so, explain.
 3. List and briefly identify each of the representatives or agents used by your company, including the territories served, the number of salesmen, lines handled, and so on.*
 4. What is the sales history of each organization for the past five years?
 5. What is the potential in each territory and how well has each been penetrated?
 6. Identify your three best rep organizations and indicate the reasons for their superior performance.
 7. Identify your three weakest rep organizations and indicate the reasons for their inferior performance.
 8. Identify any areas where you either have no representation or need to make a change. What is the market potential in each of these areas?
 9. What activities has your company taken to improve the performance of its representatives? What others have you considered? What do your major competitors do?
 10. In general, what attitudes or feelings do your reps have about your company?
 11. What is the trade reputation of your reps? Explain. What, if anything, have you done to cause this? To correct it?
 12. In what ways do you directly support your reps? In what ways do you compete with them? Are there any difficulties here?

*If your company employs its own sales force, substitute the appropriate sales management level for the terms "rep" or "agent". If wholesalers, distributors, jobbers, or dealers are also important, these same questions should be answered for each."

13. How important is your company to your rep organizations? If possible, indicate what percent of their business your company accounts for.

14. What are the current rep commission rates? Are these uniform? Do you ever split commissions with reps or between reps?

15. Describe briefly the wholesale and retail trade structure. What are the most important issues you have to deal with in connection with each type of reseller?

16. What changes in trade structure do you anticipate over the next three to five years? What threats or opportunities do these changes present?

VIII. The Advertising and Promotion

1. What is the principal purpose of your advertising?
2. What has been the amount of your advertising budget in each of the last five years?
3. How is your advertising budget determined?
4. How has the budget been allocated among media?
5. On what basis and in what amounts is the budget assigned to various products?
6. On what basis and in what amounts is the budget assigned to various market segments?
7. What has been your advertising scheduling pattern throughout the year?
8. What have been the various copy approaches that have been used over the past few years? With what results?
9. How do you measure the results of your advertising? Provide any data of this type that you may have assembled.
10. How do you determine brand names and trademarks? What is your assessment of the worth of the names and marks you are currently using?
11. Do you employ any type of advertising slogan? Has this been changed over the years?
12. What kinds of special trade and/or other types of promotion have you employed? With what results?
13. Provide examples of advertisements, catalog sheets, direct-mail pieces, advertising specialties, and any other advertising/promotional tools you may have used during the past few years.
14. What kinds of advertising assistance do you provide for your resellers?
15. Do you offer any kind of cooperative advertising program? If so, what are the details?

IX. The Pricing

1. What is your company's general approach to pricing?
2. In general, are your prices at, above, or below your competitor's?
3. What would be the effect on your sales (as specifically as you can estimate) if you: (a) raised or (b) lowered price by 10 percent?
4. How informed are your customers about competitive prices, your costs, and the value added by the products and services you sell?
5. If you develop a proprietary new product or service, how do you go about pricing it?
6. Do you price generally to produce sales volume or to generate profit margin?
7. How do you estimate or measure the costs of particular products in your line?
8. Will you charge different prices to different customers for approximately the same type and quantity of goods?
9. How are the prices charged for your products affected by their position in the product life cycle?
10. Who makes pricing decisions in your company? Who has the final authority when pricing problems arise?

Appendix 2
A Selective Bibliography on Marketing Planning

This is a selective list of books, monographs, and articles the author has found useful in building an understanding of the marketing planning process. It is a representative, not exhaustive, bibliography.

Books and Monographs

Abell, Derek F. *Defining the Business.* Englewood Cliffs, N.J.: Prentice-Hall, Inc., 1980.

———, and John S. Hammond. *Strategic Market Planning: Problems and Analytic Approaches.* Englewood Cliffs, N.J.: Prentice-Hall, Inc., 1979.

Bell, Martin L. and J. Vincze. *Managerial Marketing: Strategy and Cases.* New York: Elsevier, due 1987.

Bradway, B. M., and M. A. Frenzel. *Strategic Marketing: A Handbook for Entrepreneurs and Managers.* Reading, Mass.: Addison-Wesley, 1982.

Buell, Victor. *Marketing Management: A Strategic Planning Approach.* New York: McGraw-Hill, 1984.

Cady, J., and R. Buzzell. *Strategic Marketing.* Boston: Little, Brown, and Company, 1986.

Cox, K., and V. J. McGinnis. *Strategic Market Decisions: A Reader.* Englewood Cliffs, N.J.: Prentice-Hall, Inc., 1982.

Cravens, David W. *Strategic Marketing.* Homewood, Ill.: Richard D. Irwin, Inc., 1982.

Day, George. *Analysis for Strategic Market Decisions.* St. Paul, Minn.: West Publishing Company, 1986.

———. *Strategic Market Planning: The Pursuit of Competitive Advantage.* St. Paul, Minn.: West Publishing Company, 1984.

Drucker, Peter. *Innovation and Entrepreneurship.* New York: Harper and Row, 1985.

Foster, Richard. *Innovation: The Attacker's Advantage.* New York: Summit Books, 1986.

Henderson, Bruce D. *Henderson on Corporate Strategy*. Cambridge, Mass.: Abt Books, 1979.

————. *The Logic of Business Strategy*. Cambridge, Mass.: Abt Books, 1985.

Hofer, Charles W., and Dan E. Schendel. *Strategy Formulation: Analytical Concepts*. St. Paul, Minn.: West Publishing Company, 1978.

Hopkins, David S. *Business Strategies for Problem Products*. New York: The Conference Board, 1977.

————. *The Marketing Plan*. New York: The Conference Board, 1981.

Hurwood, D., E. Grossman, and E. Bailey. *Sales Forecasting*. New York: The Conference Board, 1978.

Jain, Subhash C. *Marketing Planning and Strategy*. Cincinnati: South-Western Publishing Company, 1985.

Kerin, Roger A., and Robert A. Peterson (eds.). *Perspectives on Strategic Marketing*. Boston: Allyn & Bacon, 1980.

Kotler, Philip. *Marketing Management: Analysis, Planning, and Control*. Englewood Cliffs, N.J.: Prentice-Hall, Inc., 1985.

Luck, David J., and O. C. Ferrell. *Marketing Strategy and Plans*. Englewood Cliffs, N.J.: Prentice-Hall, Inc., 1985.

Luther, William M. *Marketing Plan: How to Prepare and Implement It*. New York: AMACOM, 1984.

Makens, J. *Marketing Plan Workbook*. Englewood Cliffs, N.J.: Prentice-Hall, Inc., 1985.

Marrus, Stephanie. *Building the Strategic Plan*. New York: John Wiley, 1985.

O'Shaughnessy, J. *Competitive Marketing: A Strategic Approach*. Winchester, Mass.: Allen & Unwin, Inc., 1984.

Porter, M. *Competitive Advantage: Creating and Sustaining Superior Performance*. New York: The Free Press, 1985.

————. *Competitive Strategy: Techniques for Analyzing Industries and Competitors*. New York: The Free Press, 1980.

Rice, C. *Marketing Planning Strategies: A Guide for the Small or Medium-Sized Company*. New York: Dartnell Corp., 1984.

Trout, J., and A. Reis. *Marketing Warfare*. New York: McGraw-Hill, 1986.

Weitz, Barton A., and Wensley, Robin. *Strategic Marketing: Planning, Implementation, and Control*. Boston: Kent Publishing Co., 1984.

Articles

Aaker, D., and George S. Day. "The Perils of High Growth Markets." *Strategic Management Journal*, September–October 1986, 409–421.

Abell, Derek F. "Strategic Windows." *Journal of Marketing*, July 1978, 21.

Ames, B. Charles. "Trapping vs. Substance in Industrial Marketing." *Harvard Business Review*, July–August 1970, 93–102.

————. "Marketing Planning for Industrial Products." *Harvard Business Review*, September–October 1968, 100–111.

Bettis, R. A., and W. K. Hall. "The Business Portfolio Approach—Where It Falls Down in Practice." *Long Range Planning*, April 1983, 95–104.

Bloom, Paul N., and P. Kotler. "Strategies for High Share Companies." *Harvard Business Review*, November–December 1978, 95.

Bonoma, T. V. "Making Your Marketing Strategy Work." *Harvard Business Review*, March–April 1984, 68–76.

Buttle, F. "The Marketing Strategy Worksheet." *Long Range Planning*, August 1985, 80–88.

Buzzell, R. D., B. T. Gale, and R. G. M. Sulten. "Market Share—A Key to Profitability." *Harvard Business Review*, January–February 1981, 97.

———, and F. D. Wiersema. "Successful Share Building Strategies." *Harvard Business Review*, January–February 1981, 134–144.

Canning, G. "Focusing on Competition For a Winning Marketing Strategy." *Advanced Management Journal*, Winter 1986, 22–24.

Christopher, W. "Marketing Planning That Gets Things Done." *Harvard Business Review*, September–October 1970, 56–64.

Cohen, A. A. "War in the Marketplace." *Business Horizons*, March–April 1986, 20–25.

Cook, V. J. "Marketing Strategy and Differential Advantage." *Journal of Marketing*, Spring 1985, 68–75.

Cox, D., and R. Good. "How to Build a Marketing Information System." *Harvard Business Review*, May–June 1967, 145–154.

Cravens, David W. "Strategic Forces Affecting Marketing Strategy." *Business Horizons*, September–October 1986, 76–86.

———. "Strategic Marketing's New Challenge." *Business Horizons*, March–April 1983, 18.

Day, George S. "Strategic Market Analysis and Definition: An Integrated Approach." *Strategic Management Journal*, July–September 1981, 281.

———, and David B. Montgomery. "Diagnosing the Experience Curve." *Journal of Marketing*, Spring 1983, 84.

Dickinson, R., and A. Herbst. "Capital Budgeting for Marketing Managers." *Business*, April–May–June 1983, 41–45.

Dunne, Patrick M., and Harry I. Wolk. "Marketing Cost Analysis: A Modularized Contribution Approach." *Journal of Marketing*, July 1977, 83.

Fruhan, William E. "Pyrrhic Victories in the Fight for Market Share." *Harvard Business Review*, September–October 1972, 100.

Greenly, G. E. "Where Marketing Planning Fails." *Long Range Planning*, February 1983, 106.

Hall, William K. "SBU's: Hot, New Topic in the Management of Diversification." *Business Horizons*, February 1978, 17.

Hamermesh, R. G., J. J. Anderson, Jr., and J. E. Harris. "Strategies for Low Market Share Businesses." *Harvard Business Review*, May–June 1978, 95–102.

Hax, A. C., and N. S. Majluf. "The Use of the Industry Attractiveness-Business Strength Matrix in Strategic Planning." *Interfaces*, April 1983, 54–71.

Hedley, Barry. "Strategy and the 'Business Portfolio.'" *Long Range Planning*, February 1977, 9.

————. "A Fundamental Approach to Strategy Development." *Long Range Planning*, December 1976, 2.

Helmeke, T. M. "Strategic Business Unit Market Planning: An Industrial Case History." *Business Marketing*, November 1984, 42–43.

Jain, Subhash C. "The Evolution of Strategic Marketing." *Journal of Business Research*, December 1983, 409–425.

Karnani, A. "Generic Competitive Strategies." *Strategic Management*, October–December 1984, 367–380.

Kotler, Philip. "Harvesting Strategies for Weak Products." *Business Horizons*, August 1978, 15.

————, William George, and William Rogers. "The Marketing Audit Comes of Age." *Sloan Management Review*, Winter 1977, 25.

Kriegel, R. A. "Anatomy of a Marketing Communications Plan: Basics for Writing Your Objectives, Strategies, and Tactics." *Business Marketing*, July 1983, 72–74.

Larreche, J., and V. Srinivasan. "STRATPORT: A Decision Support System for Strategic Planning." *Journal of Marketing*. Fall 1981, 39.

Leontiades, M. "The Importance of Integrating Marketing Planning with Corporate Planning." *Journal of Business Research*, December 1983, 457–473.

Little, J. D. "Decision Support Systems for Marketing Managers." *Journal of Marketing*, Summer 1979, 9.

Levitt, Theodore. "Marketing Success Through Differentiation—Of Anything." *Harvard Business Review*, January–February 1980, 83.

Levy, M., et al. "Formulating Push Marketing Strategies: A Method and Application." *Journal of Marketing*, Winter 1983, 25.

Michael, George D. "Product Petrification: A New Stage in the Life Cycle Theory." *California Management Review*, Fall 1971, 88.

Porter, M. "How to Attack the Industry Leader." *Fortune*, April 29, 1985, 153–154.

Ratza, C. L. "The Strategic Marketing Process: A Practical Framework for Analytic Market Planning and Analysis." *Management Planning*, March–April 1985, 41–45.

Roberts, K. J. "How to Define Your Market Segment." *Long Range Planning*, August 1986, 53–58.

Robinson, S. J. Q. "Strategies for Declining Industrial Products." *Long Range Planning*, April 1986, 72–78.

————, R. E. Hichens, and D. P. Wade. "The Directional Policy Matrix—Tool for Strategic Planning." *Long Range Planning*, June 1978, 8.

Rothschild, William E. "Competitor Analysis: The Missing Link in Strategy." *Management Review*, July 1979, 22.

Schoeffler, S., R. Buzzell, and D. Heany. "Impact of Strategic Planning on Profit Performance." *Harvard Business Review*, March–April 1974, 137–143.

Smallwood, John E. "The Product Life Cycle: A Key to Strategic Marketing Planning." *MSU Business Topics*, Winter 1973, 19.

Stevenson, Howard H. "Defining Corporate Strengths and Weaknesses." *Sloan Management Review*, Spring 1976, 51.

Varadaragian, P. R. "Marketing Strategies in Action." *Business*, January–February–March 1986, 11–23.

Wakerly, R. G. "PIMS: A Tool for Developing Competitive Strategy." *Long Range Planning*, June 1984, 92–97.

Walker, R. F. "Portfolio Analysis in Practice." *Long Range Planning*, June 1984, 63–71.

Notes

Chapter 1   Marketing and the Marketing Plan

[1] Drucker, Peter F. *Management: Tasks, Responsibilities, Practices* (New York: Harper & Row, 1974), p. 61.

[2] Bassler, John. "Companies Want CEOs with Strong Market Vision," *Marketing News* (May 23, 1986), p. 17.

[3] ———. "Strategic Marketing: Top Priority of Chief Executives," *Marketing News* (May 23, 1986), p. 1.

[4] ———. "Apple, Part II: The No-Nonsense Era of John Sculley," *Business Week* (January 27, 1986), p. 96.

[5] Hopkins, David S. *The Marketing Plan* (New York: The Conference Board, 1981), p. 53.

Chapter 3   Prerequisites for Marketing Planning

[1] Kotler, Philip. *Marketing Management* (Englewood Cliffs, N.J.: Prentice-Hall, Inc., 1984), p. 287.

Chapter 4   The Situation Analysis

[1] Kotler, Philip. *Marketing Management* (Englewood Cliffs, N.J.: Prentice-Hall, Inc., 1984), p. 188.

[2] Mansfield, Edwin, *Statistics for Business and Economics* (New York: W. W. Norton & Co., 1980); and Plane, Donald R., and Edward B. Oppermann, *Business and Economic Statistics* (Plano, Texas: Business Publications, 1986).

[3] For example, see Bell, Martin L. *Marketing: Concepts and Strategy* (Boston: Houghton Mifflin, 1979); Engle, J. F., D. T. Kollat, and R. D. Blackwell. *Consumer Behavior* (New York: Holt, Rinehart and Winston, 1968); and Howard, J. A., and J. N. Sheth. *The Theory of Buyer Behavior* (New York: John Wiley, 1969).

[4] Chapter 8 provides additional background on the financial aspects of marketing planning.

Chapter 5   The Analytic Summaries

[1] Hartley, Robert. *Marketing Mistakes*, Third Edition (New York: John Wiley, 1986).

[2] See Abell, Derek F. "Strategic Windows," *Journal of Marketing* (July 1978), p. 21.

[3] For an excellent review of forecasting methods, see Hurwood, D. L., E. S. Grossman, and E. I. Bailey. *Sales Forecasting* (New York: The Conference Board, 1978).

[4] Ibid., p. 114.

[5] Note the similarity of this information base to the concept of the served market which was discussed previously.

[6] For three articles by John D. C. Little that incorporate the concept of the decision calculus, see "Models and Managers: The Concept of a Decision Calculus," *Management Science* (April 1970), p. 485; "BRANDAID: A Marketing-Mix Model, Parts I and II," *Operations Research* (July–August 1975), p. 628; and "Decision Support Systems for Marketing Managers," *Journal of Marketing* (Summer 1979), p. 9.

[7] Rogers, E. M. *Diffusion of Innovations* (New York: Free Press, 1962).

[8] Dhalla, Nariman K., and Sonia Yuspeh. "Forget the Product Life Cycle Concept," *Harvard Business Review* (January–February 1976), pp. 102–110.

Chapter 6   Developing a Marketing Strategy

[1] For a list of the traditional marketing mix elements, see Borden, Neil H. "The Concept of the Marketing Mix," *Journal of Advertising Research* (June 1964), p. 4. The citation of a list of 400 mix elements refers to a critical path program for the introduction of new products at Monsanto Chemical Company which had over 400 decision nodes included. Each of these decision nodes could be considered a component of the overall marketing mix.

[2] Bell, Martin L. *Marketing: Concepts and Strategy* (Boston: Houghton Mifflin, 1979), pp. 400–405.

Chapter 8   Financial Aspects of Marketing Planning

[1] This example is adapted from Cravens, David W., Gerald E. Hills, and Robert B. Woodruff. *Marketing Decision Making: Concepts and Strategy*, Revised Edition (Homewood, Ill.: Richard D. Irwin, Inc., 1980), pp. 335–336.

[2] A number of books discuss the application of profitability accounting to marketing. See Simon, S. *Managing Marketing Profitability* (New York: American Management Association, 1969); and Mossman, F. M., P. Fisher, and W. J. E. Crissy. "New Approaches to Analyzing Marketing Profitability," *Journal of Marketing* (April 1974), p. 43.

Chapter 9   The Personal Side of Planning

[1] Roseman, E. "Living Sensitively Ever After," *Sales Management* (May 13, 1974), p. 24.

[2] Gemmil, G. R., and D. L. Wileman. "The Product Manager as an Influence Agent," *Journal of Marketing* (January 1972), pp. 26–30.

Index

Abell, Derek
  on strategic windows, 101
  on "we-they" problems, 295
accounting, marketing's relations with, 292–293
accounting, types of:
  financial, 249
  managerial, 249
  profitability, 250
accounting and finance, role in marketing of, 4, 85
activity ratios, 256–257
adopter categories:
  early adopters, 132
  innovators, 132
  laggards, 132
  middle majority, 132
adoption process, 129–133
  and disadoption, 132
advertising, 98, 288–289
analytic perspectives, 54–55
analytic summaries, 100
Apple computer, shift to marketing of, 6
approval of plan, 287
asset turnover, 256–257
assumptions, accuracy of, 44
AT&T, mission of, 20

balance sheet, 250–253
basic price, 182
Bassler, John, on marketing focus of CEO, 6
brand development index, 63–64
breakeven analysis, 268–269
briefing session, 287
broadcast distribution, 164
budget, methods of setting, 177
budgeting, 4, 258–264
business planning, 25

business unit strategy, 6, 38–39
buyers' market, 68
buying power index, 61

capacity, utilization of, 67–68
capital budget, 262–264
cash cow, 138
cash flow, 257–258
census of business, 66–67
chain ratio, 64–65
channel of distribution, 71–72, 159
  see also distribution component of marketing
    mix
charter, see division charter
coercive power, 302
company capability, see SWOP Analysis, company
    strengths
company capability analysis, components of:
  advertising, 98
  distribution, 86
  financial performance, 82–85
  marketing, 86–98
  price, 98
  product/service, 86
  sales, 88
  sales analysis, 79–82
  sales promotion, 98
competitive channels, 164
competitive turbulence, stage in PLC, 126–127
competitor analysis, 72–75
  sources of information for, 75
competitors, 72–75
complementary channels, 164
computer and marketing planning, 50–53
conditional forecast, 120
constraints on marketing, 8

contingency plan, 189, 242–243
control, 241–242
core strategy, 152
corporate mission, 20–21
    change in, 24–25
corporate strategic planning, 6, 10–11, 19
    marketing's relations with, 290–291
cost, *see* marketing cost
cost standards, 283–284
CPM, 52
customer analysis, 75–78
customer profile, components of:
    demographic, 77, 78
    psychographic, 77
    usage, 77
cycle of planning and control, 244–245

data bases:
    decision support system, 49
    external, 49
    internal, 49
    marketing research, 49
    syndicated, 64
Day, George, on market share and market
        leakage, 82
dealing with conflict, steps in:
    be flexible, 301
    educate, 299
    exercise power, 302
    get general involvement, 300
    get top management involved, 299
    keep going, 302
    keep it simple, 300
    plan your planning, 302
    process before planning, 299
    remember purpose of planning, 300
    respect the numbers, 300
    use positive collaboration tools, 301
    use reward system, 300–301
    use staff assistance, 300
decision calculus, 125
decision support system, 49, 86
decline, stage in PLC, 127
delegation, 233–234
demand conditions and trend, 59–67
demand schedule, 184
demarketing, 67
demographics, 77, 78
diminishing returns, 121
directional matrix, 135–142
discounts, types of, 182–183
distinctive competence, 101
distinctive deficiency, 101

distribution, 86, 159–168
distribution component of marketing mix
    evaluation of, 168
    issues in, 163–166
    resolving issues in, 166–168
    subobjectives of, 162–163
distribution coverage, types of:
    broadcast distribution, 164
    exclusive distribution, 164
    limited distribution, 164
    selective distribution, 164
division charter, 25
divisional management, role of marketing in, 6
dog, 138
driving force, marketing as, 8
Drucker, Peter, on purpose of business, 5

environmental scan, 56
evaluation in the control process, 238–241
exclusive distribution, 164
expense budget, 259–262
experience curve, 270–271
expert power, 302

Federal Express, mission of, 20–21
financial analysis, components of:
    activity ratios, 256–257
    asset turnover, 256–257
    balance sheet, 250–253
    budgets, 258–264
    capital budget, 262–264
    capital budget-payback, 263
    capital budget-present value, 264
    capital budget-ROI, 263–264
    cash flow, 257–258
    expense budget, 259–262
    gross profit margin, 254
    income statement, 253
    inventory turnover, 256
    net profit margin, 255
    operating ratios, 253–257
    profitability ratios, 254–256
    receivables turnover, 257
    return on assets, 255
    return on assets managed, 256
    return on investment, 255–256
financial analysis, traditional, 250–264
financial performance, 82–85
fine tuning, 241
four Ps, 150, 152
frequency, 176
functional management, role of marketing in, 7–8

Gantt chart, 211
gap analysis, 117–120
G.E. Screen, 138–142
  business strengths of, 138
  market attractiveness of, 138
  procedure for using, 141–142
gross profit margin, 254
growth, stage in PLC, 126
growth/share matrix, 135–138
  cash cow, 138
  dog, 138
  problem child, 136–138
  star, 138
growth/share matrix, steps in preparing, 136

hierarchy of objectives, 29–30
human side problems, types of:
  line vs. staff, 295
  management levels, 295
  others are the problem, 294–295
  you are the problem, 293–294

IFPS, 51
implementation, 44, 216, 232–234
  and delegation, 233–234
income (P&L) statement, 253
industry, definition of, 58–59
industry analysis, components of:
  demand conditions and trend, 59–67
  supply conditions, 67–68
  trade channel arrangements, 71–72
innovation, 5
introduction, stage in PLC, 125–126
inventory turnover, 256

Kotler, Philip
  on marketing information system, 49
  on opportunity/threat matrix, 58
  on requirements of objectives, 28

leaked market, 81
legal department, role in marketing of, 4, 293
limited distribution, 164
Little, John, on decision calculus, 125
logistics, 159
Lotus 1-2-3, 52, 53

macroenvironment, 56–58, 237–238
management information, role in marketing of, 86
management levels, 295
manufacturing, role in marketing of, 3, 85
market index, 61
market manager, 7

market potential
  measurements of, 61–67
  and syndicated data, 64
  undeveloped, 80–81
market share, 81
marketing
  constraints on, 8
  definition of, 8
  as driving force, 8
  information and control system in, 8
  not a panacea, 8
marketing channels, 159
marketing cost
  behavior of, 264–268
  breakeven analysis and, 268–269
  and common cost, 271–272
  and direct cost, 275
  experience curve and, 270–271
  and fixed cost, 265, 275
  functional cost analysis and, 272–273
  long-run, 269–270
  planning curve and, 269–270
  profitability accounting for, 275–281
  and programmed cost, 277
  segment analysis in, 273–275
  segment analysis procedure and, 273
  semivariable cost and, 265
  and shared cost, 271–272
  and specific cost, 277
  and variable cost, 265, 275
marketing cost control, 281–285
  and expense budget, 281
  and profitability, 281–282
marketing cost standards, 283–284
marketing department, 7
marketing information system, 49–50, 86, 289–290
  definition of, 49
  and information and control system, 8
  see also data bases
marketing mix, 6, 150
  and core strategy, 152
  distribution component in, 159–168, *see also* distribution component of marketing mix
  logical sequence in, 151–152
  pricing component in, 180–189, *see also* pricing component of marketing mix
  product component in, 154–159, *see also* product component of marketing mix
  promotion component in, 171–180
marketing performance, 86–98
marketing plan
  definition of, 9
  need for more than one, 13

marketing planner, unique role of, 11–12
marketing planner contacts
  with advertising, 288–289
  within department, 287–289
  with marketing research, 289
  with sales, 288
  with top management, 287
marketing planner interconnections
  with accounting, 292–293
  with corporate planning, 290–291
  with legal department, 293
marketing planner relations
  with MIS, 289–290
  with other departments, 293
  with production, 291
  with R&D, 291–292
marketing planning
  information requirements of, 48–49
  linkage to corporate planning of, 10–11, 19
  types and levels of, 11
marketing planning process, steps in:
  step 1, 43–46
  step 2, 46
  step 3, 46
  step 4, 48
  step 5, 100–142
  step 6, 144–147
  step 7, 147–153
  step 8, 154–188
  step 9, 189–193
  step 10, 194–211
  step 11, 211–214
  step 12, 214–216
  step 13, 216–234
  step 14, 234–245
marketing research, 8, 49, 289
marketing strategy, 6, 148
marketing strategy statement, 148–151
maturity, stage in PLC, 127
McNair, Malcolm, on "Six Honest Serving Men,"
  75–78
measurement and monitoring
  effort, 234
  environment, 237–238
  performance results, 235–237
message platform, 174
mission, 20–21
multiple channels, uses of:
  competitive, 164
  complementary, 164

net profit margin, 255
Nielsen, A. C. Company, as data source, 64

objectives, 28
  finalizing of, 144–147
  requirements of, 28–29
operating ratios, 253–257
opportunities, 101
organization, 37–38
organization chart, 38
  line vs. staff in, 295
organizational conflict, how to deal with, *see*
  dealing with conflict, steps in
organizational conflict, reasons for:
  communications failures, 298
  competition for resources, 298
  goal differences, 296
  lack of understanding of planning, 296–297
  management style, 296
  marketing planning as threat, 297
  politics, 297–298
  reward system, 296
  short-run vs. long-run perspective, 296
  uneven distribution of knowledge, 297

payoff matrix, 193
personal computer, 51–53
personnel, role in marketing of, 4
PERT/CPM, 52, 208–211
Pet Inc., strategic planning in, 11, 19
pipeline sales, 64, 66
pitfalls in planning:
  failure to control, 304–305
  failure to develop tactics, 304
  failure to integrate steps, 303
  failure to modify the plan, 305
  hypnotized by the numbers, 304
  inadequate data base, 303
  lack of cooperation, 304
  no plan for planning, 303
  not enough time, 303
  not "selling" the plan, 305
  planning becomes a ritual, 305
  strategic drift, 304
  taking shortcuts, 304
plan for planning
  requirements of, 14
  risk of not having, 303
  steps in, 14–18
  two aspects of, 13
plan modification, types of:
  amending the document, 243–244
  contingency plan, 242–243
  effort correction, 241
  strategy change, 241–243
  tactical fine-tuning, 241

planning
  hierarchy of, 11
  purposes of, 9–10
planning prerequisites, 145, 287
  business unit strategy, 38–39
  company mission, 20–21
  division charter, 25
  objectives and subobjectives, 28
  organization, 37–38
  policies, 35–37
planning procedure, how well utilized, 46
policies, 35–37
positive collaboration, tools of, 301
power, kinds of:
  coercive power, 302
  expert power, 302
  referent power, 302
  reward power, 302
presentation
  basics of, 213–214
  outline of, 213
  purposes of, 213
  rehearsal for, 214
  visual aids in, 213–214
price
  basic, 182
  performance, 98
  relation to cost, 183
  relation to promotion, 183
price discrimination, 183–184
price level changes, 59
price-cost-volume analysis, 184–188
pricing component of marketing mix
  evaluation of, 188–189
  issues in, 181–184
  resolving issues in, 184–188
  subobjectives of, 180–181
problem child, 136–138
problems, 102
product component of marketing mix
  evaluation of, 159
  issues in, 155–156
  resolving issues in, 156–159
  subobjectives of, 154–155
product life cycle
  and adoption process, 129–133
  analysis, 125–135
  as diagnostic tool, 133
  strategies, 131
product life cycle stages:
  competitive turbulence, 126–127
  decline, 127
  growth, 126
  introduction, 125–126
  maturity, 127
product manager, 7
product/market focus, 47–48
product/market matrix, 102–113
product/service, performance of, 86
profitability accounting, 275–281
profitability ratios, 254–256
program units, 25
promotion component of marketing mix
  evaluation of, 177–180
  issues in, 171–173
  resolving issues in, 173–177
  subobjectives of, 168–171
promotion mix, 168
psychographics, 77

quality control, role in marketing of, 3
quality index, 62

reach, 176
receivables turnover, 257
referent power, 302
requirements of objectives, 28
  see also objectives, requirements of
research and development, role in marketing of,
  86
response function, 120–125
results, as compared to objectives, 43
return on assets, 255
return on assets managed, 256
return on investment, 255–256
reward power, 302
Rogers, E. M., on adoption process, 132

sales, performance of, 88
sales activity index, 62
sales analysis, 79–82
sales department, 288
sales forecast
  steps in, 114–115
  uses of, 111
sales forecasting methods:
  correlation, 116
  customer intentions, 117
  executive opinion, 116–117
  exponential smoothing, 116
  extrapolation, 115
  factor listing, 115
  moving average, 115–116
  naive methods, 115–116
  sales force composite, 117
  survey methods, 116–117

sales promotion, performance of, 98
SAMI, as data source, 64
SAS, 51, 52, 60
scanners, 64
segment cost analysis, 273–275
segmentation
    bases of, 47
    requirements of, 47–48
selective distribution, 164
sellers' market, 67
served market, 81–82
Simmons Market Research Bureau, as data source, 77, 174
situation analysis, 170
    and analytic perspectives, 54–55
    and industry analysis, 58–72
    and macroenvironment, 56–58
    procedure, 53–54
software
    analysis, 52
    data base, 52
    and decision support, 51
    presentation, 53
    word processing, 52
SPSS, 42, 51, 60
Standard Industrial Classification (SIC), 59
star, 138
Statgraphics, 60
strategic business unit, 6, 7
strategic drift, 304
strategic planning, 6
strategic window, 101
strategy
    alternatives, 147–148
    management options and, 189–190
    and product life cycle, 131
    selection of, 189–193

strategy change, 241–243
strategy choice
    and payoff matrix, 193
    and weighted criteria method, 190–192
strengths, 102
subjective probability, 56
supply conditions, 67–68
"Survey of Buying Power", 61–63
SWOP Analysis, 100–102, 170
SWOP Analysis, components of:
    company strengths, 100
    company weaknesses, 101
    external opportunities, 101
    external problems, 102
SWOP Summary, 102

tactics, 7
    fine tuning, 241
    how to prepare, 197–205
    nature of, 194–196
    using Gantt chart, 211
    using PERT/CPM, 208–211
    who should prepare, 196–197
time series analysis, 59, 79
top management, role in marketing of, 5–6, 287
tunnel planning, 189

variance analysis, 43, 44, 238–241

warehousing, role in marketing of, 4
weaknesses, 101
weighted criteria method, 190–192
writing the plan
    guidelines for, 215–216
    reasons for, 215
written marketing plan, 44

About the Author

Martin L. Bell is Professor of Marketing at the Roy E. Crummer Graduate School of Business at Rollins College in Winter Park, Florida. One of about 20 fully accredited, graduate-only business schools in the United States, the Crummer School offers full-time, part-time, and executive MBA programs, as well as non-degree executive development programs.

Prior to joining the Crummer School in 1981, Dr. Bell was for twenty-five years a member of the tenured faculty of the Graduate School of Business at Washington University in St. Louis, Missouri. He obtained his bachelor's degree in the liberal arts at Principia College and his M.B.A. and Ph.D. from the Wharton School at the University of Pennsylvania. He teaches in the areas of marketing strategy, marketing management, and advertising.

Dr. Bell has had extensive direct business experience. He worked for several years in product line accounting at General Electric Company. After obtaining his doctorate, he launched a successful teaching and consulting career. He has worked with numerous business corporations, trade associations, and not-for-profit organizations. For more than twenty years, he was affiliated with a AAAA advertising agency as director of marketing. In that capacity he participated directly in conducting marketing audits and in preparing marketing and advertising plans for clients in the industrial, consumer products, and services areas. He served for several years on the Corporate Marketing Advisory Committee at Emerson Electric Company. He developed and supervised the installation of a formal marketing planning procedure at Farmland Industries, one of the nation's largest agricultural cooperatives. In addition, he has assisted numerous other firms of various sizes engaged in industrial, consumer, or services marketing in the preparation of formal marketing plans.

Dr. Bell has had extensive experience in professional continuing education, presenting marketing management seminars on behalf of such institutions as the University of Pittsburgh, Vanderbilt University, Southern Methodist University, the Rochester Institute of Technology, Northwestern University, Michigan State University, Washington State University, and the University of Southern California. He has written numerous articles and several books, including a widely recognized M.B.A.-level text on marketing management. His most recent textbook (with Dr. Julian Vincze) is *Managerial Marketing: Strategy and Cases*, to be published by Elsevier Publishing Company in 1988. His next project will be a book on advertising strategy.

Martin Bell resides in Maitland, Florida. He and his wife, Marcie, have five grown children, including triplets, who live in various parts of the country. His hobbies are traveling, sailing off the West Coast of Florida, and collecting *Coca-Cola* memorabilia.